Around 1981

Around 1981

Academic Feminist Literary Theory

Jane Gallop

Routledge
New York • London

Published in 1992 by

Routledge
An imprint of Routledge, Chapman and Hall, Inc.
29 West 35th Street
New York, NY 10001

Published in Great Britain by

Routledge
11 New Fetter Lane
London EC4P 4EE

Library of Congress Cataloging-in-Publication Data

Gallop, Jane, 1952–
   Around 1981 : academic feminist literary theory / Jane Gallop.
     p.   cm.
   Includes bibliographical references and index.
   ISBN 0-415-90189-8.—ISBN 0-415-90190-1 (pbk.)
   Feminist literary criticism.   I. Title.
  PN98.W64G34   1991
  801'.95'082—dc20   91-24137
                                          CIP

British Library Cataloguing in Publication Data

Gallop, Jane, *1952–*
  Around 1981 academic feminist literary theory.
  I. Title
  820.99287

  ISBN 0-415-90189-8
  ISBN 0-415-90190-1 pbk

To my Students:
The bright, hot, hip (young) women who fire my thoughts, my loins, my prose. I write this to move, to please, to shake you.

Note on Permissions

Chapter one is a substantially revised version of "The Difference Within," which appeared in *Critical Inquiry,* Vol. 8, no. 4 (1982); Chapter two is a revision of "The Problem of Definition," which appeared in *Genre,* Vol. XX, no. 2 (1987); Chapter four originally appeared as "The Monster and the Mirror: The Feminist Critic's Psychoanalysis" in *Feminism and Psychoanalysis,* Feldstein and Roof eds., published by Cornell University Press (1989); Chapter five is a revised version of "Reading the Mother Tongue," which first appeared in *Critical Inquiry,* Vol. 10, no. 2 (1988). Grateful acknowledgment is made for permission to reprint.

Contents

Introduction

Late in 1981, perhaps it was actually at the MLA Convention, Elizabeth Abel invited me to write a response to the feminist issue of *Critical Inquiry* that was about to appear. The present book begins there, although of course at the time it was not yet even the hope of a book but a ten page occasional piece and a chance to get published in *Critical Inquiry*.

I had been working for nearly a decade in French Studies, doing feminist work in poststructuralist theory. As I recall, I had read no feminist literary criticism of the sort being produced in English Departments since reading *Sexual Politics* as an undergraduate. Abel's invitation produced a new conjuncture which, at the time, I experienced simply as an event in my individual trajectory. Only just today, writing this in late 1990, did I connect that invitation with the issue's title, a feminist revision of Jacques Derrida's *Writing and Difference*. "Writing and Sexual Difference" locates itself at the intersection of feminist criticism and poststructuralist theory. An encounter I experienced as individual event was in fact taking place in the volume as a whole, and represented a certain moment in American academic criticism.

Around 1981 I entered into contact with the mainstream of academic literary feminism in the United States. That is where I come in.

The end of 1981 saw a feminist issue not only of *Critical Inquiry* but also of *Yale French Studies*. Impelled by a mix of intellectual, personal, and professional motives, I decided to apply the method I had used on "Writing and Sexual Difference" to this text in the same genre located in what I still considered my "field." I had no larger project in mind but was interested in seeing if I could once again produce interesting results by reading a plural text as a whole. Unlike "The Difference Within," this took place very much where I then lived, not only in French Studies, but at the intersection of feminism and psychoanalysis. Rather than productive difference, the resulting text never moves far enough from the mirror.

Between 1984 and 1985 I began teaching and reading anthologies of American academic feminist literary criticism, at the same time

1

deciding to write a book about them. In 1984 I had not really moved from my first encounter with "Writing and Sexual Difference." Had I written the present book around 1984, it would have resembled Toril Moi's *Sexual/Textual Politics*, published in 1985, which structures itself around the difference between poststructuralist theory and American criticism. Had I written the present book around 1985, it would have been centered on the point where I came in, on the encounter between French deconstructive theory and American feminist criticism.

In 1986 I wrote a chapter on *The New Feminist Criticism*, a 1985 anthology edited by Elaine Showalter. That chapter is the first written wholly to be part of this project and is thus the actual beginning of the book as book. The encounter between French theory and American feminism is there only a subplot; the main story is about the theoretical definition and institutional establishment of feminist literary criticism. Although a different tale, this one too centers around 1981.

Between 1985 and 1987 I wrote three occasional pieces which were also meant to double as "chapters." Because of the sorts of invitations I received (based on my previously published work, on my identity as a psychoanalytic, "French" feminist) and because of my original mid-decade conception of the book's plot, all three of these were about either French feminism or psychoanalysis.

When in 1988, thanks to a year's leave, I finally had the time to devote myself to writing this book, I began by drawing up a table of contents. I immediately set to agonize over these three pieces along with the piece on *Yale French Studies*. I simply could not decide whether to chuck or to include them, and, if the latter, whether to place them in an introductory or an appendectory position.

I now wanted the book to tell the story of the main stream of American academic feminist literary criticism. What had once looked central to me now looked like a side issue which had been given all too much importance. I decided to keep these four "chapters" but also mark them as marginal. I gathered them into a section called "Side Tracks." Trying to locate a "side" in a linear progression, like a book or a history, I envisioned a structure radiating out from a center. "Around 1981," then to the side, back to the seventies, and then on in to the mid-eighties. This layout around a center disturbs the straightforward unfolding of the history, entwining the story of academic feminist criticism with the progress of the subject writing the history, herself necessarily limited by the moment(s) in which she writes. An equation with two variables: a history told by a subject in history.

Not because I presume my own story to be of major import, but because I was not the only one to see things that way. Around 1981, a good number of feminist literary academics in this country were focused on the "difference between French and American feminism," on the question of psychoanalysis or deconstruction and their usefulness or danger. "We" were not only American feminists like me who thought French psychoanalytic, deconstructive theory a great thing but also those who expended a good deal of energy attacking it. Around 1981, this conflict, this debate seemed central, and to many more academic critics than me, to feminist literary studies.

Whereas in the early eighties the project focused on the theoretical debate, by the late eighties it was organized around the institutionalization of feminist literary criticism. By which I mean its acceptance as a legitimate part of literary studies. I locate that "event" around 1981 and am interested in what led up to it and the subsequent effect it had on feminist criticism.

Although the readings that follow are undeniably textual, the framework would link text to extratextual event, institutional context, and power distribution. By power, I mean specifically the changing power of feminist criticism in relation to the institution, and of various feminist critics in relation to each other and to the institution. The institution here is the literary academy, which is at once a discursive field, a pedagogical apparatus, a place of employment, a site of cultural reproduction, an agency of cultural regulation, and an institution generally marginal to power and values in American society.

My change of focus from theoretical debate to institutional history corresponds to a shift of focus in the American literary academy between the early and the late eighties. Whereas around 1981 literary critics and English Departments were intensely concerned with the question of poststructuralism, by 1987 the theoretical action had moved to "institutions" and "history."

Not only do I as a writer undergo these small historical translocations, not only does feminist criticism's relation to the literary academy shift, but that institution itself is going through increasingly fast changes. The image of deconstruction, for example, goes from dangerous outsider to established rearguard in less than a decade. The increased attention to history in both feminist and non-feminist literary theory must certainly be related to this acceleration in critical fashions which forces upon us an awareness of living in history.

We might also map these moments onto the two major books on

feminist criticism to date: Toril Moi's in 1985 and Janet Todd's in 1988.[1] Reflecting currents of the early eighties, Moi subtitles her volume *Feminist Literary Theory* and focuses on the debate about poststructuralism, siding with "theoretical" feminism, by which she means poststructuralist. Typifying later trends, Todd entitles her contribution *Feminist Literary History*, complains of ahistoricism and calls for a historical and historicized feminist criticism. First conceived simultaneously with Moi's project, and then reconceived at the moment Todd writes, the present book could be said to move from Moi to Todd. Yet I would also hope to make explicit the relation between my perspective and its inevitable historical limitations, so as to suggest some way of understanding feminist criticism that is explicitly historical and thus not simply relativistic or reactional.

I want to stress the pain of history for those of us trying to produce knowledge. Even if we have no illusions or beliefs in the enduring, we want our understandings to last at least until they can be written, published, and read. This book, which took too long to write, not only passes through two different theoretical formations but around 1989 begins to feel the pressure of a third and grows increasingly anxious as I push to get it done and out before its power of strategic intervention is lost, before it enters a configuration different than the one for/in which it was written.

My focus is the institutionalization of feminist criticism; what, it might be asked, do I think about that? I think it is a fact. And I notice it is a fact rarely spoken of objectively. The word "institutionalization" sounds like some form of incarceration. The academicization of feminist criticism is generally discussed as if it had happened against our will.

The word "academic" itself is more often than not pejorative rather than descriptive. I notice that academic feminists accuse other academic feminists of being "academic." This sort of aggressive dissociation clouds our understanding of how we got here. None of us just woke up one day to discover that she had a Ph.D., a full-time academic job, much less tenure. This disavowal of the academic also deflects us from the question of what we ought to and could do now that we have a voice within this institution. We don't seem very able to theorize about how we speak, as feminists wanting social change, from within our positions in the academy.

My insistence that we recognize that we are, or that feminist criticism is, in the academy has sometimes been taken for a celebration of that fact. I worry that my statements will be sucked into a machine which demands that one either condemn "academic feminism" or stand accused as an "academic feminist." If I'm not bemoaning the selling-out of feminist criticism to academic respectability, then I must be one of those bourgeois feminists whose only goal is such respectability. Maybe I am; one shouldn't be too quick to deny any accusation voiced by more than the odd individual. But I continue to feel the necessity for an analysis which includes the academic location of the accusers.

I do not want to celebrate our being in. Being in something that is a transmitter of elitist values. Being in a discourse that is constituted, at this point in time, as marginal to the larger culture and society. But I do not want to bemoan it either. I want to understand why we are located here, how we got here, what we sacrificed to get here, what we gained: all as preliminaries to the question of how do we do the most good, as feminists, as social and cultural critics, speaking from this location.

Much talk about institutionalization implicitly construes institutions as monolithic, unchanging, or even inherently evil. Institutions have histories, are in history. When we conceive of them as unchanging, we have less chance of wittingly affecting their direction.

Around 1987, Meaghan Morris wrote: "Institutionalization is not another name for doom, that fate always worse than death. It's an opportunity, and in many instances a necessary condition, for serious politics."[2] Heartened by this statement, I also note that Morris writes at quite a remove from the American academic context. An Australian, although she has done various temporary teaching stints in universities, she is not "an academic" but supports herself by her writing.

I note also that her statement occurs in an anthology which debates the relation of men to feminism. That debate which drew quite a bit of energy in the mid-eighties must, I think, also be understood in relation to the academicization of feminism. A phenomenon such as men protesting their exclusion from feminist theory could only occur in the wake of some sort of institutionalization.

In 1984 a male academic begins his book on feminist criticism protesting for some two dozen pages his right to enter the field. He bases his claim on "the intervention of feminism in English studies" which makes it very much his business. Whereas Moi's book is subtitled *Feminist Literary Theory* and Todd's book is called *Feminist Literary History*, this book by K. K. Ruthven is entitled *Feminist Literary Studies*, emphasizing the academic location of the enterprise.[3] The *Men in*

Feminism debate itself must also be understood as a debate about the institutional status of feminist (literary) theory.

I don't discuss that issue in this book. But I do consider at least three other heated issues in feminist critical discourse, likewise linking them to institutionalization. I think the debate about "French feminism" or poststructuralist theory, the argument about whether feminist criticism should be defined as the study of women writers, and the acrimony and guilt around the question of race for and by white feminists must all also be understood in relation to the possibility or the fact of institutionalization.

Both the implicit definition of feminist criticism as the study of women writers and the appearance of French-style poststructuralist feminism in this country took place in the late 1970s. Both, I believe, contributed enormously to the acceptance of feminist criticism by the literary academy. The first helped define feminist criticism as a subfield, thus giving it a place within the literary academy without necessarily calling the whole into question, as well as making it seem like every department should have one. The second rode in on the coattails of the quick rise of deconstruction in American English Studies. "Theory" included a "feminist" component, although it also dismissed feminist criticism that was not properly "theoretical." These two trends have usually been opposed in feminist critical histories, but I would contend that they not only were strikingly contemporaneous but that, as separate and distinct strategies for feminist inclusion, they worked, if unwittingly, together. By the mid-eighties work on women writers based in poststructuralist theory is very widespread and constitutes the center of academic feminist criticism.

A decade later, conflict over race has taken the place of these two debates as the point of densest energy in academic feminism. This one is not a theoretical debate: no white critic claims we should ignore race or stick to writing about white women. But between feminist critics there is the same intensity, anxiety, and anger sparked by the earlier debates. Race was by and large not a question, for white literary academics, in the seventies. I would contend that one reason it is such a heated topic now is that it is also a debate about the institutional status of feminist criticism, an anxious non-encounter with the fact of our specific location as insiders.

With all this upfronting of "history,"[4] I may be giving a false impression. What follows is not contextual research but close textual analysis.

When I began using this method on the feminist issue of *Critical Inquiry*, I not only was writing about a moment still present but was unaware that there was a history of academic feminist criticism. It all seemed contemporaneous to me. By 1987 I felt that what most distinguished the various feminist critical anthologies was their alignment in some sort of chronological progression, rather than their positioning on some theoretical issue. My thematics and conceptual framework had changed, but my method did not.

The sort of reading I do could be called "symptomatic."[5] It comes out of psychoanalytic method by way of deconstruction. Its emphasis on the text resembles a tradition in American literary studies inaugurated by the old new criticism and still dominant when deconstruction hit these shores. Once here, deconstruction of course did not remain uncontaminated by the domestic variety of close reading. Where new critical close reading embraces the text in order to more fully and deeply understand its excellences, "symptomatic reading" squeezes the text tight to force it to reveal its perversities. New criticism is appreciative, even worshipful; symptomatic reading tends to be demystifying, even aggressive.

Applied to culturally powerful texts, symptomatic reading can be a tool for diminishing their power. Turned on culturally marginalized texts, it may also, because of its mixed heritage from new criticism, have the at least momentary effect of promoting the text to canonlike status. To devote such close attention to a text is to treat it as rich and powerful. "Symptomatic reading" can be at one and the same time respectful, because closely attentive, and aggressive, because it wrests secrets the author might prefer to keep.

My goal has been to chip away at certain reigning myths of what has gone on in feminist criticism. As such I have been involved in an act of demystification. Yet my hope is that what I uncover should be taken as not shameful but instructive. The necessary assumption for this is that we are all inevitably symptomatic, we are all subjects and thus speak from within a field of conflict.[6] It is not my goal to unveil the inadequacies of any individual. Reading an anthology as a whole is a method for getting at "symptoms" which recur across various authors. Rather than pointing to some individual's blind spots, these might indicate conflicts inhering in a collective situation. I am interested in the marks produced in the discourse of knowledge by a subject, not by an individual but by a collective subject, the academic feminist critic.

If we take seriously the notion of feminist criticism as a collective movement, then critical anthologies, especially those which purport to represent the entirety of that movement, may be the best place to hear that collective subject. Since anthologies not only have many voices but are organized choruses, they are good places to witness the dynamics of collectivity. Contrary to idealized or romanticized portraits of collectivity, the hard work of collective action includes individuals' attempts to speak for the whole, conflicts between centralizing and marginal discourses within the group, and the opposed pressures of solidarity and responsiveness to minority opinions.

I have joked that what I seek is some sort of "collective unconscious." Unlike the Jungian sense of the phrase, I do not mean something shared across time and cultures by all human psyches. I mean "collective" in the political sense of a specific group of individuals joined by shared interests and located together, whether explicitly or implicitly, in a field of conflicting interests. Academic feminist critics might have a collective unconscious not because women or even feminists or even academic feminists inherently have similar psyches, but because we speak within the same cultural enterprise and thus share its historical contradictions. If it is a contradiction to be an academic feminist literary critic in America in the late twentieth century then that contradiction will manifest itself in our writing. And if certain symptoms recur in a number of feminist critics, these textual symptoms may point to some sort of inner conflict, shared but not sufficiently recognized.

"I would even argue that *subjectively* the ensemble of contradictions is more basic than the background consensus, that we speak of a 'shared perspective' or 'ideology' not so much because we hold the same beliefs but because we feel the pressure of the same problems." Thus writes Patrocinio Schweickart about feminist criticism in 1985. A note offers some exemplary "contradictions": "the disciplinary requirements of literary criticism versus the demands of feminist *praxis*; aesthetic versus political concerns; the political versus the personal; integration versus separation; and so on."[7]

Although the present book looks at literary criticism, I have subtitled it "Academic Feminist Literary *Theory*." In the anthologies, I concentrate on the theoretical pieces. In the essays of practical criticism, I focus on theoretical positions and suppositions rather than on what they say about any specific text. My subject, the collective feminist critic, necessarily speaks theory since her voice is a composite of statements which recur in different specific readings. Because the symptoms are collective, they are themselves moments of theorizing, points where theory is attached to history, life, position.

The assumption tries not to be that if only these women were smarter they would not be so stuck. Rather I try to assume that they are stuck at the point where they literally are attached. We are stuck inasmuch as we speak from within history. If every knower is a subject, then her discourse will necessarily betray her subjectivity. By subject and subjectivity I do not mean an individual with idiosyncratic perception. Rather I mean someone who can only know from within history, with at best partial ideological awareness, and in specific relation to institutionalized discourses and group interests.

The danger in symptomatic reading is that it tends to constitute the reader as having superior awareness, a level of higher consciousness than the poor writers who provide grist for her mill. One of the effects of knowing in history is the ease with which we see the blind spots of an earlier formation along with the near impossibility of recognizing contemporary ones. The history of scholarship too often looks like each succeeding generation pointing out the foolishness of all who went before. "It is easy . . . to lay out the past in clear space for observation and comparison and ignore the obscured and shifting time in which it occurred."[8] As I wrote this book I have been searching for a way of understanding the past that would not lead to this sort of facile superiority. I have become more interested in the blindnesses that I share rather than those I feel superior to.

In a 1982 account of her research on the poet Alice Dunbar-Nelson, Gloria Hull writes: "Once I was dissecting an attitude of Dunbar-Nelson's of which I disapproved to a dear friend. . . . He . . . said, 'You can't stand her because you're too much like her.' . . . Then, I rose to her/my/our defense."[9] The literary historian comes to recognize the intensity of her negativity as a symptom of disavowed identification. Hull is lucky enough to have a friend to help her claim and work through that identification and honest enough to hear him and tell us. This moment of self-knowledge is presented as part of the scholarly process: "For a Black woman, being face-to-face with another Black woman makes the most cruel and beautiful mirror. This is as true of scholarly research as it is on the everyday plane."

"For an academic feminist, being face-to-face with another academic feminist makes the most cruel and beautiful mirror." Like Hull, I'm trying to learn to "rise to her/my/our defense," but along with the defense I want to learn to face the contradictions, confusions, defensiveness I find in the mirror. I want to learn how, in Myra Jehlen's words, to "join a contradiction."

"Myra Jehlen's article 'Archimedes and the paradox of feminist criticism' seems to have voiced central concerns among many American feminists: first published in the summer of 1981, it has already been anthologized twice."[10] That article speaks to me of a new praxis of contradiction:

> "There are many ways of dealing with contradictions . . . of which only one is to try to resolve them. Another way amounts to joining a contradiction— engaging it not so much for the purpose of overcoming it as to tap its energy. . . . [O]ne may recognize a point of connection by its contradictions. . . . [C]ontradictions . . . that we have tried to resolve away lest they belie our argument frequently are our firmest and most fruitful grounds."[11]

If feminist criticism is not just "academic," meaning "of no practical or useful significance," then its greatest resources are its "points of connection," points where the research, teaching, and writing are attached to actual material life. Thought detached from the world would be formally perfect. Abstract perfection of form is ruffled where thinking sticks. These "points of connection" are our "firmest and most fruitful grounds": where thought stands gnarled and rooted in life.

In 1981 I got tenure. Around the same time, American feminist literary criticism entered the heart of a contradiction. It became secure and prospered in the academy while feminism as a social movement was encountering major setbacks in a climate of new conservatism. The Reagan-Bush years began; the ERA was defeated. In the American academy feminism gets more and more respect while in the larger society women cannot call themselves feminist.

This book reads anthologies of American academic feminist literary criticism published from 1972 to 1987. Reading over a decade and a half of feminist criticism, it keeps circling back to the fictive moment I call Around 1981.

I
AROUND 1981

1
The Difference Within

At the end of 1981 the prestigious academic journal *Critical Inquiry* published its first (and to date only) feminist issue. Entitled "Writing and Sexual Difference," that special issue was "guest edited" by the feminist literary critic Elizabeth Abel, at the time an assistant professor and the only woman of the journal's six coeditors. The issue opens with Abel's Introduction which concludes: "this moment of feminist inquiry allows new figures to provide a different and enabling mythology."[1] In "this moment," Winter 1981, *Critical Inquiry* has become "feminist inquiry," and the momentary substitution of terms—"feminist" for "critical"—allows new figures (the guest editor, for example) to provide a different and en-Abel-ing mythology.

The Editor's Introduction opens with an epigraph from *The Critical Difference*. If the substitution of "feminist" for "critical" provides an enabling difference, the epigraph already occasions a return of the term "critical." Published only the year before, *The Critical Difference* was written by Barbara Johnson, another female assistant professor at another elite American university.

Johnson and *The Critical Difference* make one other appearance in the collection. Mary Jacobus describes a "love language between two women" as "a language of desire whose object . . . is that internal (in)difference which, in another context, Barbara Johnson calls 'not a difference between . . . but a difference within. Far from constituting the text's unique identity, it is that which subverts the very idea of identity'" (pp. 50–51). Writing about this internal difference, Jacobus enacts it. Johnson's words within Jacobus' text remain marked as different, marked as belonging to "another context." In its position as epigraph, *The Critical Difference* also functions as such a dis-Abel-ing difference within "Writing and Sexual Difference."

The epigraph begins by promising to repeat a commonplace about literature and sex: "If human beings were not divided into two biological sexes, there would probably be no need for literature. And if literature could truly say what the relations between the sexes are, we would doubtless not need much of it then, either." Sexual difference is a mystery; literature is concerned with that mystery. The reader expects another rendition of the refrain that literature is unable to "capture" the mystery of sex. At this point, there is an ellipsis in the epigraph; on the far side of the elision a quite startling formulation reverses the terms of the expected truism: "It is not the life of sexuality that literature cannot capture; it is literature that inhabits the very heart of what makes sexuality problematic for us speaking animals." Johnson claims that literature is already at the heart of what constitutes sex as enigma. Literature could be called the difference within sexuality.

The phrase "speaking animals" suggests that we might explain Johnson's remark by recourse to Lacanian psychoanalysis. According to Jacques Lacan, desire springs from the fact that the articulated demand always necessarily exceeds the instinctual needs one might wish to communicate.[2] The common view of language—that which underwrites the expected refrain about literature's inadequacy to capture sex—is that language is inadequate to express human needs. But according to Lacan, language is not inadequate but overabundant: it presents a surplus, always expressing more not less than we want. In a formulation closer to Johnson's, Jean Laplanche, a student of Lacan, writes that sexual excitation is an "alien internal entity" and that this entity is precisely "parental fantasies."[3] If we understand fantasies as a form of literature, then sexual excitation, for Laplanche, is the alien internal presence of literature.

Even this cursory attempt to explain Johnson's provocative remark demonstrates that any assimilation of these words necessitates a foray into "another context." My concern here, however, is not with what Johnson might have meant but rather with the effect of her remark within the bounds of the Winter 1981 issue of *Critical Inquiry* where it remains very puzzling. Abel says nothing in the Introduction to explain it, and nothing in the issue explicitly serves to assimilate this internal difference. But because of it, from the very first page, "Writing and Sexual Difference" is disturbed. Does "sexual difference" mean the *difference between* the sexes or the *difference within* sex? Are "sexual difference" and "writing" two distinct domains which intersect, or is writing interior to sexual difference?

The title "Writing and Sexual Difference" alludes to Jacques Derrida's book *Writing and Difference*. "Writing" might here function as a synonym for "difference," as it does in orthodox deconstruction. The appearance of the Derridean Johnson reinforces the reference to deconstruction. But it is noteworthy that what is usually seen as French male thought is here represented by an American woman. Such a choice avoids the usual gendering and nationalizing of the encounter between feminism and deconstruction, transposing what is usually represented as a difference between nationalities or between the sexes into a difference within American women critics.

The Introduction's second sentence makes the collection's relation to deconstruction explicit: "Deconstructive criticism has made us attend to notions of textual difference, but the complexities of sexual difference . . . have largely been confined to the edges of critical debate" (p. 1). Like deconstructive criticism, this volume will attend to difference, but it will shift the focus from the textual difference which is by 1981 so central in critical inquiry to "sexual difference." The epigraph, citing "deconstructive criticism" on the subject of sexual difference, might also enact the placement of the sexual "on the edges" by claiming textuality as the very heart of sexuality.

"Sexuality" is not synonymous with "sexual difference" although both are meanings of the word "sex." A heterosexist slippage between the two operates in the epigraph. It thus becomes one of the effects of *The Critical Difference* within Writing and Sexual Difference.

The closest the Introduction comes to stating the relation between Writing and Sexual Difference is the final sentence of the paragraph on the history of feminist literary criticism: "The analysis of female talent grappling with a male tradition translates sexual difference into literary differences" (p. 2). Literary difference is a "translation" of sexual difference which is, by implication, an original. Where *The Critical Difference* enigmatically implies that literature is already operative within sexuality, Abel suggests the standard model in which sexuality is prior to literature. But "translation" also resonates in the network of internal alterity which I am here attempting to trace.

Mentioned only twice in the issue, Johnson makes one additional appearance between its covers. In the pages of advertising at the end of the journal, in an ad for *Critical Inquiry*'s own publisher, the University of Chicago Press, we learn that Johnson has translated Jacques Derrida's *Dissemination*. From the biographical notes on the contributors, we learn that the issue includes another translator of Derrida, Gayatri Chakravorty Spivak. Spivak's contribution to "Writing and Sexual Difference" is itself a translation, of the Bengali story "Draupadi" written by Mahasveta Devi. Both in the table of contents and in the running heads, Spivak's name appears in the position of author; within the collection, the story occasions some uncertainty about the authority of original over translation.

"The analysis of female talent grappling with a male tradition translates sexual difference into literary differences." While the figure of "translation" would seem to define the sexual as anterior to the literary, the use of translation in the collection might disturb the priority of original over translation. That disturbance may be consonant with the decision to represent Derridean deconstruction by its female translators—female talent grappling with a male tradition, we might even say.

In her Critical Response to "Writing and Sexual Difference," Carolyn Heilbrun asserts that "Stimpson's article . . . concludes these essays." Since Catharine Stimpson's piece is actually penultimate in the collection, coming before Spivak's, Heilbrun adds a quick explanatory parenthesis: "(I count the powerful story Gayatri Spivak translates as fiction)" (p. 296). Heilbrun discounts Spivak's text by "counting it as fiction." Yet even her dismissal follows the volume's practice of attributing the story to the translator/critic's name. Recognizing some sort of break between Stimpson's and Spivak's contributions, Heilbrun chooses not to read beyond the break.

The editor, however, explicitly attempts to read this break as the collection's final move, not as a move out of the volume but as the volume's attempt to move out: "With this story the volume shifts from West to East, from criticism to fiction, from implicit to explicit political perspective. . . . the fragmented female body shifts from metaphor to fact" (p. 6). "From metaphor to fact": it looks like the Bengali story takes the journal from literature to life, to the real body, the real world, outside of rhetoric. This shift from metaphor to fact is in fact, however, a shift from nonfiction to fiction. When Abel says we shift from metaphor to fact, we must take "fact" as a metaphor.

Abel writes "the fragmented female body," but Draupadi (the heroine of the story) is not literally fragmented but rather mutilated. This figurative use of "fragmented" serves to link the story with Nancy J. Vickers' article on the Petrarchan tradition of fragmentary descriptions of the female body, thus connecting it to what is probably the most traditional criticism in the volume, a study of variations on a classical myth in Renaissance poetry. Petrarch and Ovid can represent the mainstream of our Western tradition, and yet they are recalled in this shift to the East.

The Introduction continues: "'Draupadi' lays bare the physical violence sublimated in metaphors of textual production." The phrase "Draupadi lays bare the physical violence" becomes black humor when we recall that the heroine, after being multiply raped and mutilated, tears up her clothes and refuses to cover her mangled, bleeding body. She literally "lays bare the physical violence," which then reminds us that the Introduction is not using the phrase literally but figuratively. Abel's sentence suggests that metaphor is a "cloth" veiling physical violence and that to expose violence demands that we tear the metaphor, render it inoperative, as Draupadi does her "cloth." Yet in order to speak this violent literalization, the editor has recourse to metaphor.

At the very moment when she would proclaim the shift from metaphor to fact, the feminist critic produces metaphors. I say "the feminist critic" rather than "Abel" because this moment recurs in several of the essays in this collection. Reaching for some nonrhetorical body, some referential body to ground sexual difference outside of writing, the critic produces a rhetorical use of the body as metaphor for the nonrhetorical.

Beginning her article on the lesbian novel, Catharine Stimpson warns that her "definition of the lesbian . . . will be . . . severely literal." The "severely literal" is the domain of the body: "She is a woman who finds other women erotically attractive and gratifying. Of course a lesbian is more than her body, more than her flesh, but lesbianism partakes of the body, partakes of the flesh. . . . Lesbianism represents a commitment of skin, blood, breast, and bone" (p. 244). Undoubtedly a bodily definition, we might well wonder how "literal" it is. The list of bodily components is highly alliterative, and each term has a long history of figurative use. She does not include more shocking, more severely unliterary terms such as kidney or even clitoris. Despite her proclamation of severe literality, her definition remains within a rhetorical tradition for designating the body.

At the moment the feminist critic would separate sexual life from literature and turn to the purely flesh, she willy-nilly produces more literature. This brings us back to the editor's epigraph. Turning to *The Critical Difference* to fill in the ellipsis, we read: "Somehow, however, it is not simply a question of literature's ability to say or not to say the truth of sexuality. For from the moment literature begins to try to set things straight on that score, literature itself becomes inextricable from the sexuality it seeks to comprehend."[4]

The first essay in the collection, Elaine Showalter's overview of feminist criticism, also tangles with the metaphoric body. The section on "Women's Writing and Woman's Body" takes up a "rhetorical question" from Sandra Gilbert and Susan Gubar's *Madwoman in the Attic*: "'If the pen is a metaphorical penis, from what organ can females generate texts?'" (p. 17). At first Showalter gives a dismissive answer: "critics . . . like myself . . . might reply that women generate texts from the brain or that the word-processor of the near future, with its compactly coded microchips, its inputs and outputs, is a metaphorical womb" (p. 17). But the dismissal does not work; the question returns in two nervously jocular parentheses: "(If to write is metaphorically to give birth, from what organ can males generate texts?)"; "(could this [the bladder] be the organ from which females generate texts?)" (pp. 18, 24).

The second of these parentheses occurs right before she discusses Lacanian psychoanalysis. Showalter recognizes that Lacanians use castration as a "total metaphor" for the subject's relation to language, but she also thinks that it refers only to the female subject, assuming that, even as a metaphor, "castration" can only refer to someone literally lacking male organs. This is a theoretical mistake and it is well taken. For as much as orthodox Lacanians protest that the phallus is not the penis, they never succeed in disentangling it from that association.[5] As much as literary paternity is a metaphor, it is also continually taken as a statement about the literal sexual equipment of authors. That the pen is imagined as a metaphorical penis turns out to produce real problems for would-be writers without literal penises.

Stimpson cannot separate the literal from the metaphoric body. Showalter cannot separate the metaphoric body from the literal. These feminist critics can no more turn to the world and leave literature behind than they can turn to literature and leave the world behind. As much as they would like, they cannot separate "writing" from "sexual difference."

Abel suggests that we read literary differences as translations of sexual difference. Translation, like metaphor, is imbued with the difference within, for it is never simply itself but must represent another text and thus includes another within its identity. Perhaps that is the lesson of Spivak's name in the place of the author.

Abel endorses Spivak's contribution to the issue as not only an explicit difference within but an unsettling one: "With this story the volume shifts. . . . Our interpretative strategies should be shaken by Draupadi" (p. 6). In fact there are two outside agitators in "Writing and

Sexual Difference": one explicitly recognized and celebrated as foreign and unsettling, the other quieter and more marginal but likewise disturbing "interpretative strategies." They appear at opposite ends of the volume and might also seem to be at opposite ends of a spectrum. "Draupadi" is literature; the epigraph, not even criticism but rarefied theory. The Bengali story is "explicitly political," not just feminist but third-world revolutionary; Johnson's statements find their context in the most esoteric achievements of first-world thought and would seem to deny feminism and other real-world concerns in favor of a formalistic attachment to literature.

Among other similarities between these two, both are resident aliens, not only differences within, but differences domesticated, translated. In the place of Devi we have Spivak; rather than Derrida we get Johnson. Both Bengali revolutionary fiction and Parisian high theory are mediated through women working in the American academy. The point of encounter with Asian history/fiction or European theory is also its intervention in the American literary academy. The exotic other is translated into a difference within.

Like Johnson, not only does Spivak teach literature in an American university, she also is a translator of Derrida. Her Translator's Foreword comments not only on Bengali language and Indian history but also on the politics of deconstruction. With Spivak this collection ends by bringing together "explicit political perspective" with deconstructive theoretical sophistication; the final move beyond Eurocentric confines also hits the heights of European high cultural production.

"Draupadi" moves "Writing and Sexual Difference" beyond the West but also figuratively back to Petrarch. "Draupadi" gives us "explicit political perspective" and, at the same time, literature, both "fact" and fiction.

The Introduction locates feminist criticism in a balancing act, trying to stave off disapproval on two opposing fronts: "concern with textual conventions dispels one litany of familiar accusations: reductiveness, dogmatism, insensitivity to literary values. . . . Such sophisticated reading . . . may also generate a litany of new accusations: that the concern with textuality augurs a return to formalism; that feminist critics have betrayed political commitments" (p. 2). "Draupadi" magically answers both accusations at once.

Spivak's contribution momentarily produces a happy ending for feminist critical inquiry. But, like most happy endings, it is a fiction. A brilliant stroke manages to silence both "litanies of accusation" at once, but both criticisms still nag the feminist literary critic. If both accusations make us squirm, it is because both feminism and literature can function as authorities for us. And their demands for commitment are more often than not opposed. In allegiance to both feminism and criticism, the feminist critic lives the at once enabling and disabling tension of a difference within.

2
The Problem of Definition

The 1985 anthology entitled *The New Feminist Criticism* never
indicates what it means by the word "new."[1] A footnote to one of the
essays uses the phrase "our current wave of New Feminism."[2] Here
"new" refers to the feminist movement of the mid-twentieth century.
This categorization, very common in histories of feminism, is not, I
believe, what "new" means in the collection's title.

We might take a clue from a roughly contemporaneous piece of
writing by the anthology's editor. In a 1984 essay, subtitled "Writing the
History of Feminist Criticism," Elaine Showalter states: "If in its origins
feminist criticism derived more from feminism than from criticism, we
could argue that today the situation is reversed. Since 1975 a *second
wave* has included many women . . . who have come to feminist
criticism via psychoanalytic, post-structuralist, or deconstructionist theory, rather than via the women's movement and women's studies."[3]
Historians of feminism conventionally use the phrase "second wave"
to indicate the twentieth century, but when Showalter sets out to "write
the history of feminist criticism," "a second wave" refers to the third
quarter of the twentieth century, post- rather than pre-1975. "The new
feminist criticism" is not the criticism produced by the "new feminism"
but a criticism which emerged in the second half of the 1970s. The
earliest article in this anthology was originally published in 1977, while
the vast majority first appeared in 1980 or 1981.

The subtitle of this collection is "Essays on Women, Literature,
and Theory." Of those three terms, printed in large type on the book's
cover, describing the subject matter of this book, two are extremely
predictable: feminist criticism has, by and large, been the attempt to
think the conjunction of "women" and "literature." The third term in
this trio is newer. Janet Todd considers the subtitle "indicative of the
progress in American criticism. Where one might expect 'society,' one
finds 'theory.'"[4] If "women" and "literature" correspond to "feminist
criticism" in the title, "theory" must be lined up with the "new." As
Showalter puts it in the passage just quoted from her history of feminist
criticism, "a second wave has included many women . . . who have

come to feminist criticism via . . . theory, rather than via the women's movement and women's studies." What is new about "the new feminist criticism" is presumably this rise of theory, which includes its usurpation of the place of the women's movement.

The prominent place of theory, given equal billing with women and literature, is what sets this anthology apart. The first page of the book's introduction declares: "While the number of feminist studies of particular writers, genres, and works is now vast, this book, *The New Feminist Criticism*, is the *first collection* of essays in *feminist critical theory*" (p. 3, emphasis added). Bookstores and libraries may be rife with anthologies of feminist literary criticism, but this collection is the first of a new genre: "feminist critical theory."

This declaration of originality poses certain problems. In 1975, Josephine Donovan edited an anthology whose full title is *Feminist Literary Criticism: Explorations in Theory*.[5] On the back cover of that earlier book, we read: "This *collection* is the *first* to deal exclusively with certain theoretical questions being raised about literature by feminists; as such, it establishes a point of departure for further development of *feminist critical theory*" (emphasis added). A decade later, Showalter would seem to repeat Donovan's gesture, thus posing the problem of a second instance of a "first collection." If, in the present reading of *The New Feminist Criticism*, we remember Donovan's book, it is not simply in order to fault Showalter's memory but to ponder why theory may seem new when it is not.

Showalter in fact cites Donovan's collection in both of her own essays in the anthology. The citation in her second essay omits the subtitle of the 1975 anthology, thus leaving out the word "theory."[6] The note to the first essay does list the complete title, but erroneously gives the publication date as 1976.[7] When "theory" does appear in the citation of Donovan's title, the book has been relocated post-1975, reassigned, albeit unwittingly, to the period appropriate for theory.

Showalter's second essay in the volume evokes the year 1975: "*Until very recently*, feminist criticism has not had a theoretical basis; it has been an empirical orphan in the theoretical storm. In 1975, I was persuaded that no theoretical manifesto could adequately account for the varied methodologies and ideologies which called themselves feminist reading or writing" (p. 244, emphasis added). At the moment of this essay, originally published in 1981, the conjoining of theory to women and literature is a "very recent" event. The passage does not actually date the arrival of theory, but these two sentences do give us the coordinates of a before and an after. As recently as 1975, Showalter "was persuaded" that the theorization of feminist criticism was impossible.[8] By the time of this essay's publication in 1981, there already is "a theoretical basis." Between the two dates falls a historical and epistemological discontinuity that irrevocably divides the moment when something is not yet foreseeable from the moment when it has already occurred.

Since over two-thirds of the articles in *The New Feminist Criticism* were originally published in either 1980 or 1981, this moment of the recent theorization of feminist criticism is the time commemorated by the book. The book, of course, actually appears later, when, as the introduction says, it can "represent the coming of age of feminist criticism as a theoretical as well as a practical enterprise" (p. 4), when theory is entitled to be on the cover with women and literature. But the book's time is essentially a moment imbued with the sense that theory is "very recent," some moment just after the arrival of theory which, however chronologically close to 1975, is a quantum leap away.

What in 1975 cannot be envisioned is a way to theoretically "account for" the entirety of feminist criticism in its breadth and diversity. It is not that it was impossible in 1975 to do feminist critical theory, but that any such theory would not have been "adequate," would only have been partial. Lack of a totalizing theory seems to be total lack of theory. What is demanded from theory is something that can adequately cover, otherwise poor feminist criticism is without protection from the "theoretical storm."

Showalter's 1981 essay is entitled "Feminist Criticism in the Wilderness." The sentence preceding the orphan in the storm passage specifies which wilderness: "the wilderness of theory" (p. 243). Theory is a wilderness, theory is a storm: theory is a threatening environment for feminist criticism. Although feminist studies may be empirical, they are not outside theory (as some empiricists would have it), but desperately, vulnerably exposed to it. Better we be pioneers in the wilderness than orphans in the storm: "*all* criticism is in the wilderness. Feminist critics may be startled to find ourselves in this band of theoretical pioneers. . . . Yet . . . we too must make [the wilderness of theory] our home" (p. 243). Theory threatens our comfort and existence, but the defense proposed is to "make it our home," to transform theory from storm to shelter. If theory is to be our wilderness home, we must make sure it is adequate to cover, no holes or gaps to let in the storm. The need for a totalizing theory stems from this essentially defensive, protective scenario.

In the volume's introduction, in the paragraph summarizing her own first essay, the editor writes:

> At that point, feminist criticism seemed to be at an impasse. Attacked by some male critics for its apparent lack of theoretical coherence, it could not seem . . . to find a way of defining its subject that included all the different modes of critical and political commentary that feminism had produced. I suggest that the study of women's writing and female creativity, which I call "gynocritics," offers the most exciting prospect for a coherent feminist literary theory. (p. 12)

The essay she is summarizing—"Toward a Feminist Poetics"—was originally delivered as a lecture in 1978. "At that point," feminist criticism was in big trouble: not only under attack but also "at an impasse"; under fire *and* at a dead end, up against the wall, no exit, no way to flee. In order to defend itself, it needed "a coherent feminist literary theory." Showalter is there to suggest one. "Gynocritics" offers us the "prospect" that soon we will not be so vulnerable. Here perhaps is the account of that moment (between 1975 and 1981) when feminist criticism made the leap from the impossibility of an adequate theory to a passably coherent theory.[9]

Up until 1978, feminist criticism could not "find a way of defining its subject." Now feminist criticism can be defined as "the study of women's writing and female creativity." Such a definition makes possible a coherent theory. As I have tried to show, *the new* feminist criticism would be different from the old not, in fact, by being theoretical but rather by being theoretically coherent. What transforms feminist criticism from orphan to pioneer is this advent of an adequate definition.

The only text in the anthology published later than 1981 bears out this sense that feminist criticism is now defined as the study of women's writing. In an essay originally published in 1983, Lillian Robinson writes that "the very definition of feminist criticism has come increasingly to mean scholarship and criticism devoted to women writers" (p. 108). This definition has allowed the pioneers to stake out a territory of their own, not only finding shelter, but fencing off a "field." According to Robinson, "to the extent that feminist criticism has *defined itself as a subfield* of literary studies—as distinguished from an approach or method—it has tended to concentrate on writing by women" (p. 107). Not only has feminist criticism specifically defined itself as a (sub)field, but perhaps the very gesture of defining (from Latin *definire*, to set bounds to) always implies fencing off a field.

Sharing the sense that defining feminist criticism involves taking women's writing as its object, Robinson points out that, however coherent, this definition is exclusive: "In fact, as the very definition of feminist criticism has come increasingly to mean scholarship and criticism devoted to women writers, work on the male tradition has continued" (p. 108). The "definition" does not include all the feminist criticism that exists "in fact" but rather poses an ideal border that would render feminist criticism coherent provided it did not stray out of bounds.

This dilemma of definition in feminist criticism, the choice between being coherent but exclusive or vague but inclusive, is, I believe, a central question for *The New Feminist Criticism*. And it is most articulately and most seriously explored in the theorizing of what may seem to be but a subfield of a "subfield"—lesbian feminist criticism. Bonnie Zimmerman's contribution to the anthology—"What Has Never Been: An Overview of Lesbian Feminist Literary Criticism"—confronts this dilemma so centrally that it could have been entitled "The Problem of Definition." Zimmerman's article, which dates from 1981, shows us that—at the very moment when mainstream, heterosexual feminist criticism was increasingly fixing its definition—for lesbian criticism, definition grew more explicitly and interestingly problematic.

In her concluding paragraph, Zimmerman writes: "Many of the issues that face lesbian critics . . . are the interests of all feminist critics. . . . [A]ll women would grow by adopting for themselves a lesbian vision. Disenfranchised groups have had to adopt a double vision for survival; one of the political transformations of recent decades has been the realization that enfranchised groups—men, whites, heterosexuals, the middle class—would do well to adopt that double vision for the survival of us all" (p. 219). Ordinarily we assume that the enfranchised have something (enfranchisement) that the disenfranchised lack. In this "transformation," that traditional assumption remains, of course, nonetheless correct; but along with that assumption is a reversal by which we see that the disenfranchised also have something (a perspective, an invaluable knowledge) that the enfranchised lack. Rather than simply complaining about heterosexism and demanding inclusion in the mainstream, Zimmerman inverts our understanding of the distribution of critical wealth and need by suggesting that heterosexual feminists should listen to lesbian critics not just for the sake of the latter but also for the good of the former.

Precisely *because of* their special problems, lesbians have something to offer mainstream feminist criticism. According to Zimmerman, "lesbians are faced with [a] *special problem of definition*" (p. 204, emphasis added). I would contend that all feminist critics would do well to attend to the contours of this supposedly special lesbian problem, and that we would benefit from the lesson of Zimmerman's "double vision" at work as she tackles that problem.

"Lesbians are faced with this special problem of definition . . . we have to determine how inclusively or exclusively we define 'lesbian'" (p. 204). The exclusive definition, in this case, is "women for whom sexual experience with other women can be proven" (p. 204). The inclusive definition follows, for example, Adrienne Rich's wish to "expand [the definition] to embrace many more forms of primary intensity between and among women."[10] Zimmerman feels that the inclusive definition "is of mixed value to those who are developing lesbian criticism and theory and who may need limited and precise definitions" (p. 205). She thus makes explicit the connection between a need for limited definition and the establishment of a theory, that same connection we saw at work in the prospectus for gynocritics. On the other hand, although the exclusive definition would certainly lead to a more clearly demarcated "subfield," to a stronger and more coherent "criticism and theory," Zimmerman remarks that it "can be an overly defensive and suspect strategy" (p. 205).

Rather than choose sides, Zimmerman's "Overview" makes it possible to think through the relation between the two positions. Exclusive definition is not only a "suspect strategy," but a *suspicious* strategy, "overly defensive" as befits a young criticism, orphan in the theoretical wilderness. Zimmerman's "double vision" can appreciate the need for such a strategy, without relinquishing the sense that it is also finally "limited," as definition and as theory.

A theory whose position is essentially defensive cannot afford to wander far afield. Lillian Robinson finds feminist criticism "sticking to its own turf": "[feminist criticism] has been more successful in defining and sticking to its own intellectual turf, the female counter-canon, than in gaining general canonical recognition for [women writers]. *In one sense*, the more coherent our sense of the female tradition is, *the stronger* will be our eventual *case. Yet* the longer we wait, *the more comfortable* the women's literature *ghetto*—separate, apparently autonomous, and far from equal—may begin to feel" (p. 118, emphasis added). "In one sense," coherence and remaining within exclusive definitions are tied to the necessity of making a "case," that is, defending. "Yet," Robinson comes to consider this "an overly defensive and suspect strategy." "In one sense. . . . Yet . . .": exercising "double vision," Robinson is close to Zimmerman in her appreciation of the advantages and drawbacks of an exclusive definition.

Now, of course, Zimmerman is talking about the definition of "lesbian" whereas Robinson is interested in the definition of "feminist criticism." However, with Zimmerman, I would argue that "the issues that face lesbian critics . . . are the interests of all feminist critics" (p. 219). Although discussing feminist criticism in general, at one point Robinson does specifically consider lesbian criticism: "Much lesbian feminist criticism has addressed theoretical questions about *which* literature is actually part of the lesbian tradition, all writing by lesbians, for example, or all writing by women about women's relations with one another" (p. 115). As Robinson construes the lesbian definition issue, the choice is between "writing by lesbians" and "writing by [all] women." In the latter case, although lesbian critics might only consider certain themes in writing by all women, they would nonetheless take the entire body of women's writing as their object. This echoes the question of whether feminist criticism will restrict itself to writing by women or whether it will consider, as it in fact has from the beginning, all writing.

This problem of the boundaries of a field cannot be just a question of choice between a larger all-inclusive field and a smaller exclusive subfield. Were it just a question of choice, each individual critic could choose her field, narrow or broad. Were it just a question of choice, it would not be a "theoretical question"; it would not be a "problem of definition." Zimmerman's lucid analysis illustrates the extent to which this problem cannot be transcended. Analyzing the pitfalls of both sides, she considers the argument not only unavoidable but central to lesbian critical theory. "Nevertheless," she writes after a thorough assessment of the weaknesses of both positions, "lesbian criticism continues to be plagued with the problem of definition" (p. 205).

The irresolvable argument between narrow and broad constructions is a symptom of the impossibility of defining the lesbian corpus: impossible first of all because, in many cases, we literally do not know whether certain women were or are lesbians. This "special problem of definition," presumably, does not plague the mainstream feminist critic who generally knows which writers are women and which are men. I am reminded of Freud's remark: "When you meet a human being; the first distinction you make is 'male or female?' and you are accustomed to make the distinction with unhesitating certainty."[11] Although many people, straight and gay, pride themselves on their ability to guess sexual preference from appearance, that their acumen should be a cause for pride simply demonstrates that the sort of first-glance, "unhesitating certainty" to which Freud refers is nonetheless not generally associated with deciding whether a woman is lesbian or heterosexual.

It is not only that we lack such certainty in specifically identifying lesbians but, beyond that special problem, the lesbian may also be— historically, fantasmatically, or theoretically—a locus where Freud's "first distinction" begins to "hesitate." As Zimmerman points out, "heterosexuals often have difficulty accepting that a lesbian, especially a role-playing 'butch,' is in fact a woman" (p. 203). A lesbian, then: not without hesitation identified as a woman, but still not a man either. In the early years of this century, homosexuals were called "the third sex." And fantasmatically, in our homophobia, a woman may fear that her desires for other women will make her less a woman, will turn her into a man. Now, homophobia is, of course, to be combated; lesbians must, certainly, be recognized as women. But rather than just this movement of inclusion into the mainstream of unhesitating sexual difference, we might benefit from the vision afforded by lesbians' special problems.

According to Zimmerman, "lesbian critics have had to begin with a *special* question: "When is a text a 'lesbian text' or its writer a 'lesbian writer?" Lesbians are faced with this *special* problem of definition: *presumably we know* when a writer is a 'Victorian writer' or a 'Canadian writer.'"[12] Are lesbian critics truly faced with "a special question"? Or are lesbians, precisely inasmuch as they are located at the point where certainty hesitates, forced to articulate questions crucial for us all that the enfranchised may be allowed to overlook?

The notion that lesbian critics have a special question, a special problem, is based upon the presumption ("presumably") that "*we know* when a writer is a 'Victorian writer' or a 'Canadian writer.'" Although no one in this anthology ever takes up the problem of determining the boundaries of those two fields, the volume does include Nina Baym's brilliant analysis of what goes into the definition of the "American writer."

Baym looks at the formation of the American literary canon and discovers that the definition of an American writer is very much a "theoretical question." She finds that the canon is, in fact, created through critical theory, which in the case of the American canon turns out to be theories of what constitutes "Americanness" (pp. 65–66). Critics of American literature, in creating a new "subfield" within the field of English literature, "have had to begin with a special question": What is American?

According to Baym, "the earliest American literary critics began to talk about the 'most American' work rather than the 'best' work because they knew no way to find out the best other than by comparing American with British writing. . . . We had thrown off the political shackles of England; it would not do for us to be servile in our literature" (p. 65). Like the fields of women's or lesbian literature, American literature defines itself in a highly politicized context: America is politically and culturally breaking away from British hegemony. We can certainly sympathize with this rejection of criteria which, although supposedly aesthetic, in fact, simply continue the traditional dominance of British cultural ideology, and we also understand the concomitant need for a coherent definition of Americanness at the moment of establishing a young criticism. Yet the result of this exclusive definition is quite disturbing: "Before he is through, the critic has had to insist that some works in America are much more American than others, and he is as busy excluding certain writers as 'un-American' as he is including others. . . . [I]t is odd indeed to argue that only a handful of American works are really American" (pp. 66–67). Odd indeed. If not all American works are American than we have a problem of definition. At least in this context, we *cannot* "presum[e] we know when a writer is an '[American] writer.'"

Something quite similar to this exclusion can go on in lesbian critical theory. Zimmerman enthusiastically cites various theories of what might constitute a lesbian text but then also warns: "*There is a danger* in this attempt to establish a characteristic lesbian vision or literary value system. . . . In an *attempt to define* a lesbian literature, we are *easily tempted* to read selectively, omitting what is *foreign to our theories*" (p. 214, emphasis added). There is a danger to theory: theory threatens to bring on chauvinism, xenophobia. The urge to resolve the problem of definition tempts us to exclude "foreigners" from the Lesbian Nation.[13]

"Beginning as a nationalistic enterprise," writes Baym, "American literary criticism and theory has retained a nationalistic orientation to this day" (p. 66). Now, of course, it is true that all the disciplines whose object is the study of a national literature are profoundly nationalistic, in origin and principle. For example, considering "the era of the academic establishment of English," Terry Eagleton writes: "What was at stake in English studies was less English *literature* than *English* literature: our great 'national poets' Shakespeare and Milton, the sense of an 'organic' national tradition and identity."[14] But beyond the literal nationalism of the national literatures, it might be that the fencing off of a field of literature always involves glorifying and strengthening the territory in a defensive relation to the outside, keeping out the foreign element. And beyond that, such nationalism, whether now literal or figurative (as in the Lesbian Nation), involves a theoretical definition of the "national" character which not only excludes foreigners but searches to purify the interior by expelling the alien within: "excluding certain writers as 'un-American,'" "omitting what is foreign to our theories." "Odd indeed," yet a structure that is very tempting whenever one is establishing a canon and/or theorizing a nascent field.

Baym's explicit "concern is with the fact that the theories control-ling our reading of American literature have led to the exclusion of women authors from the canon" (p. 63). Her essay is, in fact, a good example of that feminist criticism which ventures beyond the bound-aries of the subfield in order to examine the male tradition. Yet the similarities between the exclusive definition of the American writer and the theoretically coherent definition of the lesbian writer suggest that Baym's reading might also prove useful *within the bounds* of the sub-field theoretically under construction by "the new feminist criticism."

Nancy Miller suggests, by way of T. S. Eliot and Elizabeth Janeway, that we construct a women's literature on the model of American literature.[15] We saw with Baym that American literature, precisely inas-much as it must, for political reasons, be independent from British literature, needed to generate a theoretically coherent notion of Ameri-canness. Following this model, women's literature would not be merely the conglomerate of writing by women but, in the process of mapping its field and constructing the canon, would generate a theory of femininity.

Although all the essays in *The New Feminist Criticism* are theoreti-cal, the word "theory" only appears in the title of the third and last section: "Women's Writing and Feminist Critical Theories." "Feminist critical theory" would seem, in this book, to mean theories about women's writing. Part III of the anthology is headed off by the editor's "Feminist Criticism in the Wilderness" which has a section entitled

"Defining the Feminine" that begins: "In the past decade, I believe, this process of defining the feminine has started to take place" (p. 248).

We cannot simply have an empirical sense of women's writing (writing by those who biographically happen to be women); we must have a theory of what constitutes women's writing. And so, the subfield of gynocritics is involved precisely in defining the feminine. Critical theory here functions as Baym has taught us to see it in the constitution of American literature.

Baym complains that the notions of Americanness which shape the canon of American literature exclude those who are not white, middle-class, of Anglo-Saxon derivation, and male. Deborah McDowell points out that "early theorists and practitioners of feminist literary criticism . . . *perpetrated* against the Black woman writer *the same exclusive practices* they so vehemently decried in white male scholars. Seeing the experiences of . . . white middle-class women as normative, white female scholars proceeded *blindly to exclude* the work of Black women writers from literary anthologies and critical studies" (p. 186, emphasis added). In this second example, what is once again at stake is a canon, this time the female (counter)canon, which—like any canon according to Baym's persuasive argument—is based in theory. In this case, an implicit definition of femininity (what McDowell refers to as "normative experience") is leaving out (in the storm) some who might empirically belong to the category (of women).

In the highly moralized context of feminist criticism, it is devastating to discover that white feminists "perpetrated" the same sort of exclusions as the male critics against whom we were protesting. Yet, following the logic of Zimmerman's investigation of the problem of definition for lesbian critics, we might want to consider this perpetration of exclusion not so much as an ethical failing but rather as the effect of a certain structure, the recurrent tendency in the establishment of a subfield to generate exclusionary definitions.

McDowell's article, "New Directions for Black Feminist Criticism," immediately precedes Zimmerman's in the collection. Centrally concerned with problems of definition, she also has occasion specifically to consider the definition of the lesbian. Her essay, originally published in 1980, is in part a response to Barbara Smith's 1977 "Toward a Black Feminist Criticism," which immediately precedes it in this anthology. Smith presents the following definition: "if in a woman writer's work a sentence refuses to do what it is supposed to do, if there are strong images of women and if there is a refusal to be linear, the result is innately lesbian literature."[16] McDowell comments: "This definition of lesbianism . . . subsumes far more Black women writers . . . than not into the canon of Lesbian writers. . . . Further, if we apply Smith's definition of lesbianism, there are probably a few Black male writers who qualify as well" (p. 190). Smith's theorizing of "national character" is faulted not for excluding some people, but for including too many. Like Zimmerman's, McDowell's contribution reminds us that there are two, seemingly opposed, problems of definition: not only over-exclusion but also over-inclusion.

Although Baym is primarily concerned with *ex*clusionary notions of Americanness, her account ends with a surprising twist in the direction of all-*in*clusiveness: "Ironically . . . in pushing the theory of American fiction to this extreme, critics have 'deconstructed' it by creating a tool with no particular American reference. In pursuit of the uniquely American, they have arrived at a place where Americanness has vanished into the depths of what is alleged to be the universal male psyche" (p. 79).

Baym found exclusionary definitions functioning in "the earliest American literary critics" (p. 65). But by the end of her essay, when she uncovers the ironic twist into the all-inclusive, she is considering contemporary critics (Harold Bloom and Edward Said). If exclusion seems necessary at the moment of establishing the new field of American literature, by the time of Bloom and Said, American literature is sufficiently strong for those critics to have little or no interest in its boundaries in one way or another. It is time that may be at stake here: different moments in the political history of a criticism.

Zimmerman suggests that a *"developing* lesbian criticism and theory may need limited and precise definitions" (p. 205, emphasis added). Definitions do not function in the abstract; they find their place in history. A "developing" criticism, a young theory, a new field, needs and generates precise, rigid, limited definitions. A young criticism is vulnerable, needs shelter and boundaries for survival and defense.

Robinson, too, ties definition to a temporal scheme. Earlier, considering spatial questions, we read in her essay that feminist criticism "has been more successful in defining and sticking to its own intellectual turf, the female counter-canon, than in gaining general canonical recognition for [women writers]. In one sense, the more coherent our sense of the female tradition is, the stronger will be our eventual case. Yet the longer we wait, the more comfortable the women's literature ghetto . . . may begin to feel" (p.118). "The stronger *will be* our *eventual* case": for Robinson, the act of definition is merely prefatory. This preparatory stage of exclusive and coherent definition is necessary because we are still weak, because we must become "stronger." Yet the movement from exclusion (the ghetto) to inclusion is not the inevitable course of history. In her scenario, time could defeat us. An early moment of constructing fences and remaining within bounds is necessary, yes, but we must beware lest that early moment quickly become too late. "The longer we wait, the more comfortable the ghetto may begin to feel."[17]

Like Zimmerman, Robinson recognizes that a developing criticism needs limited definitions. In her account, however, there is a serious threat to development if the exclusive phase lasts too long. In order to be secure enough to grow, a young criticism needs firm limits, but if sheltered too long, it will stultify and never reach maturity. The problem all too quickly becomes how do we know when it is no longer early but already too late.

One cannot simply decide between exclusive and inclusive definitions because, as Zimmerman and McDowell make clear, there are serious drawbacks to either choice. Following our temporal schemes, it does seem that one could at least say that an exclusive definition is necessary to a *new* criticism. Although that promises to make our choice easier, at least for a while, we are still left with the problem of knowing when a new criticism is no longer so new, when it is old enough to be stifled by its sheltering definitions. How soon after the definition is adequate to cover does the growing young criticism begin to suffocate under that very cover?

With this question in mind, let us return to the historiography of feminist criticism. In 1981, the date of Showalter's "Feminist Criticism in the Wilderness," the arrival of theory, the definition of feminist criticism is "very recent." The new feminist criticism is still new. Robinson's essay, published in 1983, is the only post-1981 essay in the book. Has this brief two year interval been sufficient for the women's literature ghetto to begin to feel too comfortable?

Robinson specifically says "the more comfortable the women's literature ghetto *may begin* to feel." Robinson is just starting to envision a later moment when gynocritics may become a gilded cage. We are dealing here, nonetheless, with an extremely accelerated time frame. In 1975, it was impossible to imagine an adequate theoretical definition of feminist criticism. In 1981, Showalter is celebrating the recent arrival of such a definition. By 1983, Robinson sees that definition as firmly installed and threatening to begin to stifle feminist criticism. If 1980–81 is, as I said, the real moment of Showalter's anthology, then the inclusion of this single post-1981 text threatens to undo the triumph of that moment, by beginning to point to the process by which the new feminist criticism could rapidly become old.

In the anthology, two Black feminist critics accuse feminist criticism of operating under too exclusive a definition. Following Robinson, one could also complain that the coherent definition of feminist criticism as gynocritics excludes those feminists working on the male tradition. But if we imagine Women's Literature along the model of American Literature, then Baym's essay should lead us to expect that at some point in the future the dangers of over-exclusion will give way to the threat of over-inclusion. If, in its beginnings, feminist criticism needs the well-defined borders of gynocritics to survive and prosper, there could come a time when Women's Literature is so well-recognized a territory that it would include anyone writing about women authors and their texts, whatever the critic's position. At that point gynocritics would no longer be restrictively narrower than feminist criticism but would extend far beyond its bounds and in its all-inclusiveness might threaten to render feminist criticism a meaningless category.

In 1983, Robinson can just barely imagine a future when Women's Literature *might begin* to be too comfortable. And, as I write this in 1986, that moment has still not yet come. Women's Literature certainly does not go without saying as American Literature does. But the lesson to be learned from Baym's account of the history of American literary theory is that *the very same theoretical position* can swerve from defensively exclusive to vague and over-inclusive.

There are serious difficulties to assuming either an exclusive or an inclusive definition. But perhaps the greatest danger in these definitions of national character is the way they can swerve from too exclusive to too inclusive, thus affording us, in turn, the disadvantages of both positions. All these problems of definition are perhaps best outlined in Zimmerman's account of the debate in lesbian critical theory over the definition of the term "lesbian." But Zimmerman may also be offering us a way out of this dilemma precisely by her refusal to choose either position. Along with her acute analysis of the difficulties of either, she continues to emphasize the necessity for both. This is a terrific example, I believe, of what she calls "double vision."[18]

Showalter has her own version of "double vision." In the conclusion of "Feminist Criticism in the Wilderness" we read: "If a man's text . . . is fathered, then a woman's text is not only mothered but parented; it . . . *must deal with* the problems and advantages of *both* lines of inheritance. . . . [O]nly male writers can forget or mute half of their parentage" (p. 265, emphasis added). Their enfranchisement affords men the luxury of forgetting half of what is double, thus rendering their vision single and their self-definition homogeneous, coherent, and strong. Women "must deal with both." Their disenfranchisement compels them to double vision. The enfranchised thus have the mixed privilege of not wholly knowing who they are and where they come from. For the woman writer, as for the lesbian, double vision poses special problems, but that someone is forced to see double may also prove to be an advantage, as Zimmerman puts it, "for the survival of us all" (p. 219).

"Women's writing," according to Showalter, "is a 'double-voiced discourse' that always embodies the . . . heritages of both the muted and the dominant."[19] "Writing the history of feminist criticism," during the same period she is putting together her anthology, Showalter explicitly brings the "double-voiced discourse" home: "Insofar as feminist criticism is a kind of women's writing, it is a double-voiced discourse that is influenced by both the muted and dominant cultures."[20] Showalter's own critical writing, for example, must itself "deal with the problems and advantages" of more than one voice.

All the sections of her landmark 1981 essay, "Feminist Criticism in the Wilderness," are headed by a single quotation with the sole exception of the second section which begins with two. Such use of quotations is normally the most domesticated sort of polyphony, the other voice serving only as an authorizing chorus, echoing and deepening the author's voice. But in this case the different voices do not exactly harmonize. Here the double-(or triple-)voiced discourse of the feminist critic poses a special problem.

The first epigraph is from Virginia Woolf: "A woman's writing is always feminine; it cannot help being feminine; at its best it is most feminine; the only difficulty lies in defining what we mean by feminine" (p. 247). Woolf has no difficulty characterizing women's writing, but that only leads us to a second definition which does present a problem. Woolf's words posted at the entry to this section entitled "Defining the Feminine" warn us that progress within will be "difficult."

The second quotation comes from Hélène Cixous: "It is impossible to define a feminine practice of writing, and this is an impossibility that will remain, for this practice will never be theorized, enclosed, encoded—which doesn't mean that it doesn't exist" (pp. 247–48). Not merely difficult, definition here is impossible, and not just momentarily: "this is an impossibility that will remain." Cixous's position, or at least her rhetoric, would seem to be more extreme than Woolf's. However, when Woolf's sentence is coupled with Cixous's, we can envision the possibility that Woolf is exercising characteristically British understatement so that when she writes "the only difficulty lies in defining what we mean by feminine," it is not out of the question that this sole difficulty might in fact pose an insuperable stumbling block in the way of defining women's writing.

Showalter, in fact, does read the two quotations together as saying essentially the same thing. But rather than read Woolf's "difficulty" as an understatement meaning impossibility, she reads Cixous's "impossibility" as a—perhaps characteristically French—hyperbole meaning "difficulty." And so, summing up toward the end of the section, she remarks: "Defining the unique difference of women's writing, as Woolf and Cixous have warned, must present a slippery and demanding task" (p. 249). "Slippery and demanding" might be satisfactory as a gloss of Woolf's "difficulty," but they inject a hint of positivity where Cixous sees only radical "impossibility." If we are cautious enough and clever enough, if we work long and hard enough, we might succeed in defining women's writing.

Cixous links definition to theorizing and enclosing. Let us recall how Showalter's definition would shelter us from the stormy wilderness. For Cixous, enclosure is contrary to "practice" and "existence" rather than protective of them. Definition, here, is an oppressive theoretical force that tames and restricts the wild energy of feminine practice, once again theorizing to confine women. For Cixous, the impossibility of definition is not a problem but an advantage.

Cixous's extreme distrust of definition cannot help but subvert the statement that immediately succeeds it in Showalter's text. After the epigraphs Showalter opens the section with this sentence: "In the past decade, I believe, this process of defining the feminine has started to take place" (p. 248). "*This* process"? The one just referred to? The process Cixous, and perhaps Woolf too, make so unattractive? Why does Showalter include this voice which mocks her own?

The quotation from Woolf might have been tamed and integrated into an echo of Showalter's discourse. Why then, in this sole exceptional instance, add a second epigraph? Showalter is American; Woolf

British; Cixous French. Is the double epigraph a gesturing beyond national and even linguistic boundaries?

In this same section of her essay, Showalter gives a rapid biblio-graphical history of American feminist criticism, tracing the progress "from androcentrism to gynocentrism," then writes: "This shift in em-phasis has also taken place in European feminist criticism" (p. 248). That sentence introduces a paragraph on French feminist critical dis-course. Finally, there is one sentence on English feminist criticism and then the following summation: "The emphasis in each country falls somewhat differently: English feminist criticism, essentially Marxist, stresses oppression; French feminist criticism, essentially psychoana-lytic, stresses repression; American feminist criticism, essentially tex-tual, stresses expression. All, however, have become gynocentric" (p. 249).

Although Marxist, psychoanalytic, and textual criticism can be widely disparate methodologies, the wonderful rhetorical find of "op-pression, repression, expression" transforms large conceptual differ-ences into near sameness through the insistent repetition of the signi-fier. All feminist criticism, whatever its differences, is gynocentric, that is, falls within the bounds of gynocritics, within her exclusive definition of feminist criticism.

It is right after this round-up of the feminist criticism of three countries that we find the sentence already quoted which states that Woolf and Cixous warn that defining women's writing is "a slippery and demanding task." This is the only mention of either Woolf or Cixous in this section headed by their epigraphs. If they appear here it is because, having given time to national differences, Showalter has worked her way to an international consensus. Or rather she would like it to be a consensus. But, as we saw, the French critic, in particular, seems to be contradicting the American critic's assertions.

Earlier, with the help of Baym and Zimmerman, I tried to show how there is an at least figurative nationalism at work in any definitional fencing off of literary territory. Showalter proposes an exclusive defini-tion of feminist criticism, but she would like that definition not to be exclusive, and so she rhetorically suggests it to be internationally all-inclusive. Ironically, it turns out that her token gesture beyond national bounds actually does take us outside the well-defended territory of her definition. Wishing to include the French critic, she ends up including a second voice which is destroying the walls of her definition while she is in the very process of constructing them.

The feminist critic thus publishes a *truly* double-voiced discourse and its irredeemable doubleness prevents any simple resolution to the problem of definition. On the one hand, a theoretical definition of feminist criticism is necessary for its survival; on the other, that very same definition threatens to stifle feminist critical practice. The two voices, separately, assert the two sides of the question, together affording us the double vision necessary "for the survival of us all."

"Lesbian criticism," writes Zimmerman, "continues to be plagued with the problem of definition" (p. 205). There was a time, there still is a time in many a place, when lesbianism itself was/is considered a plague, a disease, an affliction. Yet in the new wave of feminism which arose in the second half of the twentieth century, lesbianism came to be considered a particularly liberated position, in the vanguard of existential challenges to established definitions of womanhood. If lesbian critics see themselves as afflicted with a new "plague," a special handicap of definition, perhaps in the new wave of feminist criticism we must once again transvaluatively see this lesbian plague too as a particularly enviable vanguard position, setting an example for all feminist critics who must juggle two opposing demands: both the need for the security of a well-built shelter *and* the desire for the exhilaration of intellectual adventure.

II

SIDETRACKS

3
"French Feminism"

In the second half of the 1970s, academic literary critics in the United States began to talk about something called "French feminism." Like many other countries, France had witnessed a surge of feminist consciousness and activity in the late 1960s and early 1970s. The phrase "French feminism" referred, however, to only a narrow sector of feminist activity in France, a sector we perceived as peculiarly French. "French feminism" is a body of thought and writing by some women in France which is named and thus *constituted* as a movement *here* in the American academy. Its most effective context may thus be American literary studies where it became a force to be reckoned with by most critics, feminist and non-feminist alike. Accounts of feminist criticism published in the mid-1980s give ample time to "French feminism."[1] Thus it seemed necessary to take this brief *détour* outside of American feminist literary criticism.

The 1980 publication of the anthology *New French Feminisms* in effect represented and canonized the phenomenon. Elaine Marks and Isabelle de Courtivron's collection of translations of texts from the 1970s culminates in Keith Cohen and Paula Cohen's translation of Hélène Cixous's "Le rire de la méduse." Not only is Cixous's "Laugh" last, it is also the longest piece in the collection, the only text near its length left unabridged, even though this same translation had already been published in the most widely read American academic feminist journal. If "French feminism" is a movement constituted in the transmission of certain French women's writing into America, its central text is the Cohens' translation, first published in 1976 in *Signs*.[2]

By 1981 Elaine Showalter feels the need to incorporate "French feminism" into her overview of feminist literary criticism. Her 1978 text, "Toward a Feminist Poetics," made no mention of feminist work in France. By 1981, four of the six epigraphs in Showalter's "Feminist Criticism in the Wilderness" are from French writers. In our last chapter we considered the disturbance caused when Showalter on one occasion doubled her epigraph, adding Cixous's words after Woolf's. That is not the only way in which Cixous's "Laugh" is excessive in Showalter's

"Wilderness." Although no other author rates more than one, there are two epigraphs among the six total from that same essay by Cixous. If any text represents the "French feminism" with which Showalter would contend, it most insistently is "The Laugh of the Medusa."

As organized by Showalter, feminist criticism was tending more and more toward the topic of "women's writing." In its American context, "French feminism" is also called *écriture féminine*, a phrase which generally remains untranslated, but which functions as a rather loose cognate of "women's writing." More than any other text, "The Laugh of the Medusa" defines *écriture féminine*. It also asserts that "it is impossible to *define* a feminine practice of writing" (p. 253): *define* here connotes limitation and containment. Cixous's woman writes from her "libidinal economy," an economy of abundance that overflows the tight, patrolled boundaries of masculine thrift. Man's libido is phallocentric; woman's libido has another economy: her various bodily drives are not dominated by any one center. Cixous imagines the revolution in thought and living that will be produced by a writing that carries such prodigious female sexuality: bodily, multiple, and insubordinate. This *écriture féminine* is more an ideal than a description of how women have written; Cixous can name only two women who have achieved this truly feminine writing.

In the mid-1970s a number of French women's texts explored this analogy between female sexuality and writing.[3] These women were all responding to the concept of *écriture* afloat in male French literary theory at the time. In the late 1960s and early 1970s theorists like Roland Barthes and Jacques Derrida were promoting a notion of *écriture* as something insubordinate to "logocentric" discourse, discourse in the service of a governing idea. The politics of *écriture féminine* involved wresting *écriture* away from this high male avant-garde and claiming it for the common woman. For example, Irigaray writes: "Her sexuality . . . is *plural*. Is this the way culture is seeking to characterize itself now?" (*This Sex*, p. 28). The great male literary movements of modernity are trying to get where women already are. Rather than bang at the gates of high literary culture, a token woman let in now and then, *écriture féminine* would make women the insiders, construe male high culture as the parvenu.

When it reached these shores, what got called "French feminism" was what seemed strikingly different from the feminism which arose in the United States in the late sixties and early seventies. That feminism,

"American feminism" was in fact centrally influenced by a French writer, Simone de Beauvoir. Thus when Americans began to talk about the difference between "French and American feminism," we were also talking about the difference, say, between Cixous and Beauvoir.

Yet if we leave the American context of "French feminism" and follow its exemplary text back to its original 1975 French publication, we find Cixous's Medusa in the middle of an issue of the Parisian intellectual journal *L'Arc* devoted to Simone de Beauvoir.[4]

"It has often been claimed that the new generation of French feminist theorists have rejected Simone de Beauvoir's . . . feminism entirely. . . . The picture, however, is somewhat more complex than this. . . . Simone de Beauvoir remains the great mother-figure for French feminists, and the symbolic value of her public support for the new women's movement was enormous."[5]

In the mid-1970s, in response to the burgeoning of feminist consciousness, a large number of French intellectual journals published special women's issues. The women's issue of *L'Arc* had to contend with the quarterly's format. Though a journal of ideas, not personalities, *L'Arc* organizes the presentation of those ideas around or through what the editors of the sixty-first issue, Catherine Clément and Bernard Pingaud, call "figures, names, 'great' names" (p. 1). Each issue is devoted to a cultural hero, artist or intellectual; so the 1975 issue on feminism is inscribed under the name Simone de Beauvoir.

Following a list of some fifty men, Beauvoir is the first woman to rate an issue of *L'Arc*. Yet entering a woman's name in the roster of great men entails a contradiction, foregrounded by the issue's editors: "Now never, in the history of the journal, will the choice have been more appropriate [*juste*]; but also never will it have been more questionable in its very principle" (p. 1). It is only "just" finally to include women in history, but this inclusion ends up challenging the very principles behind this sort of history. The feminist issue of *L'Arc* raises two general questions: What does it mean for a woman to become a "name"? And what does it mean to organize the history of ideas around such names?

The editors center Beauvoir's contradictory status on the "name": "for Simone de Beauvoir is a historic name, but today in this issue, her choice . . . is to be . . . a woman among others, nameless [*anonyme*]" (p. 1). Beauvoir is represented in *L'Arc* 61 by two texts, both conversations. In the first she "interrogates" Jean-Paul Sartre about feminism: throughout he is known only as "Sartre," she as "Simone de Beauvoir."

In the second conversation she discusses feminism with four women who choose to identify themselves by first name only, with what in French is called not a name but a *prénom*, a "prename." Unlike the other women, Beauvoir is identified throughout this discussion as "S. de Beauvoir." In contrast to Sartre, she has a *prénom*; in contrast to the women, she has a name. She belongs both with the man who *is* a name (her boyfriend who already had his issue of *L'Arc*) and with the women who choose to remain prename, and not quite with either.

Beauvoir's two interviews are placed together at the beginning of the journal, separated by one short essay, Catherine Clément's "Enclave esclave."[6] By thus positioning her own writing, the woman of the two editors places herself within Beauvoir's dilemma. Clément recounts an experience as a podium speaker: in the audience, passion "circulates anonymously [*anonyme*] from woman to woman. At the podium, one is necessarily in a contrary position: nonymous [*nonyme*], called to the podium because of one's name. . . . '*Bravo, sir.*' A woman, among others, sends forth this salutation from the balcony" (pp. 132–35). At the podium, Clément is cut off from what circulates "from woman to woman." From the perspective of "a woman, among others," the nonymous woman is on the opposite side, on the side of the men. Like Beauvoir, Clément appears in *L'Arc* as the only woman in a list of men: in her case, the editorial board on the masthead.

L'Arc 61 begins: "The position taken [*parti pris*] by this journal has been, for a long time, to choose figures, names, 'great' names: those names [*noms*, nouns] that are called proper" (p. 1). "Le rire de la méduse" has something to say about the name and the "proper": "if, by means of laws, lies, blackmail, and marriage . . . her name has been extorted . . . she has been able . . . to see more closely the inanity of the 'proper'" (pp. 258–59, translation modified). The word *propre* (proper) set off in quotes has a sense of propriety (the sexual insubordination of "Laugh"), a sense of property (the attack on masculine thrift), and, in resonance with patriarchal "extortion" of woman's name, a sense of *nom propre*, the proper noun. If *L'Arc* has, "for a long time," taken its stand on the *nom propre*, within the covers of this 1975 issue, "Medusa" is laughing at precisely what the journal takes very seriously.

As name that would be nameless, with the man and with the women, Beauvoir assumes a double position in *L'Arc*. Clément is likewise doubly represented in the issue: as editor with a man in the introduction, and in her own article as one woman among women writing. "The token woman . . . is an ambiguous creature," says Sartre in *L'Arc* 61 (p. 11).

The woman chosen to join the ranks of men disproves the exclusion of women, "so that it may appear that any truly qualified woman can gain access to leadership, recognition, and reward; hence that justice based on merits actually prevails."[7] "The . . . center welcomes selective inhabitants of the margin in order better to exclude the margin."[8] But the "token woman" is not only coopted, she is double, "ambiguous," she is also there as a token of, a marker for, all the women excluded. A year earlier, in the women's issue of *Les Temps Modernes*, Beauvoir recognized that she had "more or less played the role of the token woman."[9] In her issue of *L'Arc* she undoubtedly plays that role, but this time she wants to play it knowingly, assuming her place in high male culture as token, and thus reminder, of the nameless women.

The token woman is not the only woman Sartre terms "ambiguous." He finds a similar doubleness in the bourgeois wife's relation to her cleaning woman: as women they share confidences and a certain female complicity, but through her relation to her husband the affluent woman has authority over the other woman. Whether through entry into marriage or into the boardroom, into the ruling class or into history, a woman's access to name and power puts her in an ambiguous position, unless she denies her connection to other women.

There is a third ambiguous creature in *L'Arc* 61, this one not particularly a woman. According to the editors, the "names, 'great' names: those names that are called proper . . . are most often . . . in an ambiguous position: innovators, but already recognized enough to be the stake of a special issue" (p. 1). It might seem to be originality that makes a thinker historic, but it also must be the widespread influence of his thought. If the thought were literally "proper" to him, belonging to him alone, it would have no effect. If he is a historic thinker, then his work must be widely shared. The great names in the history of ideas are also tokens, markers of all the nameless who shared their ideas, both those influenced by and those influencing the "name."

If Beauvoir is a "historic name" it is because *The Second Sex* nourished the international feminist movement of the second half of the twentieth century. It had this broad effect because masses of women reading that book recognized their own knowledge there. Had her knowledge been truly singular, she would not have become a "name."

The first woman chosen to be a "name" by *L'Arc* makes a difference.

The nonymous woman insists on keeping her connection to the name-less women who have entitled her. Chosen in keeping with the journal's format, Beauvoir ends up calling that format into question. Breaking with its usual practice of the lone name, the sixty-first issue of *L'Arc* has in fact a double title: "Simone de Beauvoir and the Women's Struggle."

Virginia Woolf had a similar view of the token status of great works: "Masterpieces . . . are the outcome of many years of thinking in common, of thinking by the body of the people, so that the experience of the mass is behind the single voice."[10] When Beauvoir shares her title with "the Women's Struggle," she is using her position to give authorial recognition to "the mass behind" her voice.

According to Adrienne Rich, "the token woman is encouraged to see herself as different from most other women, as exceptionally tal-ented and deserving; and to separate herself from the wider female condition; and she is perceived by 'ordinary' women as separate also: even as stronger than themselves" ("Privilege," p. 43). Beauvoir strug-gles against that exceptionality by using her status to betoken other women.

Woolf, Rich, Beauvoir, and Cixous, all women successful and recognized in the realm of high literary culture. All "names" grappling with the token status of the woman of genius, great writer. All attempted to contravene the encouragement and the rewards for separation "from the wider female condition."

We associate *écriture féminine* with the body, but we do not often associate it with what Woolf calls "the body of the people," with "the body of women." Yet the strategy of *écriture féminine* was in fact to claim high vanguard culture (postmodern *écriture*) for the ordinary woman, to associate it with what in women was most "common," the body. Rather than vying for token status, trying to be recognized as good as men (and thus "different from most other women"), "French feminism" claimed that Everywoman already could produce the high culturally privileged writing.

Here in America, we associate "French feminism" not with the body of women, but in fact frequently with a "body" that seemed to separate the French feminists from other women. We worried about clitorises and vaginas; they went on about their lips.[11] We struggled with orgasms; they had that ineffable, untranslatable *jouissance*.[12] We groped for our "sexuality"; they had "libidinal economies."

As "French feminism" installed itself in the American literary academy, it arrived as a short list of names—Cixous, Irigaray, Kristeva[13]—separated off from any larger body or movement or struggle of women. Separated off, they quickly began to function as token feminists par excellence, in the American literary academy.

By 1981 or so, French-style literary theory had become the most prestigious, the "highest" discourse in American literary studies. That is "the wilderness of theory" where Elaine Showalter locates us in 1981.[14] And that is why the American feminist critic had to contend with "French feminism," had to pay disproportionate attention to three or four women writing in the mid-1970s in Paris. Literary theory seminars in American universities which had never included any women much less feminist authors suddenly were reading Kristeva or Irigaray or Cixous.

In the American literary academy "French feminism" became the token feminism: "in order better to exclude" the body of feminist critics. Those of us American feminist academics who were clever enough or lucky enough to be associated with "French feminism" were rewarded and accepted as literary theorists: "encouraged to see [ourselves] as different from most other [feminist critics], as exceptionally talented and deserving; and to separate [ourselves] from the wider [feminist] condition." If I use the first person plural here, it is precisely and pointedly to interrogate the career that goes by the name Jane Gallop.

4

The Monster in the Mirror

In 1981, *Yale French Studies*, at the time the most prestigious American journal of French, published its first and, to date, only feminist issue. The volume successfully combines engaged feminist analysis with sophisticated literary and psychoanalytic theory. But the first sentence disturbs me.

YFS 62 (as I will henceforth refer to it) opens thus: "This is a very unusual issue of *Yale French Studies*, in that its guest editor is a seven-headed monster from Dartmouth."[1] The notion is quite funny: nonhuman it might be, but nonetheless Ivy League.

Seven Dartmouth faculty women edit YFS 62. The monster is a figure for the seven individuals working together as one body. Appearing in the Introduction signed by the editors, the image is a self-portrait and is followed by a glowing description of their collaboration. The editors are saying: we are horrifying, we are inhumanly ugly. This is an ironic way of saying: we are "very unusual," we are extraordinary, we are beautiful.

The image of the monster thinly disguises a monstrous narcissism. This reader, for one, recoils from such unseemly self-congratulation. The irony of this irony is that when the editors say they are ugly to mean they are beautiful, they become ugly.

But let us consider this vivid image as something more interesting than an infelicity of taste, as something even more interesting than a witty example of speakers betrayed by their own rhetoric. We will read this as a symptom, in the psychoanalytic sense, by assuming, as Freud does in *The Psychopathology of Everyday Life*, that in every infelicity of language something is quite successfully getting said. In other words, I would like here to check my impulse to recoil and rather try to understand this monster, perhaps at the risk of encountering my own horror.

The monster represents the collectivity, a new kind of being in which seven individuals are neither totally merged nor totally separate. The first section of the introduction describes how, despite the "skepticism" and "amazement" of their "male colleagues," collaboration was a totally positive experience— "productive," "rigorous," "audacious" (p. 3). Others warned them of inefficiency or reductive thinking but, as it turned out, there was nothing to fear.

The praise of collectivity ends thus: "We have not, of course, abandoned our 'individual' research; but we have found it enriched by the reverberations between the two styles of work" (p. 3). The word "individual" in this sentence is placed in quotation marks; "individual" research does not quite exist. The anguish a scholar feels about those writing on the same topic, or what Harold Bloom calls the "anxiety of influence," for example, bespeak the suspicion that individual work is at least irremediably uncertain if not downright impossible. The we who speaks for the collectivity recognizes that all research is in conversation with other research, so the boundaries which separate one individual's contribution from another can never be absolutely clear. This monster knows that.

But, if ultimately illusory, something called "'individual' research" nonetheless exists. And the purport of the sentence is not just to call individuality into question through its quotation marks, but to alert us to the deeper connections, the "reverberations" between individual and collective work.

Only one of the seven members of the collective, Marianne Hirsch, published an article in YFS 62. In her article, we find the word "monstrous":

> To study the relationship between mother and daughter is not to study the relationship between two separate differentiated individuals, but to plunge into a network of complex ties, to attempt to untangle the strands of a double self, a continuous multiple being of *monstrous* proportions stretched across generations, parts of which try desperately to separate and delineate their own boundaries.[2]

"Monstrous" here refers to a "continuous multiple being," which is to say that *this* monster *too* represents a being whose multiple parts are neither totally merged nor totally separate. There are many different forms of monstrosity, but the same type figures in both the Editors' Introduction and Hirsch's text: a conglomerate being where boundaries between individuals are inadequately differentiated.

Hirsch's "monstrous" specifically refers to the mother and daughter who are not "two separate individuals" but a "double self." This notion of the lack of separation between mother and daughter derives from feminist psychoanalytic theory. Particularly important is the work of Nancy Chodorow who—drawing on the English school of psycho-analysis called object relations theory—has posited that the female self is less individuated than the male self since, although both are formed in relation to the mother, the male self can use sexual difference to institute and insure differentiation.[3]

Whereas, in the Introduction, the monster is the sole hint of something frightening, in Hirsch's article the connotations of "monstrous" are amplified by the phrase: "parts of which try *desperately* to separate and delineate their own boundaries." Does the individual's text voice the need for individuation which the collective we suppresses in order to pronounce itself?

The adverb "desperately" also appears in Hirsch's description of a book by French feminist psychoanalyst Luce Irigaray: "In *Et l'une ne bouge pas sans l'autre*, a lyrical and personal address to her mother . . . Irigaray pleads for distance and separation, laments the paralysis she feels as a result of the interpenetration between mother and daughter, calls *desperately* for a new kind of closeness possible only between two separate individuals."[4] Although Chodorow has made the most extensive theoretical contribution to the study of the mother-daughter bond, Irigaray's little lyrical text, explicitly speaking from the daughter's position, most effectively conveys the desperation of the daughter's situation.

The American translation of *Et l'une ne bouge pas sans l'autre* appears in a 1981 issue of *Signs* which also contains a review article on "Mothers and Daughters" by Marianne Hirsch. Discussing *Et l'une. . .*, Hirsch here uses the same adverb: "desperately trying to untangle herself from within her mother and her mother from within herself."[5] This review article begins and ends with Adrienne Rich and finds in Rich's 1976 *Of Woman Born* the matrix of feminist work on mothers and daughters: "Rich's chapter on 'Motherhood and Daughterhood' contains, in fact, the germs of many of the other studies I shall mention in this essay" (p. 202). Rich's chapter is the mother text, "contains the germs of" the theoretical work which Hirsch applies in her contribution to YFS 62. It also contains the adjective "desperate": "Our personalities seem dangerously to blur and overlap with our mothers'; and in a desperate attempt to know where mother ends and daughter begins, we perform radical surgery."[6] Writing from the daughter's position, Rich articulates the same desperate need for boundaries as Irigaray a few years later.

The title of Irigaray's 1979 book—which I would translate as "And One Cannot Move Without the Other"—could recall the plight of the seven-headed monster. Alerted by the editors to look for "reverberations," I read Hirsch's article not merely as a separate contribution but also as a continuation of the collaborative text of the Introduction. Her elaboration of the daughter's bind may also give voice to the dilemma of the individual member of the collective. The female collective functions as nurturing and stifling mother, as body of monstrous proportions, whereas, whatever her reproductive history, the individual in relation to the collective plays the role of daughter.

This is, I believe, more than a clever analogy. According to Hirsch and Chodorow, any daughter, that is, any woman, has a self that is not completely individuated but rather is constitutively connected to another woman. The formation of groups of women draw upon the permeability of female self-boundaries.[7] The collectivity reactivates the mother-daughter bond. One monster cannot be separated from the other.

"To study the relationship between mother and daughter is not to study the relationship between two separate differentiated individuals, but to *plunge* into a network of complex ties" (YFS 62, p. 73, emphasis added). Although Hirsch here appears to be saying that in studying the mother-daughter relationship the object of study is different than one would suppose, this sentence also says: "To study the relationship between mother and daughter is not to study . . . but to plunge." The scholar is, so to speak, immersed in her work. The "being of monstrous proportions" threatens to envelop whatever would stand outside and observe.

The sentence then adds one more verb phrase: "To study the relationship between mother and daughter is not to study . . . but to plunge . . . *to attempt to untangle* the strands of a double self, a continuous multiple being . . . parts of which try desperately to separate and delineate their boundaries." In "attempt[ing] to untangle," the student comes to resemble the "parts" which "try to separate and delineate." What she studies would seem to mirror her. And although not yet "desperate" herself, there is something threatening in the mirror.

Two sentences later, Hirsch writes: "This basic and continued relatedness and multiplicity, this mirroring which seems to be unique to women have to be factors in any study of female development in fiction." Here we have a second figure for the mother-daughter bond: "this basic and continued relatedness and multiplicity," in other words, "this mirroring." If the relationship being studied is itself a mirroring, then when the scholar who "attempts to untangle" is reflected in the parts which "try to separate and delineate," she is both observing a mirroring and enacting one. When Hirsch writes that "this mirroring ha[s] to be [a] factor in any study of female development in fiction," we might take it to mean, not only does it have to be discussed, but that it has to be a "factor in any study," something that takes place in the study, something that happens to the student.

That "this mirroring . . . seems to be unique to women" then could lead us to pose some questions as to whether women's studies, studies by women, differ from those performed by male scholars in that women, based perhaps on our more permeable self-boundaries, tend to get entangled in a mirroring with the object of study. And, whether or not this is "unique to women," we might also go on to ponder the more epistemologically radical question of whether this is a good or a bad thing, which is another way to ask whether the monster in *our* self-portrait is ugly or beautiful.

(My emphasized use of the first person plural here, like the reference to "my own horror" at the end of the first section, is meant to mark, probably much too subtly, my own identifications and entanglements with the monsters I am studying. I call this piece "The Monster in the Mirror" likewise to signal where I locate the monster that disturbs me, that compels me to write this piece. This chapter is always also about the monster I observe in my mirror. When in 1983 I first tried to write this, I began to realize my resemblance to those figures who most repelled me. I tried to incorporate that recognition in my writing but, overcome by anxiety, I could no longer write. Everything I started would quickly boil down to writing about myself and to a particularly distasteful image of myself as totally trapped in narcissistic mirroring. In a last self-reflexive twist, writing about that became simply a reprehensible example of it. I would begin a paragraph and then throw it away, through ten or so false starts until suddenly I was pacing my apartment, screaming. In order to write, I gave up the idea of self-implication. I also felt that all the threads of what I wanted to say were entangled together and I could not separate them sufficiently to progress along any line of thought at all. I am sure that is one reason why the text I did finally write is so very fragmentary. In order to separate lines enough for articulation, I had to "perform radical surgery," detach ideas from their articulation to the whole.[8])

"Mirroring" in the mother-daughter relation is central to the article immediately following Hirsch's in YFS 62. Ronnie Scharfman derives the term "mirroring" from the work of D. W. Winnicott, an object-relations theorist: "Winnicott asks what a baby sees upon looking at the mother's face . . . 'ordinarily, what the baby sees is himself or herself.'"[9] Scharfman describes an "unsuccessful mirroring bond": "When a mother reflects her own mood or the 'rigidity of her own defenses' rather than her child's, what the baby sees is the mother's face, and the 'mother's face is not a mirror.' The consequences are tragic" (p. 99).

Scharfman applies this theory to two Caribbean novels, finding in them examples of good and bad mothering. Of the mother figure (actually the grandmother) in Simone Schwarz-Bart's *Pluie et Vent sur Télumée Miracle*, Scharfman writes: "grandmother is not other, but rather same. She encourages the narcissism which psychoanalytic theory assures us is fundamental to the healthy constitution of an autonomous self" (p. 91). I quote from her account of Jean Rhys's *Wide Sargasso Sea*: "Self-absorbed, [the mother] is imprisoned in a destructive narcissism. [The daughter] . . . watches her look at herself in the mirror. . . . But she never sees herself reflected there. [The] mother's concern for [the daughter] is mainly as a disappointing narcissistic extension of herself" (p. 100). A daughter's narcissism is good; a mother's is bad.

At the beginning of the essay, Scharfman asks: "Is the kind of mirroring which this bond implies *reflected* in the writing itself, and, perhaps in reading as well?" (p. 88, emphasis added). Is mirroring *reflected*? Her answer is yes. Reading as mirroring turns out to be the final point of Scharfman's article: "a feminist aesthetic can . . . dramatiz[e] . . . the possible bonds between the text as mother, and the daughter-reader it produces" (p. 106).

The text will be mother. The question of mirroring is finally here a question about reading. The daughter-reader considers one of these novels a better "mother" than the other. She complains, for example, that Rhys's text "keeps us at a distance, rejects our efforts to be present in it" (p. 106). A good text, like a good mother, will reflect the reader: the text will provide the reader's self-portrait. If the reader does not see herself but perceives something other, that will be tragic.

And so I want to recoil from this daughter-reader, her monstrosity yet another case of unseemly narcissism.

(As reader of YFS 62, I recognize myself in Scharfman's response to Rhys's novel. In 1979 I received a letter from seven Dartmouth women inviting me to contribute to a feminist issue of *Yale French Studies* they were editing. Jumping at the chance to be published in the top journal in what was then my field, I immediately sent them an abstract of a text on Irigaray and Freud. I never received an answer. This absolute lack of response was, for me, worse than rejection. Pointing to the editorial collective's self-regard, I am the disregarded daughter "watching her look at herself in the mirror." The seven-headed monster "rejected [my] efforts to be present in it." If I am particularly harsh on Scharfman, perhaps I cannot bear this reflection of my daughterly resentment.)

When Hirsch writes about the "parts" which "try desperately to delineate their own boundaries," the plural implies that both daughter and mother are anxious for autonomy. We tend however to think of "mother" not as one of the parts but as the whole monster. Actually, any mother is also an individual trying to untangle herself from the mothering web.

According to Chodorow, "male theorists ignore the mother's involvements outside of her relationship to her infant and her possible interest in mitigating its intensity. Instead, they contrast the infant's moves toward differentiation and separation to the mother's attempts to retain symbiosis."[10] When the theorist attempts to untangle the double being mother-daughter, he assigns the desire for autonomy (an attribute of both individuals inasmuch as they are individuals) to the daughter term and the desire for symbiosis (which both parts, inasmuch as they are connected, share) to the mother term. Not just male theorists, I would add, but any theorist who writes from a position of identification with the child rather than the mother.

In her contribution to YFS 62, Naomi Schor touches on the psychology of theory. Following Freud's lead, she links theory to paranoia. Rereading Freud's only case history of a female paranoiac, Schor reminds us that the female paranoiac fears another woman who resembles her mother.[11] Her feeling of persecution is the other side of "the daughter's bond with her mother": inextricably linked to the daughter's self, the mother is always there to witness. Paranoia, and theory which is its more socially acceptable form, thus bespeak a daughter's terror of the ubiquitous mother, a particularly desperate form of this terror.

A few years after YFS 62, Jane Marcus also psychologizes a certain "theory" as fearful need for separation from the mother.[12] In the same issue of *Tulsa Studies in Women's Literature*, and in much the same vein, Nina Baym expresses her distress that mother-daughter theory not only speaks from the daughter's perspective, but "provides testimony, often unwitting and in contradiction to its stated intentions, of the deep-seated hostility of daughters to mothers." She goes on to say: "If the speaking woman sees other women as her mother, sees herself but not her mother as a woman, then she can see her mother (other women) only as men or monsters."[13] The lack of agreement between the singular "mother" and the plural "men or monsters" probably arises from the very tangle Baym would untie, where it is difficult to see mother as "a woman," as an individual.

Baym's discussion of the matricidal impulse in feminist theory cites the feminist treatment of Bertha Mason in *Jane Eyre*: "Who, after all, might Bertha Mason be—she to whom Rochester *is already married*? . . . another woman, who is made repulsive and ridiculous so that the reader must reject her; and is killed before the narrative is out, so that the daughter can replace her." A few years later, Gayatri Spivak likewise complains about the treatment of Bertha: "Sandra Gilbert and Susan Gubar . . . have seen Bertha Mason only in psychological terms as Jane's dark double."[14] In this landmark feminist reading, the "dark double," Bertha Mason is only a mirror or, perhaps more precisely, the monster in the mirror.

Around 1980, feminists identified with Jane, the exemplary daughter-reader. A decade or two earlier, Jean Rhys "was moved by Bertha Mason; 'I thought I'd try to write her a life.' *Wide Sargasso Sea* . . . is that 'life.'"[15] *Wide Sargasso Sea* is also the novel Scharfman resents for not mirroring her.

"There are, noticeably, many images of mirroring in the text."[16] Spivak and Scharfman quote the same one. In this passage, the speaker is "Bertha Mason" as a young white creole girl; the other girl is a little black servant: "When I was close I saw the jagged stone in her hand but I did not see her throw it. . . . We stared at each other, blood on my face, tears on hers. It was as if I saw myself. Like in a looking glass."[17]

This white girl is the daughter of the narcissistic mother who will not mirror her. "What [her] mother cannot give, the girl seeks from . . . the faithful black woman who runs the household and represents the nurturing, maternal figure" (p. 101). Within the analogy of reader to daughter, Rhys's text is the bad, Schwarz-Bart's the good mother. The former "keeps us at a distance"; the latter "generously allows us . . . to incorporate it and assimilate it and make what use of it we may" (p. 106). Introducing the two Caribbean novels, Scharfman specifies that Rhys is white, Schwarz-Bart is black. I am somewhat troubled by the historical reverberations of the cold white mother, the generous black mother. I am more troubled by the assumption, here readerly, that good mothering is mirroring and that what we demand from a text is an image of ourself.

In her contribution to YFS 62, Spivak writes: "However unfeasible and inefficient it may sound, I see no way to avoid insisting that there has to be a simultaneous other focus: not merely who am I? but who is the other woman?"[18]

5
Reading the Mother Tongue

In 1985 the first anthology of psychoanalytic feminist criticism was published.[1] The title of that collection, *The (M)other Tongue*, is not easy to pronounce: both "The Mother Tongue" and "The Other Tongue," or perhaps not quite the mother tongue nor quite the other tongue. The title is not quite in *our* mother tongue (spoken English), although not in any other. It brings out the other in the mother.

The play on mother and other reminds us that in psychoanalytic theory the mother is the subject's first other, the other in opposition to which the self is constituted. Or rather, as becomes clear in object-relations theory and particularly in the work of Nancy Chodorow, the mother is the site of something which is both other and not quite other, of the other as self and the self as other.[2] Thus the monstrous word—"Mother-other"—in its double identity could be said to body forth the borderline status of the powerful, early mother, so central to psychoanalytic feminist theory.

Yet the title of the book is not "The (M)other" but "The (M)other Tongue." The book would appear to be not just about Mother but about language. The title phrase is nowhere glossed, or even used in the book, at least not with the M in parentheses. But we do find the simpler phrase, "The Mother Tongue" (without parentheses). In fact, the Editors' Introduction concludes on that more familiar phrase: "Feminists working from a number of critical approaches are concluding that it is time to learn, to begin to speak our mother tongue" (p. 29).

Although not marked in any way by unpronounceable punctuation, the phrase "mother tongue" in this sentence clearly does not mean what it usually means in *our* mother tongue. If it is only now time "to learn, to *begin* to speak" this language, then this is not what we usually refer to as our native language. It may look familiar on the page, but this is not the same old mother tongue, but precisely an other mother tongue.

However "other" we can imagine this tongue to be, in this unmarked version it still looks like the idiomatic phrase. No mark forces the reader to see the otherness in this "mother tongue." This lack of marking may be part of a tendency, in this concluding sentence, to cover over an alterity that is, elsewhere, carefully noted. In this last sentence of the Introduction, "feminists working from a number of critical approaches are" jointly, in a plural, inclusive verb, "concluding." The triumphant conclusion forgets a difference articulated earlier in the Introduction between two "critical approaches." In the "mother tongue," we are not divided.

From object-relations theory we learn that, for the infant, differentiation *is* differentiation *from the mother*. Imagining that the mother demands symbiosis, the infant experiences the drive toward separation as a guilty betrayal of the mother. Guilty to see the mother as other, to see the other in the mother; guilty thus to differentiate within the oceanic symbiosis. According to Chodorow, this atmosphere particularly characterizes the daughter's relation to the mother, long past infancy, and carries over into adult relations between women. This feminine lack of rigid separation has been celebrated by feminists, but let us not forget the corollary uneasiness that attends the drive toward differentiation, never wholly absent from this complex. In the vicinity of the "mother" there may be a tendency to cover over difference.

The Introduction's conclusion, with its lack of marked alterity, might be read as a happy ending. According to generic convention, comedy concludes with the resolution of previous differences in a joining of all parties. But earlier in the narrative when the pressure of conclusion does not yet weigh so heavily, the differences between "critical approaches" can be delineated.

Rehearsing the history of psychoanalytic feminism, the Introduction finds that the French feminists have, like their American sisters, "turned to the preoedipal relation." The editors then carefully add: "Although this shift to the mother has brought some degree of rapprochement between this line of French feminist concern and Anglo-American theory, the French detour through Lacan results in a difference. The insertion of the question of language introduces the notion of a form of expressivity outside the dominant discourse" (pp. 22–23).

Whereas "the mother" brings rapprochement, a lessening of difference, "the question of language," the mother *tongue*, introduces difference. The question of the mother tongue inserts itself in the very reading of this passage. The word "rapprochement" can be found in an English dictionary, yet it is pronounced in such a manner as not to let us forget that it is a French import. The French and English versions of the word remain close, so that "rapprochement" itself may be said to function as a point of rapprochement between the two languages. The appearance of this word in the text wishfully enacts a closing of the gap between the French and the "Anglo-Americans."[3] The book itself represents a wish to close up that gap, to be able to speak the mother tongue and the other tongue simultaneously. But however ardent that wish, it is also true that the relation between the mother tongue and the other tongue involves us with material difference so that the book's title cannot simply be pronounced.

The title of the book is "a form of expressivity outside the dominant discourse." The play of its parenthesis, using the material of language to reflect on the language, resembles the stylistic devices of poststructuralist writers such as Jacques Derrida and Luce Irigaray as well as American feminists such as Mary Daly. The feminists and the poststructuralists are trying to find a mode of expressivity which is not already shackled by the ideological weight of standard language. Standard language can be called the mother tongue; the attempt to write outside the dominant discourse could be construed as a try for the other rather than the mother tongue. But as the title of our anthology makes us see, "the other tongue" is already inscribed in "the mother tongue." These feminist and poststructuralist attempts at new expressivity do not go outside the dominant discourse but rather bring out what deconstructionists such as Barbara Johnson have called "the difference within."[4] We are not looking for a new language, a radical outside, but for "the other within," the alterity that has lain silent, unmarked and invisible within the mother tongue.

In the Introduction, the editors write: "At this juncture . . . the tendency of Anglo-American psychoanalytic feminism to focus on the drama of the preoedipal relationship between mother and daughter intersects with French feminist dreams of another mode of discourse, another side of language whose authority is the mother" (p. 24). A mode of language where mother not father is authority—matriarchal discourse—is not an object of "focus" but a "dream," that is to say, in psychoanalytic terms, the fulfillment of a wish. Another mode, another side: the mother tongue as other tongue, a dream devoutly to be wished.

Anglo-Americans focus; French dream. On one side, "the drama of the preoedipal relationship"; across, "another mode of discourse." The only term repeated on both sides: "mother." Hitching the "expressivity outside the dominant discourse" to the mother seems to promise a lessening of difference, a rapprochement on various fronts. This "juncture," this "intersection": paths that seemed to run parallel are crossing. In "mother," we are not divided.

If "French feminist dreams" come down to the mother, then perhaps we can ignore the differences between "focus" and "dream." To focus (telescope or microscope) is the classic mode of empiricist scientific investigation. The "drama of the preoedipal" is treated as an object of positivist study. That it is then, figuratively, a "drama" renders the pre-Oedipal relationship (figuratively) literary and preps it for use in analogical operations on literary works.

On the other side, to dream is to become, oneself, the classic object of psychoanalytic study, the dreamer's psyche. If Freud invented psychoanalysis through interpreting his own dreams, then psychoanalysis may be the locus of an uncanny self-knowledge where subject and object are neither identical nor different, where the subject and object of knowledge are aspects of "the same person" separated by the opaque materiality of the dream. Such study no longer partakes of the positivist objectivity of the focusing lens, but rather inevitably implicates the subject's desires and defenses in the investigation.[5]

In *The Interpretation of Dreams*, Freud provides us with a method of interpretation that involves attention to details we overlook when we reduce a story to its central drama. That aspect of Freud's work has influenced a different sort of literary criticism, one indebted to psychoanalysis for its interpretive methods rather than its dramatic analogies.

This other sort of psychoanalytic reading might be applied to our dream of the mother tongue. For example, the word "patriarchal" is actually spelled five different ways in this book: aside from its standard spelling, we can read "partriarchial" (p. 16), "patriarchial" (p. 22), "partiarchal" (p. 105), and "partriarchal" (p. 264 n. 11). Presumably these are typographical errors, yet no other word in the book is so frequently misspelled, as if some unconscious (author's? editors'? typist's? typesetter's?) was insistently trying to speak something other than patriarchal.[6] This is not a language "whose authority is the mother," not matriarchal, but other than patriarchal. This is clearly no one's mother tongue, but it may be the other tongue, perhaps what Jacques Lacan calls the discourse of the Other, that speaks in and through the mother tongue.[7]

The mother tongue, the language we learn at our mother's breast, *is* patriarchal language, the language which feminism has taught us to see as full of masculinist bias. In trying to move beyond the father, the mother looks like an alternative, but if we are trying to move beyond patriarchy, the mother is not outside. As Chodorow—among others[8]—has shown us, the institution of motherhood is a cornerstone of patriarchy. Although the father may be absent from the pre-Oedipal, patriarchy constitutes the very structure of the mother-child dyad.[9] The early mother may seem to be outside patriarchy, but that very idea of the mother as outside of culture, society, and politics is an essential ideological component of patriarchy.

There is a drive, in this book, to speak outside of patriarchal discourse. But to the extent that drive fixes on "the figure of the mother" and/or glorifies the pre-Oedipal, the book risks losing its title to diacritical marks and settling for a mother tongue that is not recognizably an other tongue.

In the Preface, the editors write: "It is clear that fascination by the preoedipal period and a corresponding focus on the figure of the mother in theories of human development have had a profound impact on the discipline of psychoanalysis and on the feminist interpretation of literature" (p. 10) "The discipline of psychoanalysis" and "the feminist interpretation of literature" are widely separated realms. Opposed here are not only Freudian and feminist ways of thinking but also a quasi-medical practice of healing and a mode of literary interpretation. And yet these two domains are simply conjoined under the aegis of "the preoedipal period" and "the figure of the mother." The pre-Oedipal is the realm of fusion and indifferentiation; its "impact" may include a preference for merger over distinction.

Or rather not the impact of the pre-Oedipal, but the impact of "fascination by the preoedipal." Coppélia Kahn, in her contribution to the anthology, speaks of the "charmed preoedipal dyad" (p. 74). From the Preface, we might infer that the pre-Oedipal period is not only a magical moment for infant and early mother but exercises a charm over those who contemplate it, who study and theorize. Fascinate: "1. To be an object of intense interest to; attract irresistibly. 2. To hold motionless; to spellbind or mesmerize. 3. *Obsolete.* To bewitch; cast under a spell. [Latin *fascinare*, to enchant, bewitch, from *fascinus*, a bewitching, amulet in the shape of a phallus.]"[10] The pre-Oedipal attracts us irresistibly and holds us motionless, and in place of the phallic amulet, we are bewitched by the figure of the mother. The maternal having replaced the phallic, the early seventies' opposition between psychoanalysis and feminism can give way to a charmed union.

The first section of the editor's Introduction to *The (M)other*

Tongue is a history of the encounters between psychoanalysis and feminism. The last paragraph of that history begins: "So far we have traced the ways in which feminism has reacted to psychoanalysis. . . . But there may be another story here, that of the response of psychoanalysis to feminism" (p. 25). For ten pages they have traced feminism's response to psychoanalysis, and now with but one paragraph left, they are just beginning to imagine the other side ("there *may be* another story"). This relationship seems far too one-sided: one party has done all the talking, the other all the listening.

In a psychoanalytic context, however, we know of a relationship in which knowledge and authority derive from the one who listens. Perhaps, after all, psychoanalysis has been doing all its talking in relation to the knowledge it presumes feminism (or women) to have. That may be why feminism has been willing to listen. But that other story, the influence of feminism on psychoanalysis, remains to be told.

That story would have to begin with what the first story has left out, what psychoanalysis for all its talking could not say. For if feminism, in its listening posture, is in the place of the analyst, then when it speaks it will intervene in response to some marked gap in the story of the one who does all the talking. In the last paragraph of the historical introduction, the editors start to imagine that intervention: "Psychoanalysis, whether it posits in the beginning maternal presence or absence, has yet to develop a story of the mother as other than object of the infant's desire or the matrix from which he or she develops an infant subjectivity" (p. 25). "Whether it posits in the beginning maternal presence or absence": that is, whether we are dealing with object-relations or Lacanian theory. In Lacanian models she is the prohibited object of desire; in object-relations she is the mirror where the infant can find his or her subjectivity. In either case her role is to complement the infant's subjectivity; in neither story is she a subject. It is not mother that is missing from psychoanalytic accounts, but precisely mother as other ("Psychoanalysis . . . has yet to develop a story of the mother as other").

In *The Reproduction of Mothering*, Chodorow begins to notice this blind spot in psychoanalysis, but she appears to attribute it to the gender of the theorists: "male theorists . . . ignore the mother's involvements outside her relationship to her infant and her possible interest in mitigating its intensity. Instead, they contrast the infant's moves toward differentiation and separation to the mother's attempts to retain symbiosis" (p. 87). Since the subject of both sentences is "male theorists," we might infer that women theorizing will not make the same mistake. Such a supposition about female theorists is kin to the assumption that the mother is outside patriarchy.

The last essay in the anthology begins with an account of the same syndrome in psychoanalytic theory: "It is as if, for psychoanalysis, the only self worth worrying about in the mother-child relationship were that of the child" (p. 356). Explicitly following Chodorow's lead, this essay by Susan Suleiman gives examples (from Helene Deutsch, Melanie Klein, Alice Balint, and Karen Horney) which expose this bias not (merely) in the fathers but in the mothers of psychoanalytic theory. Suleiman remarks in a footnote: "It will certainly be noticed that almost all of the analysts I have been quoting are women" (p. 356 n. 8).

Remarking this only in a footnote, Suleiman makes no prolonged attempt to understand why these women might perpetrate such patriarchal bias. It might be argued that, although women, these theorists are not, strictly speaking, feminists, or at least are not in a position to benefit from the work done in the contemporary field of psychoanalytic feminism. It might also be argued that they are all practicing psychoanalysts and therefore have an investment in the discipline of psychoanalysis that a literary critic, for example, need not share. Yet I think the problem might be more pervasive, that the maternal figure may move many of us to wish for an embrace that obliterates otherness. And those of us who are attracted to psychoanalytic theory may be particularly susceptible to the mother's charming figure, the dream of the mother without otherness.

For example, in an article we considered in the last chapter, Ronnie Scharfman echoes D. W. Winnicott's position that the child looking at the mother should see not the mother's face but him- or herself.[11] Producing an agile literary application of Winnicott's position, the feminist literary critic accepts the notion that it is tragic to see the mother's subjectivity, to see the mother as other. Scharfman writes explicitly from the daughter's point of view; Nina Baym has asserted that all feminist psychoanalytic theory is from the daughter's point of view.[12]

Suleiman writes that "psychoanalysis is nothing if not a theory of childhood. We should not be surprised if it locates . . . every . . . aspect of adult personality in the child the adult once was, and often continues to be" (p. 358). Psychoanalysis is "a theory of childhood," that is, not merely about childhood, but theorized from the child's point of view. Baym comes to the same conclusion: "one can wonder what a theory deliberately developed from childhood fantasies describes other than childish fantasies" (p. 59). Baym's statement is meant to discredit psychoanalysis. Essentially agreeing with her observation, I would however add that this description of "childish fantasies" is psychoanalysis's great strength, giving us access to what is denied by any psychology that assumes that the child simply becomes an "adult": rational, civilized.

Childishness is psychoanalysis's insight and its blindness. It can see from the child's point of view and it can only see from the child's point of view. The child's particular blind spot is an inability to have a realistic notion of the mother as an other subjectivity.[13] The child the adult continues to be shares this blind spot: "people continue not to recognize their mother's interests while developing capacities for 'altruistic love' in the process of growing up. They support their egoism, moreover, by idealizing mothers and by the creation of social ideology" (Chodorow, p. 81). This child the adult continues to be is the source of psychoanalytic theory.

If one of the major goals of feminism has been to put a stop to women's self-sacrifice, their exploitation through the ideology of maternal altruism, then it must counter every adult child's wish for the mother to be the perfect selfless mirror. That is where psychoanalysis and feminism part company: one taking the child's wishes into account, the other defending the mother's side of the story. The coupling of psychoanalysis-and-feminism might then represent a wish we all, mother and/or daughter, hold dear: that whatever is in the daughter's interest is also in the interest of the mother, and vice versa.

Pointing us toward this opposition between psychoanalysis and feminism, Suleiman's essay stands out from the rest of the anthology. Thus by the time we reach the end of the first anthology of psychoanalytic feminist criticism, we have in some way gone beyond the boundaries of the new field into a critique of its very possibility. That such an essay should be included and positioned last suggests that perhaps such a move is inevitable. Since *The (M)other Tongue* ends with Suleiman's text, we are, in some ways, forced to rethink what has come before.

Earlier, looking at the Editors' Introduction, I said that *The (M)other Tongue* seemed to follow the generic code for comedy, culminating in a procession of couples marching hand in hand (psychoanalysis with feminism, Anglo-American theory with French feminism, the discipline of psychoanalysis with the feminist interpretation of literature). But an Editors' Introduction is a secondary revision (in the psychoanalytic sense of the term)[14] of the unruly material of an anthology. Ending with Suleiman's text, the volume actually concludes not with marriage but divorce.

And the accusations we hear typify the contemporary subgenre of the feminist divorce tale. Psychoanalysis does not allow mother her selfhood, makes her an object of service, and expects her to sacrifice herself to her partner's fantasies of her.[15] If "the figure of the mother" blesses the marriage of psychoanalysis and feminism, the mother as other presides over their divorce.

The anthology thus leads us from the mother (fantasy figure and ideological construction) to the (m)other . . . But what of the (m)other tongue? It seems that the question of language, in this book, is always tied to that other tongue, French, and to those "French feminists." Suleiman discusses French woman writer Chantal Chawaf, who "has tied the practice of feminine writing to the biological fact of motherhood" (p. 370). Like other women of the French school, Chawaf is trying to practice *écriture féminine*, but more explicitly than with the other practitioners, her practice would be a mother tongue: "Chawaf has stated in interviews and commentaries on her work that for her motherhood is the only access to literary creation" (p. 370).

When Suleiman quotes from a novel by Chawaf entitled *Maternité* (French cognate for "maternity"), the footnote reads: "*Manternité*" (p. 370 n. 42). In the text the title is correct, but at the bottom of the page we find an alien in the mother tongue. Perhaps the monstrous word "manternité" includes the English word "man" in the French word, producing a composite that is in no one's mother tongue, that cannot simply be pronounced.[16]

In the classic psychoanalytic story, the "man" comes to disrupt the charmed pre-Oedipal dyad. As Janet Adelman puts it in another footnote in the anthology, this Oedipal intrusion of the man is but a late form, a repetition of an otherness already there in the early mother: "For the infant, the mother's separateness constitutes the first betrayal; insofar as she is not merely his, she is promiscuously other. I suspect that this sense of otherness itself as promiscuous betrayal antedates the more specific oedipal jealousies and is retrospectively sexualized by them" (p. 134 n. 17). Those of us under the fascination of the pre-Oedipal often see the man's entry as the fall from Eden. In a Lacanian version of that story, the man's intrusion saves us from symbiotic fusion, from the mother's engulfment. Adelman (and Chodorow and Suleiman) reminds us however that both the positive and the negative valuations of the pre-Oedipal equally ignore the fact that the pre-Oedipal mother is already other.

The disruptive appearance of the word "man" within maternity may also remind us that the masculine is already inscribed in motherhood; patriarchal discourse structures the institution and the experience of motherhood as we know it. In any case, whether suppressed wish for separation or unauthorized critique, the n in Suleiman's footnote continues the legacy of the title's parentheses, interrupting the mother tongue by an other tongue.

The (m)other tongue is hard to pronounce. Maybe psychoanalytic and feminist criticism can teach us not how to speak the mother tongue, not *only* how to see the mother as other and not mirror, but how to read the other within the mother tongue.

6

The Coloration of Academic Feminism

The 1982 publication of *Writing and Sexual Difference* represented feminism's arrival in the increasingly powerful academic circle of literary theory. At the time, the most prestigious theory was either a Paris original or a good copy. Two years later, Columbia University's *Maison Française* devoted its Eighth International Poetics Colloquium to the Poetics of Gender; this Ivy League, Frenchy institution recognized feminism as belonging in the realm of Poetics. I spoke, at that 1984 colloquium, of the anthology *Writing and Sexual Difference*, and of its color, which I called "mauve."

"One of those colors whose name in English is still in French," mauve, for me, was almost pink but, importantly, not quite pink: "not the blatant little-girl color, unseemly in its explicit, infantile femininity but a stylish, sophisticated version of that color, one that bespeaks not the messy, carnal world of the nursery but high culture, high feminine culture, the realms of interior decoration and *haute couture*."[1] The last phrase literally means "high sewing" but, pronounced with an American accent, sounds an awful lot like the French for high culture. The idea of high sewing might remind us that in the world of American female culture, French has held the place of the high.

As I was soon, and repeatedly, informed, it was not correct to call that color "mauve." According to *The American Heritage Dictionary* "mauve" is "brilliant violet to strong or brilliant purple to moderate reddish purple." I guess, for me, "mauve" simply meant fancy pink, a "fanciness" exemplified by its French name.[2] My "mauve" points to high feminine culture at the same time that its incorrect use marks me as outside that realm. I belong as little to the world of "high sewing" as I do to masculine high culture. My fantasy geography locates both in Paris. No wonder I went into French.

Fancy or not, at the *Maison Française*, pink, I argued, "unlike its diacritical partner blue, remains—way past the nursery—marked as feminine. If blue, outside the infantile realm, is no longer a particularly masculine color, might not that relate to the phallocentrism which . . . raises the masculine to the universal, beyond gender, so that the feminine alone must bear the burden of sexual difference? Pink then becomes THE color of sexual difference, carrying alone within it the diacritical distinction pink/blue" (pp. 138–39). In 1986 Columbia University Press published the papers from the Poetics of Gender Conference in a book edited by Nancy K. Miller. Its cover is precisely what inside the book gets called "blatant little-girl pink."

If the cover of the anthology *The Poetics of Gender* is pink, it is relevant to ask how pink functions within. The color appears not only in my paper but also in the one immediately preceding it, in a sentence Susan Suleiman quotes from Georges Bataille's *Story of the Eye*: "Then I lay down at her feet without her having moved and, for the first time, I saw her 'pink and black' flesh cooling itself in the white milk."[3]

Andrea Dworkin, who considers *The Story of the Eye* in her book on pornography, glosses the last phrase as "He saw her cunt in the milk."[4] Suleiman agrees with Dworkin but also draws our attention to the three words "rose et noire" which Bataille puts in quotation marks. Whereas Dworkin heads directly for the bottom line, Suleiman would also have us look at what she calls the "periphrasis," the way Bataille skirts the organ's name, the style which drapes "her cunt" in "pink and black." This attempt to balance politicized reading with sophisticated rhetorical play might exemplify the act of a feminist in the ring of poetics.

The quotation marks "suggest a literary or pictorial allusion": "The allusion is to Baudelaire's famous verses about Lola de Valence, who was also represented in a famous painting by Manet: 'Mais on voit scintiller en Lola de Valence/Le charme inattendu d'un bijou rose et noir' ['But one sees scintillate in Lola de Valence/The unexpected charm of a pink and black jewel']" (p. 126). Suleiman goes on to delineate an elaborate play of rhetorical substitutions between Bataille's and Baudelaire's texts. But the passing reference to Manet and the "literary *or pictorial* allusion" suggest that "pink and black" open not only onto a realm of words but might also indicate an equally elaborate world of colors to be seen.

During the discussion following her paper Suleiman was asked what it meant that she was wearing a black skirt and a pink blouse. She laughed but did not answer. Her ingenious and careful reading of that quoted periphrasis seemed to demand that her clothing be read. Yet she could not account for wearing that pair of colors.

This allusion to Suleiman's clothing is only available to those of us actually present at the conference. In the preface to the anthology,

Miller makes it clear that she would like the book to carry as much as possible of the event: "And because that frame of reference . . . lent, I think, so particular a *coloration* to the work . . . I in the end decided to present the papers in the volume according to the order (however arbitrary) in which they were presented at the conference itself" (p. xiv, emphasis added). Through her editorial decisions, Miller hopes to transmit from conference to book what she here calls "coloration." Although the reader of *The Poetics of Gender* does not have Suleiman's black leather skirt and pink silk blouse to look at, Suleiman's paper does appear in a volume whose cover is precisely pink *and* black.

"That frame of reference lent so particular a coloration to the work": Miller is concerned here with the mark of context in the text. The papers in *The Poetics of Gender* insist upon the necessity of reading both text and context, in other words, upon both formal and socio-historical criticism. Yet none of us are very clear on how to join those domains. That join functions as the obscure object of desire, assiduously sought and nonetheless obscure. Trying to talk about the effect of context on this text, Miller proffers the word "coloration."

The word appears one other time in *The Poetics of Gender*, in the final paragraph of Monique Wittig's paper: "To close my discussion of the notion of gender in language, I will say it is . . . the unique lexical symbol that refers to an oppressed group. No other has left its trace within language to such a degree that to eradicate it . . . would change the coloration of words in relation to each other."[5]

Concluding, Wittig compares gender to other oppressive hierarchies and proclaims that it is "unique." Another paper in *The Poetics of Gender* concludes with a warning against privileging gender. Elizabeth Berg writes: "Finally, in the context of this encounter as feminists, it is important . . . to remind oneself . . . that the move to privilege gender . . . participates in the same logic of oppression as the masculine philosophy one criticizes, for by that gesture one subsumes what is different from oneself (a different color, a different class, a different sexual orientation, a different belief) into a universal that denies that other even as it pretends to represent it."[6]

The first entry in Berg's list reminds us that the word "color" can refer to racial difference. Where Berg reminds us not to forget "a different color," Wittig, claiming the uniqueness of gender as the only oppressive hierarchy so marked in language, uses the word "coloration." Could that word be the trace within Wittig's language of another oppressed group?

My contribution to *The Poetics of Gender* has its own tinge of unconscious coloration. In order to talk about the academic feminist's relation to women who serve us, I identify with the French philosopher Annie Leclerc who identifies with the bourgeoise in the Vermeer painting "Lady Writing a Letter, with her Maid." Leclerc associates Vermeer's maid with her own mother. I wrote: "We need to understand how our relation to the mother *colors* our relation to women of the class who work for us" (p. 152, emphasis added).

Audre Lorde: "If white american feminist theory need not deal with the differences between us, and the resulting difference in our oppressions, then how do you deal with the fact that the women who clean your houses and tend your children while you attend conferences on feminist theory are, for the most part, poor women and women of color?[7]

Hortense Spillers: "That the care of Anglo-American families in certain communities has been entrusted over time to black women largely remains unspoken in feminist discourse."[8]

Angela Davis: "The condition of white women workers is often tied to the oppressive predicament of women of color. Thus the wages received by white women domestics have always been fixed by the racist criteria used to calculate the wages of Black women servants."[9]

My paper addressed class differences between women, most specifically the way that academic feminists as bourgeois writing women forget the women who do our "women's work" and make our writing possible. While the maid in Vermeer's painting is of the same race as her mistress, my use of the word "colors" might recall that Rosie who cleans my house is black.

"Rose et noire." According to Suleiman, Dworkin's "deadpan summary" of *The Story of the Eye* ends with Simone and the narrator "embarking on a schooner from Gibraltar to sail to further adventures." In fact, Dworkin's plot summary ends: "They leave town to find new adventures with a sailing crew of Negroes on Sir Edmond's new yacht."[10] This crew is essential to Dworkin's ultimate analysis of the story: "The challenge of savage sexuality in a black crew in service to a wealthy English aristocrat provides a new context for conquest. . . . Conquest . . . is carried in pornography . . . inevitably into the racial realm" (p. 177).

Suleiman never mentions the context in which *The Story of the Eye* appears in *Pornography*. Bataille's story is the last of four pornographic texts analyzed in Dworkin's fifth chapter: all four explicitly eroticize racial difference. This same fifth chapter which culminates with the analysis of Bataille begins by considering a pictorial text: "there are two women. . . . The white woman is the whore, the sexual object of the moment. The woman of color is the menial."[11]

Studying Bataille's "pink and black," Suleiman mentions the painter Manet in passing. Bataille has, in fact, written a book on Manet which cites Baudelaire's line, "The unexpected charm of a pink and black jewel." But although Baudelaire wrote the verse as a tribute to Manet's painting *Lola de Valence*, Bataille contends: "it is certainly *Olympia*, not *Lola de Valence*, in which we see the scintillation of '*Le charme inattendu d'un bijou rose et noir*. . .'"[12]

The black cat with pink eyes, the play of flowers: *Olympia* is undoubtedly a meditation on pink and black. Behind its European female flesh adorned with a black ribbon and a pink flower is an African maid in a pink dress. Which is the pink and black jewel?

("Mr. Dizzy was, to be quite honest, not very clever. If you were to ask Mr. Dizzy what the opposite of black was, he'd say, 'Er, the opposite of black is . . . er . . . pink!' . . . One of Mr. Dizzy's problems was that he lived in a country where everybody else was terribly clever. Cleverland!")[13]

Pink does not just have a gender connotation. European flesh is sometimes referred to as pink, a color with other implications than the purity connoted by white. Beneath its pink jacket the hardbound cover of *The Poetics of Gender* is white and black. If this anthology of academic feminist criticism recovers the ideologically oppressive polarity with the sexier pair, positions pink in the place held by white, is there any chance we can take this gesture up seriously? Can we begin to talk explicitly about our own colors and those of the women in the background of our proud Olympian display?

"That frame of reference—Columbia University, the Maison Française, the history of the other colloquia—lent so particular a coloration to" *The Poetics of Gender*. Columbia's Maison Française is the site of French cultural events, including all the so-called "International" Poetics colloquia. In this context, "international" has a rather particular sense: meaning both French and American speakers.

Elaine Showalter begins her paper with a profound sense of how this frame colors her work: "As one of the critics from an English department to have invaded the hitherto French space of the poetics conference, I am faced with some special anxieties. I am going to look at the development of women's writing within a framework that is both historical and American—a critical position that may make me about as authentic in the Maison Française as a Pepperidge Farm croissant."[14] Her marvelous, self-conscious performance of the last word—a gawky, decidedly American pronunciation—played out those anxieties to our delighted recognition.

Showalter continues: "my purpose is in fact to ask about the difference of American women's writing . . . through the use of a down-home, downright Yankee historical approach." "Downhome, downright Yankee" draws on the cultural commonplace opposing America and Europe, European finesse versus American homeliness. America is here insistently "down," to be contrasted with European "*high* sewing" in this article which wraps literary culture in the "American women's tradition" of the patchwork quilt.

"If we move away," Showalter goes on, "from some of the universal, even global, constructs of psychoanalytical feminist criticism to consider American women's writing, will we find a literature of *our* own and an American poetics of gender?" She wants to "move away from universal, global constructs." Berg warns us about a tendency to universalize which denies difference: this tendency toward universal constructs might be called cultural imperialism. It, for example, underwrote an enterprise in which Western European man set out to impose a culture which he thought of as universal upon the rest of the globe.

Showalter, who italicizes the word "our" in the phrase "a literature of *our* own," wrote a book called *A Literature of Their Own* about British women writers. Turning from British to American women's writing, Showalter links finding "a literature of *our* own" to finding "an American poetics of gender," links America's difference from Britain to Yankee difference in the Maison Française. The difference between English and French or, as it too often gets put in feminist and literary theory, between French and Anglo-American is a national difference with a long history within European culture. When we emphasize that difference we remain within the frame which takes Western European culture for the world. But Showalter's sentence locates the difference elsewhere: not Anglo-American versus French but American as opposed to European.

American culture enjoys a rich tradition of turning away from Europe. When that gesture simply affirms the "downhome, downright Yankee" it lines up all too well with a traditional European image of America. We run the risk of taking up our place as Europe's specular other, thus continuing to accept a Eurocentric view of America and the globe.

American academic culture continues to face Europe which we think of as facing West even though Europe is to our East. For example, Rice University, where I taught until recently, in 1988 instituted a course in "Western Civilization" as *the* foundation Humanities course to be required of all Science and Engineering majors. The growing percentage of Asian-Americans studying science and engineering at Rice will be required to take a Eurocentric conception of humanity all the while the university's Texas location renders especially ironic the idea of Europe as the West.

Although widely used today by American intellectuals trying to criticize ethnocentrism, the phrase "Western culture" continues to map the world from the standpoint of Europe. Denoting a patrimonial line moving ever westward from the Biblical Middle East through Classical Greece and Rome to modern Western Europe, crossing to North America to pursue its manifest destiny and reach Hollywood, "Western culture" is the ideology which not only justifies our taking this land from the so-called Indians (the misnomer appropriately locating them East of Europe, of civilization) but also determines the true Americans as those who, like our cultural heritage, descend from the East (e.g. Europe) rather than those who descend from the West (e.g. Asia). This Eurocentrism is certainly part of the coloration lent feminist criticism by the academic frame of reference.

In *The Poetics of Gender*, trying to talk about differences between women, I quote Gayatri Spivak: "However unfeasible and inefficient it may sound, I see no way to avoid insisting that there has to be a simultaneous other focus: not merely who am I? but who is the other woman?"[15] Early in 1983 I used this quotation to end my reading of the issue of *Yale French Studies* where it appeared, not commenting on the quotation, not integrating it into the text.[16] At the end of 1984, I used the very same quotation in my talk at the Poetics of Gender Colloquium. Although there it appeared in the middle of the text, it remains unglossed, undigested.

Rereading Spivak's essay in 1989, I notice the line immediately preceding my favorite quote: "let me insist that here, the difference between 'French' and 'Anglo-American' feminism is superficial." "Here" refers to the context of Spivak's essay, "French Feminism in an International Frame," which is precisely a recontextualizing. The 1981 feminist issue of *Yale French Studies* was subtitled "French Texts/American Contexts." Within that volume, Spivak's essay would recontextualize French texts from an American to a global frame. Perhaps the present chapter, as originally drafted in 1987, was the beginning of a gloss on this line of Spivak's which I forgot even as I feel compelled to repeat the line immediately following it, always out of context.

III
GOING BACK

7

Writing About Ourselves

In 1972, the first anthology of feminist literary criticism was published by Bowling Green University Popular Press. The press presents contradictory images: the university press, publishing for a small, highly-educated audience, conflicts with "popular," its suggestion of a broad, demotic audience. Of the contributors to that anthology, the editor, Susan Koppelman Cornillon, writes: "Some of us haven't gone in formal education beyond high school and some of us have Ph. D.'s."[1] The essays range from theoretically sophisticated articles with full scholarly apparatus reprinted from prestigious, mainstream academic journals (*American Quarterly*, *New Literary History*) to impressionistic pieces from feminist counterculture newspapers (*Off Our Backs*). The contributors to later feminist critical anthologies will all be trained academics; the other anthologies more solidly and traditionally located within academic criticism and theory. This path-breaking 1972 book, *Images of Women in Fiction: Feminist Perspectives*, nonetheless, shares most of the characteristics of the genre it will have founded: feminist writing which takes the academic study of literature as its field of struggle.

In the preface, Koppelman Cornillon writes: "People are beginning to see literature in new perspectives which have been opened up by the Women's Liberation Movement" (p. ix). Beginnings: the verb "begin" appears four times in the first two paragraphs; some form of the word occurs seven times in the first two pages. Yet the book is not and could not literally be a beginning. It is not the first book of feminist literary criticism: an honor probably due to Virginia Woolf's *A Room of One's Own*. Nor is it the first book of academic feminist criticism: a place usually conceded to Kate Millett's *Sexual Politics*. The essays in the volume were preceded by others: for example, those by Vivian Gornick, Wendy Martin, Cynthia Ozick, and Elaine Showalter collected in the classic 1971 anthology, *Woman in Sexist Society*.[2] That 1971 collection of feminist analyses, however, was neither strictly academic nor, more importantly for our purposes, strictly literary. Other influential articles of feminist literary criticism had appeared in various periodicals: mainstream, academic, or feminist. In point of fact, a first anthology could not possibly be an origin point. As opposed to Woolf's or Millett's solitary achievements, as opposed even to the single articles scattered here or there, the first anthology marks the moment when feminist study of literature has spread sufficiently to call for a representative gathering. Koppelman Cornillon's first sentence brings the good news: "*Female Studies I–IV* lists over eight hundred new courses in women's studies in the past few years, and more than half of these are being taught with their focus on literature" (p. ix). By 1972, "people are beginning to see literature" in feminist perspectives, not just a few vanguard critics, but "people," the collective noun implying masses.

If I take this history of feminist literary study back no further than the first anthology, it is because I am interested in this collective subject, "people" considering literature through the "perspectives opened up by the Women's Liberation Movement." There have been many stunning individual achievements in this field; some are mentioned in passing in my study. Too many, I'm afraid, are necessarily slighted as I pursue the subject of this history: the study of and theorizing about literature by that collective subject, the academic feminist.

By 1981 or so, that collective subject had reached her majority, become a full-fledged member of the literary academy. By 1981 or so, the academic feminist critic was no longer reading Koppelman Cornillon's anthology. Elaine Showalter's 1981 survey of the field, "Feminist Criticism in the Wilderness," makes no mention of it; nor do any of the essays in *Writing and Sexual Difference* (1980–82) or in *The New Feminist Criticism* (1977–85), although the latter anthology includes it in its comprehensive bibliography. *Images of Women in Fiction* is all but forgotten. It is generally assumed that we know what is in it, that we have gone far beyond it, that we have nothing to learn from it; so there is no reason to read it.

As someone who started seriously reading American feminist literary criticism around 1981, I did not read Koppelman Cornillon's anthology until 1987. I would start my seminar on feminist criticism with Josephine Donovan's 1975 anthology, *Feminist Literary Criticism*. I knew of the existence of *Images of Women in Fiction* but, since no one seemed to refer to it, there seemed little reason to consider it. When I finally read it, I found myself surprised. It was much more diverse, sophisticated, complex, and interesting than I had imagined. Joanna Russ was using Aristotle to explore literary convention; Lillian Robinson and Lise Vogel were reading Marx and Engels to piece out a politics of culture and a reinscription of modernism into history; Nina Baym was drawing on Lévi-Strauss for a structuralist reading of marriage.[3] The insight, conflict, and wisdom found in that 1972 anthology are not at all represented by our notion of the Images of Women phase of criticism.

Usually cited as the first phase of feminist literary study, considerations of Images of Women in literature are generally treated as juvenilia, of archival value at best. At play is a notion of our history as a simple progress from primitive criticism to ever better and more sophisticated. Some of us question what we have sacrificed to gain sophistication: populist appeal, political commitment, authenticity. But we rarely question our assumption that this stuff is primitive. Just two decades old, we already have a myth of our early years: a heroic, simpler time, when we were bold but crude.

> One striking feature of feminist metacriticism has been its attempt to describe the different types of feminist criticism . . . as constituting an evolutionary sequence. By the time "our" feminism was only ten years old it was already spoken of as being in its third phase. . . . This supersessional model of feminist criticism implies that feminism has progressed in a linear fashion, driven (like everything else) by the demon of progress from early crudities to later sophistications.[4]

> In my concentration on the legacy of and development from the earliest socio-historical feminists, I have tried to avoid nostalgia, the location of some utopia in the past, mine or anyone else's as well as the idealization it causes. But I agree with Cora Kaplan . . . who remarks . . . that brutal rejection of the past . . . "sets up another mythology in which these decades appear as a naïve political childhood assessed from a realistic adult perspective." I want to hold onto the past and to historicize it, while avoiding any premature consigning of it to history.[5]

Like all myths, this one serves to consolidate and justify some notion of who we are now. Yet unlike most golden ages, this one is neither prehistoric nor preliterate; we do not need oral history or ancient artifacts or esoteric archives. *Images of Women in Fiction* is not only in our university libraries, it is still in print. If we read it, we may find something whose shape does not simply fit the myth.

The fact that it is still in print suggests that, for some readers this is not the remote past but the present. "This supersessional model of feminist criticism implies that feminism has progressed in a linear fashion. . . . Yet to browse through current feminist journals is to realise that . . . many women who think of themselves as in some way feminist still engage energetically in first-phase exposés of androtexts" (Ruthven, p. 21). In writing this history of feminist literary criticism, I am at times reminded that there is no single history of some homogeneous national body of feminist readers.

When, in 1987, I opened *Images of Women in Fiction*, I was doubly surprised. First, because it was different than I had expected. But also, because it was deeply familiar. As much as I found myself excited by and enjoying some of the more sophisticated essays (taking notes, learning, finding phrases and ideas from them appearing in my speaking and writing), I was extremely embarrassed by some of the articles which I took to be written by undergraduates. Responding in a superior, professorial mode as if a nearly infinite expanse of knowledge and experience divided me from these writers, I found them naive, self-important, immature. Whereas I was pleased to identify with Joanna Russ or Nina Baym, I rejected with energetic disgust any identification with Johanna Leuchter as she disclosed the sexism in Hermann Hesse's novels or Nancy Burr Evans as she told what she had learned from her experience as a female undergraduate English major. And then I realized: this book, this moment of academic feminism, unread until 1987, was not wholly new to me.

Joanna Russ is an exemplary figure in this 1972 anthology: the author of the first essay, the only author to rate two articles. In the Spring of 1971, as an undergraduate, I took my first women's studies course. Entitled "Images of Women in Literature," it was taught by Joanna Russ. I loved the course.

In 1984 I wrote: "In the first phase of feminist criticism, literary critics schooled in the tradition of male authors turned on that male canon to show how the great authors were sexist pigs, that is to say, that the images of women in literature were distorting stereotypes that contributed to women's oppression and our alienation from self." Although I recognized that this characterization was reductive, it nonetheless fairly well represents what I expected to find in *Images of Women*. My schema went on: "In a second phase, feminists turned to women writers—the few already in the canon, the rediscovery of lost women writers from the past, and contemporary literary progeny of the women's movement. Feminist criticism moved from negation to affirmation. . . . A feminist can enjoy her identification with the heroine of Kate Chopin's *The Awakening* or Virginia Woolf's *Orlando*."[6]

Images of Women in Fiction includes not just the first but both of these "phases." In fact, the book is structured by a progress from the first to the second. Koppelman Cornillon writes in the Preface: "This book is divided into four sections depicting the roles women have been forced to assume in society and are now beginning to occupy, beginning with the most desiccated and lifeless traditional stereotypes of woman as heroine, and as invisible person, progressing through an awakening to reality, wherein the woman is treated as person, and ending with the newest insistence by women that we are equal in all respects to men" (p. x). The book moves from "The Woman as Heroine," title of the first section, to "The Woman as Hero," title of the third.

The center of the book, the turning point, occurring between the second and the third section, perfectly conforms to and confirms my expectations. Section Two ends with Johanna R. Leuchter's "Sex Roles in Three of Hermann Hesse's Novels." Although Hesse may not be canonical, he was a great influence on undergraduates at the time. Leuchter exposes this (counter)cultural hero as traditional and worse as far as sex roles go. The essay immediately following Leuchter's is equally marked by this historical moment, concluding with a celebratory summary of Alix Kates Shulman's *Memoirs of an Ex-Prom Queen*, which in 1972 was hot off the presses. Section Three, "The Woman as Hero," opens with Ellen Morgan's "Humanbecoming: Form and Focus in the Neo-Feminist Novel" which along with Shulman's novel, presents and praises June Arnold's *Applesauce* and Virginia Woolf's *Orlando*. Whereas Leuchter's piece is almost certainly an undergraduate paper, Morgan's text is "adapted from an unpublished dissertation, University of Pennsylvania, 1972" (p. 205). Does the progress from heroine to hero parallel this passage from student to Ph. D.?

All but one of the essays in "The Woman as Hero" section treat fiction written by women; the sole exception looks at novels written by men that depict feminists. "The Woman as Hero" thus fully meets our expectations, but we might be surprised to find that "The Woman as Heroine" section likewise contains only one article on male-authored fiction. The article that does treat a male novelist is written by a man, so nothing in the first section of the anthology answers to my first phase stereotype of women critics trashing male writers. True, the second section includes Leuchter's study of Hesse and two essays studying female characters by nineteenth-century male American novelists. Yet the second section also features an essay by Susan Koppelman Cornillon herself which rails at women novelists' failure to express women's reality in their female characters, finding particular fault with Joyce Carol Oates' 1969 novel, *them*.

Koppelman Cornillon's article is unusually vehement, but, especially since she is the volume's editor, we might also read it for the particular stamp of this anthology.[7] Kathleen Conway McGrath believes that Susanna Rowson, the woman who wrote the first American bestseller back at the end of the eighteenth century, reinforces conservative social ideology. Susan Gorsky finds mainly stereotypical female characters, albeit a predominance of "angels" rather than "demons," in the novels written by Englishwomen between 1840 and 1920. Madonna Marsden shows how the popular novelist Elizabeth Goudge uses her talents to recontain disgruntled female characters within the bounds of woman's conventional role as wife and mother. Even Nan Bauer Maglin, who is mainly concerned with novels by Henry James and George Gissing, begins by contrasting James's and Gissing's novels which give us feminist role models with works by Jane Austen and George Eliot which offer us only "women in traditionally male-dependent relationships."[8] I expected the 1972 collection to go from trashing men to praising women. Although it does in fact conclude by celebrating women writers, it begins by trashing *them*.

In the anthology, Florence Howe says: "In several hundred women's studies courses in literature this year, students are searching for images of women or classifying the stereotypes they find. . . . This is not, perhaps I should add, an effort to damage the reputations of male writers; that's not the point."[9] Howe points to a connection between studying images of women and trashing male authors in order to deny that connection. At the same time, her gesture shows her awareness that such a connection, however inaccurate, is being made. In the context of the Koppelman Cornillon anthology, however, it is noteworthy that Howe never questions that the literature "students are searching," where they are finding these "stereotypes," is written by men. She might, for example, have cleared up the question of whether feminists were trying to damage male reputations by pointing out that they are also finding stereotypes in women's writing. Later in her essay when Howe discusses the classroom effect of reading women writers, it is clear they are not being read for the study of stereotypes. Howe presents two types of feminist reading: reading male authors for stereotypes, reading females for pleasurable identification.

Howe recounts what has already happened in the feminist class-room. Koppelman Cornillon alludes to this prior feminist practice in a note explaining the specific focus of her own article: "I will not attempt to deal with the reasons male novelists misrepresent female characters in their work, i.e., create inauthentic females (much has been said about this topic, particularly in relation to the fiction of Hemingway), but I will attempt to deal with this problem in the work of female novelists."[10] "Much" has already been said about male novelists. Kop-pelman Cornillon will look at inauthentic characters by female novelists precisely because that has not been done, taking the study of images of women onto new territory.

Koppelman Cornillon's anthology takes us to a deeper level of literary sexism. According to Marcia R. Lieberman,

[s]exism affects literature at three levels, of which the easiest to detect is criticism. . . . It is also apparent that some male writers impose sexist views of female psychology upon the characters they create. . . . The most subtle, pervasive level at which sexism affects literature, however, is that of literary convention. The treatment and fate of the heroine, for example, may be controlled by conventions that inherently impose a sexist view on the author and the reader, male or female.[11]

Critical prejudice is "easiest to detect"; male writers' prejudices are "also apparent." Beyond authorial sexism is "the most subtle, pervasive level" of sexism. Lieberman's third level takes us to the most literary sort of sexism, that which inheres in literary structures themselves, not in extraliterary ideas imposed upon or contained in literature. Literary conventions can impose sexism on readers and authors, "male *or female*." Women writers, even those with explicitly feminist loyalties, may, unwittingly, perpetrate sexism when invoking the conventions which afford their work recognition as literature.

Lieberman gives one example of such a literary convention: "the treatment and fate of the heroine." That specific convention is precisely the focus of the anthology's first essay: Joanna Russ's marvelous "What Can a Heroine Do?" "Novels, especially," writes Russ, "depend upon what central action can be imagined as being performed by the protago-nist—i.e., what can a central character *do* in a book? . . . [O]f all the possible actions people can do in fiction, very few can be done by women" (pp. 4–5). What a heroine can do is not in the author's power to determine, but is largely controlled by what Lieberman calls "literary convention." According to Russ, "writers . . . do not make up their stories out of whole cloth; they are pretty much restricted to the attitudes, the beliefs, the expectations, and above all the plots, that are 'in the air'—'plot' being what Aristotle called *mythos*; and in fact it is probably most accurate to call the plot-patterns *myths*. They are dramatic embodiments of what a culture believes to be true—or what it would like to be true—or what it is mortally afraid may be true" (p. 4). Literature is made from conventional plots and those plots carry "what a culture believes" or wants or fears; in other words, conventional plots are "dramatic embodiments" of ideology.

The formal structures of literature are themselves the bearers of the most profound sexism, one we can only get at if we go beyond the sexism that can simply be ascribed to the author. When feminist critics find stereotypes in male-authored works, it is easy to rest with an explanation in the author's gender, his investments, his fears and prejudices. Expanding the study of stereotypes to women's writing leads feminist criticism to a truly literary problem, sexism as structurally inscribed in literary form.

Lieberman's specific example of a deep sexist structure is the subject of the first section of *Images of Women in Fiction*. Joanna Russ's "What Can a Heroine Do?" provides the theoretical framework for this consideration of the heroine. Russ literally provides the frame for "The Woman as Heroine" since she is the author not only of the first but also of the last essay of the section.

Russ's second essay, "The Image of Women in Science Fiction," begins by showing the gender stereotypes that have pervaded science fiction written by men. The last third of the article then turns to fiction written by women; according to Russ, "the usual faults show up just as often" (p. 89). Like Koppelman Cornillon, Russ focuses her disappointment in particular on a 1969 novel by a highly-esteemed and successful female author. "The Image of Women in Science Fiction" concludes with an attack on Ursula K. LeGuin's *Left Hand of Darkness*.

Russ also expresses her admiration for the novel: "a fine book . . . a beautifully written book" (p. 89). Unlike Koppelman Cornillon on Oates, Russ is self-conscious about her relation to LeGuin. "I am too hard on the book," she writes in a note at the end of her discussion of *The Left Hand of Darkness*, seeking to soften the attack. The note goes on to offer three possible justifications for the novel's apparent failings: "one could make out a good case that the author is trying to criticize [the narrator's] viewpoint. There is also a technical problem . . . han-

dling *two* unknowns in one novel would present insuperable difficulties. Moreover, Miss LeGuin wishes us to contrast Winter with our own
world, not with some hypothetical, different society." Yet after three
sentences of trying to be fair to LeGuin, the lengthy note closes with
the most damning statement Russ makes about the other woman:
"However, her earlier novel, *City of Illusions* . . . is surprisingly close
to the space opera, he-man ethos—either anti-feminism or resentment
at being feminine, depending on how you look at it" (p. 94 n. 29).
The condemnation is, in a sense, more devastating because Russ is
apparently going out of her way to be fair.

Russ's ambivalent note shows an affective intensity about criticizing a woman writer, absent elsewhere in the book. Whereas McGrath,
Gorsky, Marsden, and Koppelman Cornillon are female critics considering women fiction writers, Russ is herself a science fiction writer
judging a more successful sister. The psychological scenario is more
apt to involve the aggressive aspects of identification: a complex we
can call rivalry.[12]

I do not want to reduce the consideration of sexism in women's
writing to female rivalry or any other psychological mode. I have tried
first to emphasize the theoretical advances such a move implies. Finding stereotypes in women's writing takes us beyond the more "apparent"
male-authored sexism to encounter a gender bias that is both more
intrinsically literary and more pervasively ideological. Yet I also believe
it is worth attending, although not exclusively, to psychological dynamics that may shape criticism in order better to understand what we
are doing and why. Recently, feminists have begun to discuss rivalry
between women and even between feminists; we have begun to consider those aspects of "sisterhood" which mean not solidarity but hostile competition.[13] It may be useful to think of Russ's troubled note to
LeGuin—displaying a combination of admiration, guilt, and aggression—as speaking a certain kind of woman to woman relation: the
view of a more established woman by a woman with ambitions in the
same field. We might call this the little sister's discourse on the big
sister.

In *Images of Women in Fiction*, the most dramatic occurrence of
this discourse is certainly Russ's discussion of LeGuin. The instance
most important for our study of feminist criticism, however, occurs in
Linda Ray Pratt's article. One of the collection's few studies of men's
writing, Pratt's essay nonetheless criticizes women writers, not authors
of fiction but feminist literary critics.

Pratt begins: "A number of recent feminist critics have indicated the two dimensional nature of women in the nineteenth-century American novel."[14] She then appends a page long note to this first sentence, citing, "for example," articles from 1971–72 by Carolyn Heilbrun, Judith H. Montgomery, and Wendy Martin, and stating: "My argument for the superior humanity of these heroines suggests the opposite" (pp. 171–72 n. 1). The critic begins by citing other feminist critics in order to assert her opposition to them. Although this is a common strategy in non-feminist academic writing, it is, to my knowledge, the earliest instance of it in feminist criticism.

The note would seem to call into question the findings of "recent feminist critics." The text, however, treats the findings as indubitable, but wants to know the explanation for them. The opening paragraph concludes: "Part of the explanation no doubt lies in the answers offered by such generalized studies as Kate Millett's *Sexual Politics*, or Carolyn Heilbrun's forthcoming *Androgyny: A Literary Essay*. From the standpoint of literary criticism, however, such explanations as 'patriarchy' or 'anti-androgynous' 'male-fantasy' novels, or any of several other offerings, are often unsatisfying and occasionally inaccurate" (p. 155). By the end of her first paragraph, Pratt has already, twice, taken her distance from recent feminist criticism.

Note where she stands. "From the standpoint of literary criticism," Pratt goes on to examine "the inadequacy of this criticism." "First, assumptions regarding the two dimensional nature of women in certain novelists often ignore the fact that the male characters in those novels may *suffer* the same lack of fully human delineation. . . . Critics who *slight* this general characteristic of American novels . . . are less than entirely convincing" (pp. 155–56, emphasis added). Critics who complain about flat women characters "ignore the fact" that male characters also "suffer" and in the same way. These critics thus not only fail to be "entirely convincing"; they also "slight" the novels. Feminists complain of female suffering and injustice to women. Pratt picks up the vocabulary of injustice, but she is concerned with the "suffering" of characters and "slights" to literature.

Worry about "slighting" novels is not as marginal to this anthology or to feminist criticism as one might assume. In her summary of the "Woman as Heroine" section, Koppelman Cornillon writes: "This section consists of analyses of traditional views of women, of the 'sugar 'n' spice and everything nice' stereotype that insults most fiction" (Preface, p. x). The complaint about the stereotype here is not that it oppresses women but that it "insults fiction." The feminist literary academic speaks not only as a woman but also from a professional identity she has invested much time and effort to acquire. We should perhaps not be surprised to find that the feminist *literary* critic speaks out of a vested interest in literature, speaks "from the standpoint of literary criticism."

"The second shortcoming of some recent criticism," writes Pratt,

> is in analyses and interpretations which depart widely from the context of both the understood critical vocabulary and the controlling worlds of the novels themselves. Such criticism extracts from the novel the image of a two-dimensional woman and then proceeds to measure her by such innovative terminology as 'patriarchy' or 'anti-androgyny,' or even 'Galetea.' Here the chief thrust of the criticism is to illuminate certain societal attitudes toward women rather than the function of women characters within the context of a specific novel. (p. 156)

The quoted phrases are from Millett, Heilbrun, and Montgomery. These critics are called out-of-bounds on two counts: they "depart widely" from the discourse of the critical community and from "the controlling worlds of the novels." Interested in "societal attitudes" rather than the novel itself, this "recent criticism" is extrinsic rather than intrinsic.

René Wellek and Austin Warren divide their book, *Theory of Literature*, into "The Extrinsic Approach to the Study of Literature" and "The Intrinsic Study of Literature." Note the lack of parallel structure to the two section titles: only *approaching* "the study of literature," the extrinsic approach is itself outside literary study; the "intrinsic" is "the study of literature" proper. In the "Literature and Society" chapter of the extrinsic section, Wellek and Warren assert that "extrinsic approaches to literature" cannot "do justice to the analysis, description, and evaluation of a literary work."[15] Wellek and Warren's book was certainly the canonical theory of literature for those in graduate school in the sixties and early seventies. Their preference for the "intrinsic study" of literature is tied to a demand that we "do justice" to literature, a demand echoed in Koppelman Cornillon's Preface and Pratt's critique.

Pratt's critique closes thus: "As feminist critics of literature, we must now take our new understanding of women back into the works themselves and re-examine the characters within the controlling values of the novel" (p. 156). However harsh she is toward feminist critics, however much allegiance she displays to the ruling values of the literary academy, Pratt fully considers herself a feminist critic. She wants to ring in a new era in feminist literary study. From the Women's Liberation Movement, we have gained a "new understanding of women." "Now" we must take that understanding "back into the works themselves." She wants an intrinsic feminist criticism, one no less feminist but which will remain "within the controlling values of the novel."[16]

In her 1980 survey of feminist literary criticism, Cheri Register writes: "From the start, feminist criticism was identified as a contextual criticism, a reaction against the strict formalism in vogue in midcentury. Many of us avoided close textual examinations. . . . Our training, however, predisposed us to watch style, structure, and imagery. The benefits of that training are becoming visible again in the attention to formal characteristics."[17]

In 1981, Elizabeth Abel begins her Introduction to *Writing and Sexual Difference* with a brief history of feminist criticism. "Initially," she writes, "literary criticism . . . focused primarily on blind spots in male texts, cataloged [sic] masculine stereotypes of women. . . . Feminist readings . . . typically progressed from text to author to society."[18] By 1981, Abel finds, feminist literary study has shifted to more properly literary or textual concerns. Abel's description of the initial phase of feminist reading (cataloguing stereotypes in male texts) does not fit our 1972 collection with its images of women in women's fiction. Already beyond the initial stage, the first anthology is already moving toward the more truly *literary* criticism that a decade later will have arrived.

According to Abel, the later feminist "concern with textual conventions dispels one litany of familiar accusations," such as "insensitivity to literary values" (p. 2). Pratt's accusation belongs to this litany. Finding feminist study insufficiently literary, Pratt proposes or promotes a feminist criticism that will do justice to literature. Her gesture will be repeated through the next decade. I was surprised to find it so early, almost as soon as feminist criticism was established. Again and again the academic feminist critic will strive for a synthesis of feminism and intrinsic literary study, trying to resolve a conflict between her feminist identity and her institutional identity, between valuing women and valuing literature.

Abel continues: "Such sophisticated reading may belatedly accord the feminist critic a position closer to the mainstream of critical debate.

It may also generate a litany of new accusations: that the concern with textuality augurs a return to formalism; that feminist critics have betrayed political commitments in pursuit of academic credibility." By 1981 something has decidedly changed. No longer "insensitive to literary values," feminist criticism is now in danger of insensitivity to feminist values. It is precisely the thesis of the present book that this change helped to "accord the feminist critic a position closer to the mainstream of critical debate" around 1981.

In 1983, Elaine Showalter asserts a similar shift in feminist criticism: "If in its origins feminist criticism derived more from feminism than from criticism, we could argue that today the situation is reversed."[19] Showalter dates this switch around 1975. Both Abel and Showalter line up an allegiance to feminism with a first stage of feminist criticism, an allegiance to literary criticism with a second stage. Looking at *Images of Women in Fiction*, we see the switch already begun. Pratt is already, in 1972, turning on an earlier "stage" of feminist criticism, already speaking "from the standpoint of literary criticism." At the very least, we must conclude that the initial stage was extremely brief, the reversal began very early. Or we might want to consider this division into stages a simplification of what has been, from the beginning and up to the present, an ongoing history of divided loyalties.

"[T]he real or apparent conflict between critical standards and political engagement recurs in various guises in the writings of feminist critics throughout the 1970s and early 1980s" (Moi, pp. 23–24). In the 1972 anthology, Lieberman expresses this conflict thus: "The feminist critic has to struggle with her dual consciousness of the inaccuracy or distortion of the depiction of women in novels, poems and plays which she considers to be great works of art" (p. 338). In the mid-eighties, when the privileged discourse in the literary academy has shifted from great art to critical theory, Elizabeth Meese expresses this dual consciousness thus: "I begin here in indecision because I cannot reconcile the terms, the differences within myself, feminist criticism and critical theory."[20]

A year after the publication of *Images of Women in Fiction*, Carolyn Heilbrun and Catharine Stimpson performed a dialogue between feminist critics in which "X" speaks from a primary commitment to literature while "Y" has a primary commitment to the interests of women. Whenever I read the dialogue, I find myself siding with Y against X. I and my students always want to identify X simply with Heilbrun, Y directly with

Stimpson, want to locate and name the good and the bad feminist critic. The paragraph introducing the debate, however, specifically states:

> In the dialogue that follows, Heilbrun and Stimpson have isolated the essential differences between two distinct approaches to the feminist critical process, and presented them in the form of a debate between two feminist critics, designated "X" and "Y." Obviously, a certain amount of abstraction was necessary to develop the two positions as a working dialogue. . . . The authors intend it to represent the sort of dialogue going on not only *among* feminists but within the individual feminist critic herself.[21]

Our wish simply to distinguish the radical from the domestic feminist critic leads us to ignore what this introductory paragraph clearly says. When we take this as a debate between two critics rather than as something "presented in the form of a debate between two critics," we do not need to consider this as "the sort of dialogue going on within the individual feminist critic herself."

X explicitly states: "for the purposes of this dialogue, I am going to put aside what I know of the politics of literature, and suggest the ways in which even the despised New Criticism can become feminist criticism" (p. 62). In order better to contrast with Y, X, whom I persist in confusing with Carolyn Heilbrun, embraces the possibility of a feminist New Criticism, choosing formalism and textuality over the politics of literature. A year earlier, Linda Pratt sees Carolyn Heilbrun as too concerned with the socio-historical, positioning Heilbrun in the role of Y in contrast to Pratt's own attempt to "suggest the ways in which New Criticism can become feminist criticism." If Heilbrun switches sides depending on whether paired with Pratt or with Stimpson, let that lead us to remember the dramatized polarization of these debates which tend to transform differences within the academic feminist critic into differences between us.

Not that certain individual critics have not been more clearly either on the side of feminism or the side of the literary institution. But our collective subject, the academic feminist critic, has perhaps necessarily expressed, in different ways, throughout her history, a double viewpoint, linked to her contradictory identity as both a feminist and a literary academic.

* * *

Earlier, I said that *Images of Women in Fiction* progresses from "The Woman as Heroine," title of the first section, to "The Woman as Hero," title of the third. I never mentioned the title of the intervening second section: "The Invisible Woman." Recalling Ralph Ellison's *Invisible Man*, this title points to something which pervades the 1972 anthology.

Ellen Morgan makes one of the volume's two explicit references to Ellison's novel: "although movements such as neo-feminism are particularly inclined to produce polemical writing . . . their natural inclination toward polemic should not be thought to imply that neo-feminist writing is, or will be, primarily of this type. . . . Obviously, to use Ellison's *Invisible Man* as just one case in point, passionate consciousness of oppression does not preclude the creation of art" (pp. 187–88). Relying on an analogy between women and blacks, Morgan offers *The Invisible Man* as model for what feminist writing could be. The analogy fulfills a wish.

In this collection, Florence Howe recounts her experience as a teacher. The turning point of her story occurs in the summer of 1964 when she "went to Mississippi to teach in a freedom school" (p. 258). Howe writes dramatically: "it had taken Mississippi to make clear to me the need for a new connection: between learning and life. Black students needed to feel and love blackness, to want liberation enough to struggle, even die for it. Maybe it would have to be the same for women" (p. 259). The next summer, she taught black high school students in an experimental N.D.E.A. Institute. Reading Richard Wright's novel *Native Son*, they identified with the hero, Bigger Thomas. In 1972 she read *The Awakening* with a class of adult women who identified with Chopin's protagonist, Edna Pontellier. "It is certainly arguable," writes Howe, "that, like black students who saw themselves as Biggers with a difference, these women recognized their relationship to Edna and drew strength . . . from it" (p. 274). Her phrase "it is certainly arguable" conveys both certitude and contentiousness, marking the intensity of her stake in the analogy. Teaching women's literature to women students is, hopefully, like teaching black literature to black students. The analogy functions here as a precedent. Blacks in 1965 provide the model for women in 1972.

Analogy implies a parallel. The two classrooms are not strictly parallel; they intersect in the teacher, the same white woman. Not only does the 1972 class recall 1965, but, in this account, the 1964 experience already prefigures 1972: "Maybe it would have to be the same for women." Mid-sixties black consciousness made this white woman feel *we* ought to get to where *they* are. When she finds 1972 women students resemble 1965 black students, we cannot view what she finds as separate from her earlier wish to find precisely that.

I am not trying to say either that as historical observer she simply found what she was looking for or that as historical agent she simply created her women students in the image of her black students. Howe makes perfectly clear that her story belongs to the genre of autobiography; yet she also gives it the absolutely general title "Feminism and Literature." She thus explicitly takes her reader to a place where history cannot be simply disentangled from the anticipatory desires and retrospective longings of subjectivity. Trying to write the history of feminist literary study from the subjective position, Howe offers her autobiography as the story of our collective subject: "I use my life because it is an ordinary one and because I have been mainly not a writer but a teacher of literature" (p. 255). She uses her life for two reasons: it is "ordinary," that is, can be taken as representative of a collective and her main identity is as "teacher of literature."

Howe's drama centers on the teacher-student relation. In 1964 she goes to Mississippi, "to teach," but, in fact, she *learns something* from her students. The tables are turned; "I date this experience as the turning point in my life," she writes (p. 259); the teacher becomes her students' student. In 1965 her students identify with Bigger Thomas; in 1972 they identify with Edna Pontellier. Howe, however, does not identify with Edna; no more than she does with Bigger. Throughout her account, her unswerving identification is as teacher of literature. What she learned in Mississippi in 1964 was how to improve that role, how to make the teaching of literature seem important, essential, alive. The analogy leads her to hope that, what teaching literature felt like with those black students, it could also be with white women students, the students she mainly teaches, the students we mainly teach. Then, as now, the vast majority of students of literature are white women. Howe's "arguable" analogy would make teaching them as exciting and important as going down to Mississippi Freedom Summer. The feminist teacher of literature has a lot to gain from the analogy.

In their contribution to the collection, Lillian Robinson and Lise Vogel help us see why feminists might find the sex to race analogy so attractive. Considering race, sex, and class exclusion from culture, they begin with, and devote the least time to, racial exclusion. "Racial exclusion," they write, "presents the clearest case. . . . At least nobody doubts the reality of racial exclusion. Those whose exclusion from the cultural tradition is based on sex or class have a more ambiguous problem of consciousness."[22] Because racial exclusion is clearest, it need not be demonstrated; so they spend much more time persuading us of the reality of sex and class exclusion. Because racial exclusion is clearest, it is most persuasive; so they begin there.

Robinson and Vogel do not invoke the race to sex analogy, but they do use a race to class analogy: "a working-class person acquiring 'culture' . . . is rejecting what the working class *knows* to be true and, in this sense, 'changing race.'"[23] American Marxists, like feminists, envy the success of the Black movement in raising consciousness about oppression. As Robinson and Vogel put it, "nobody doubts the reality of racial exclusion." The analogy to race is a way to be taken seriously.

Lieberman complains of the "laughter and scorn of male colleagues who reject . . . feminist criticism . . . as being silly" (p. 338). She contrasts our lot with that of our black colleagues: "the same unease which is permitted to the Black critic or teacher, and even respected in him (when he deals with Faulkner, for example) is treated as a joke when expressed by women." The black critic or teacher already is where we would like to be.

Lieberman's pronouns make the black critic or teacher's gender clear; it is equally clear that "women" here is a parallel category that does not intersect with "black." In 1982, bell hooks began her *Ain't I a Woman* by pointing out that in analogies between women and blacks, so dear to feminist thinking, the assumption is that women are white and blacks are men. That same year Gloria T. Hull, Patricia Bell Scott, and Barbara Smith edited an anthology of Black Women's Studies entitled *All the Women Are White, All the Blacks Are Men, But Some of Us Are Brave.*[24] White feminists may finally have begun to listen to black feminists such as these, however minimally. In 1972, white feminist critics blithely propose to join black men, offering "the invisible woman" as counterpart to "the invisible man." Looking back, thanks to the impact of black feminist writing, we now know to ask what place that gesture leaves for the black woman.

Nowhere in its four sections does *Images of Women in Fiction* consider writing by black women. There is, however, a pretty good list of black women's fiction at the back of the book. Although omitted from the Preface's delineation of the volume, an extensive annotated bibliography constitutes in fact a fifth section of the anthology.

Compiled by six women who "started a seminar on Women and

Literature at the Cambridge-Goddard Graduate School" in Fall 1971,[25] the bibliography, in at least one specific, differs markedly from the editor's perspective. The bibliography considers Joyce Carol Oates' *them* "[a]n excellent book [which] examines in a sympathetic way the complexities of violence, sexism, and racism that are perpetuated by a system in which some people are hopelessly trapped in poverty and ignorance" (p. 376). Compare Koppelman Cornillon on the same novel: "Although it may be appropriate for her characters to express [sexist] ideas . . . it is not appropriate for Oates to share them. . . . [A]t no time does Miss Oates separate herself from her characters and say, 'This sexism, like their racism, their ignorance . . ., their poverty, is part of their victimization'" (p. 120).

The bibliography has four sections: I. Women Writers Before the Twentieth Century; II. Twentieth Century Women Writers of Fiction; III. Works About Literature; IV. Summary Reference Lists. The fourth section is made up of two lists: A. Books by Black Women, and B. Books Presenting Lesbian Relationships. We are informed that the books on the lists in this last section are all, unless otherwise stated, annotated in the second section. The bibliography thus deploys a double strategy in its treatment of these women marginalized by race or sexual preference. The marginalized women are both included *and* separated; these books are in the general section on women writers *and* on separate lists. These minority groups ought to be included in any general notion of women but also need particular mention in order not to be erased by the tendency to construct a group portrait based on the white, heterosexual majority.

In the fourth section of the bibliography we find a book by Toni Cade, entitled *The Black Woman*. Turning to the second section, we find that this book, published by Signet in 1970, is actually edited by Cade: "An exciting collection of essays, short stories, and poems written by black women concerning the lives of black women in America" (p. 365). *The Black Woman* also shows up in the third section of the bibliography, although neither the entry in section II nor in section IV gives us this cross-reference. When treated as non-fiction, *The Black Woman* is more than just "exciting":

A solid and well put together collection of political, historical, and critical essays by black women. . . . In her introduction Cade says, "there have been women who have been able to think better than they've been trained and have produced the canon of literature fondly referred to as 'feminist literature'; Anais Nin, Simone de Beauvoir, Doris Lessing, Betty Friedan, etc. And the question for us arises how relevant are the truth, the experiences, the findings of white women to Black women?" (p. 384)

Nothing in the bibliography section explicitly devoted to black women leads us to this disturbing question. This question cannot simply be integrated into a composite of primarily white women writers; nor can it simply be appended as an addendum for further reflection. Either of those two strategies, and even both of them taken together, still assume that *The Black Woman* can be included in women's experience or feminist literature as formulated by white women. Cade's quotation in section III of the bibliography suggests that, rather than including or appending, the real consideration of black women will demand rethinking our findings about "women" and recognizing them as findings by and about white women.

Actually, there is one name on the bibliography's list of black women writers that does show up in the text of the anthology, in The Invisible Woman section, in the one article that was reprinted from a nonacademic feminist periodical. In "Why Aren't We Writing About Ourselves?", originally published in *Off Our Backs*, Carole Zonis Yee wonders "where are all the Jewish women writers who can tell us the reality of what it feels like to be a woman and Jewish. And [she] beg[ins] to imagine characters and plots: For instance . . . a young Jewish Angela Davis" (pp. 132–33).

Remarking our non- or mis-representation in contemporary literature by gentile women and Jewish men, Yee asks "Why Aren't We Writing About Ourselves?" Ourselves?: "the names of some of the most prominent writers in the women's movement . . . bear the unmistakable mark of the twelve tribes of Israel." Ourselves?: "of those academicians teaching literature and writing criticism of literature, many seem to be women and Jewish" (p. 131).

The shortest piece in the volume and the furthest from academic discourse, Yee's essay is placed immediately after the editor's own article. If Koppelman Cornillon chose to reprint and include it, despite its marginality to the genre, it must, in some way, be central. Here is another of Yee's imaginary protagonists: "a young, brilliant, attractive Jewess who sees herself climb to fame and reputation as a university professor, giving speeches at MLA conventions, publishing articles, adored by her students" (p. 133). Although not itself academic discourse, "Why Aren't We Writing About Ourselves?" has something to say about academic feminism.

The names of some of the contributors to *Images of Women in Fiction* "bear," as Yee puts it, "the unmistakable mark of the twelve tribes of Israel." Some of them even acknowledge the identity. Howe begins her life story with her grandfather, an orthodox Rabbi, teaching her Hebrew and Yiddish (p. 255). Robinson and Vogel, in their exploration of racism in literature, briefly discuss anti-Semitism, mentioning in passing that they are Jewish (p. 290).

In the anthology, Charles Blinderman demonstrates that Anthony Trollope "adapted [the] Dark Lady archetype to symbolize the Victorian woman liberationist and her reductio ad absurdum, the Jewess."[26] For the Victorian novelist, "[t]he complete Dark Lady is the Jewess" (p. 63). Trollope used the Dark Lady "for the political purpose of confounding the aspirations of the women's rights movement" (p. 58). The connection between Jewess and feminist is able, thanks to anti-Semitism, to make the feminist seem absurd.

According to Blinderman, Trollope's use of the Jewess supports "Leslie Fiedler's thesis that in the historical treatment of the Dark Lady, is apparent 'the Northern European wish to glorify the fair and debase the black.'"[27] Robinson and Vogel connect anti-Semitism with racist literary treatment of blacks, but they also believe that, in America, anti-Semitism is a thing of the past, "never a material force in our lives" (p. 290). Feminists have debated whether Jewish women are victims of racism or holders of white privilege. Most likely, the correct answer is both. In any case, Koppelman Cornillon's inclusion of Yee's essay opens the possibility of endowing "The Invisible Woman" with more specificity, of writing, not about some universal woman with no attributes but gender, but "writing about ourselves."

At a few points, *Images of Women in Fiction* moves beyond analogy to remember that everyone belongs both to a sex and a race. Considering those two categories along with socio-economic class, Robinson and Vogel write: "Obviously . . . a single individual possesses all three characteristics. The white woman may share all the tastes and concerns of the bourgeoisie if she is born or marries into it. . . . Her experience is not wholly excluded from the world of art, because she does participate in the experience of her class and also because she has learned to interpret that experience the way the dominant culture does" (p. 283). Having "learned to interpret" according to "dominant culture," the white woman, "not wholly excluded," can function inside institutions like the literary academy.

"North American culture is not only male in its point of view; it is also Western European," writes Joanna Russ in the first article of the anthology (p. 14). To demonstrate her central thesis that "culture is male," Russ too makes use of the sex to race analogy, but her version of this familiar story has a different twist:

> what is an American Black writer to make of our accepted myths? For example, what is she or he to make of the still-current myth (so prominent in *King Lear*) that Suffering Brings Wisdom? . . . Does suffering bring wisdom to *The Invisible Man*? When critics do not find what they expect, they cannot imagine that the fault may lie in their expectations. I know of a case in which the critics (white and female) decided after long, nervous discussion that Baldwin was "not really a novelist" but that Orwell was. (p. 15)

Although the only black writers she names are male, Russ's pronouns at least leave open the possibility of a black woman writer. The more visible females in the passage are white critics not suffering exclusion but subjecting a black male writer to it. Here where blacks come in two genders and females belong to different races, the sex to race analogy breaks down. Whereas the Dark Lady might stand beside The Invisible Man, the white female critic could well find herself on the opposite side.

I have yet to mention the title of the fourth section of *Images of Women in Fiction*. "Feminist Aesthetics" seems appropriate enough as the title for this section comprised of theory rather than applied criticism. What is surprising is what Koppelman Cornillon does and does not say about the section.

Here is the Preface's description: "*Feminist Aesthetics.* In these determined and courageous statements are revealed portions of the credo and manifesto of women, in which is made patently clear women's desires and determinations and their abilities to achieve, at least as much as men do, their goals" (p. xi). "Credo and manifesto" do give some sense that these are theoretical statements rather than practical applications, yet nothing (and I have quoted the complete description) makes any reference at all to "aesthetics."

Let us now look again at the Preface's overview of the collection's progress: "This book is divided into four sections depicting the roles women have been forced to assume in society and are now beginning to occupy, beginning with the most desiccated and lifeless traditional stereotypes of woman as heroine, and as invisible person, progressing through an awakening to reality, wherein the woman is treated as person, and ending with the newest insistence by women that we are equal in all respects to men" (p. x). This sentence is immediately followed by a paragraph on each section, ending with the just-cited description of the fourth section. It is possible to gloss this sentence by lining up a phrase with each of the sections, but we get into trouble when we come to section four. "Beginning with the most desiccated and lifeless traditional stereotypes of woman as heroine" is easily aligned with the first section, "The Woman as Heroine." "And as invisible person" just as surely refers to the second section, "The Invisible Woman." "Progressing through an awakening to reality, wherein the woman is treated as person" would then refer to the third section, "The Woman as Hero." "And ending with the newest insistence by women that we are equal in all respects to men" is left to cover "Feminist Aesthetics."

Casting her book as a progress narrative, maybe the editor could not figure out how to fit the final section in; so she neglected it, plotting just the first three sections. Koppelman Cornillon tells it as the most general story of women's progress: "the roles women have been forced to assume in society and are now beginning to occupy." The book would belong to Morgan's genre of the neo-feminist novel, the story of Everywoman's progress from sex-role to liberation. But if the narrative includes the fourth section, the anthology may really be "writing about ourselves." Progressing from her traditional circumscribed role, the "teacher of literature" ends up doing aesthetics, thus becoming "equal in all respects" to her male colleagues in the literary academy.

The book's final essay is Josephine Donovan's "Feminist Style Criticism." Following a suggestion Virginia Woolf makes in *A Room of One's Own*, Donovan seeks to determine what constitutes feminine style. She examines sentences by Austen, Eliot, Chopin, Richardson, and Woolf herself. Working with her last example, Donovan remarks: "I do not presume here to do a thorough analysis of Woolf's magnificent style" (p. 351). She shows no such compunction about subjecting the other four novelists to stylistic analysis. Functioning here as both theoretical authority and supreme stylist, Woolf represents the aesthetic summit of the last essay, the terminus of the book's progress.

Like any good telos, she is sighted at the beginning of the story. In the collection's first article, Russ suggests "lyricism" as a way out for the writer trapped in sexist plot conventions. Her example for this "alternative" is Woolf whom she terms a "lyric novelist" (pp. 13–14). The term "lyric," usually associated with poetry, locates Woolf somewhere near the edge of prose fiction. Donovan concurs: "The impeccable design of the sentences, that not a word could be changed, creates an aesthetic control over the 'events' narrated that makes this great work [*To the Lighthouse*] more like a poem than the series of dramatic encounters of the traditional novel" (p. 351).

The first anthology of feminist literary criticism is entitled "Images of Women in *Fiction*." In the preface, Koppelman Cornillon states: "I have limited the panorama to fiction because to have attempted to cover other forms of literature would have made a huge task unmanageably large" (p. x). Poetry is beyond this book's horizon. The editor treats that boundary as merely heuristic. Yet when we read this volume as a narrative progress toward the "aesthetic control" which makes Woolf's novel "more like a poem," this horizon begins to beckon.

"One might wish indeed," writes Donovan, "that had anyone attempted Flaubert's great ambition, to write a novel about nothing, it might have been Virginia Woolf" (p. 351). Indeed! The father of the modernist novel's "great ambition" would free form of any encumbering content. "Feminist style criticism" leads us to wish for this great formalist triumph, only achieved by a woman.

Toril Moi's *Sexual/Textual Politics* shares Donovan's admiration for Woolf. Moi's account of the 1972 anthology singles out Donovan's article: "all the contributors to Cornillon's volume (with the notable exception of Josephine Donovan) adhere to a rather simple form of content analysis when confronted with the literary text. . . . The wider question at issue here is clearly the problem of realism as opposed to modernism. Predictably enough, several essays in the volume lash out against modernism" (p. 46). Donovan remarks that Woolf is "of course, part of the larger literary movement against 19th century realism which was to dominate early 20th century literature as 'Modernism'" (p. 344). I do not share Moi's conviction that modernism is intrinsically more politically progressive than realism, but I do agree that what singles Donovan out from *Images of Women in Fiction* and what is "at issue" there is "the problem of realism as opposed to modernism." Two of the other articles in the final section of the anthology attack modernism as politically regressive.[28] Feminist aesthetics, in the first anthology of feminist literary criticism, could be seen as a debate between modernist and realist aesthetics.

Whereas "realism" privileges prose fiction, "modernism" places poetry at the center of literature. Realism tends toward an extrinsic literary aesthetic; modernism has promoted and benefited from the emphasis on an "intrinsic" appraisal of literature.

Like Linda Ray Pratt, Donovan is proposing an "intrinsic" feminist criticism. Following Donovan's direction, the study of women's literature would become "equal in all respects" to the study of men's literature, with like emphasis on language and rhetoric, style rather than societal attitudes. It is fitting that this first anthology end with Donovan, not only because she will edit the next anthology of feminist literary criticism, but also because the following decade will see more and more feminist criticism devoted to the question of women's style.

8
An Idea Presented Before Its Time

The second anthology of academic feminist criticism, published in 1975, sports the absolutely generic title, *Feminist Literary Criticism*. While *Images of Women in Fiction* actually opens the genre, this anthology, edited by Josephine Donovan, first makes it explicit, claiming in its title to stand for the entirety of "feminist literary criticism."

The 1975 anthology begins with Cheri Register's "Bibliographical Introduction" which, according to the editor, is an "interpretive introduction to the body of existing feminist criticism."[1] 1975 also sees the launching of the journal *Signs*, which includes yearly "review essays, assessing the status of the study of women in the various disciplines."[2] Elaine Showalter writes the first review essay on literary criticism. Although subsequent review writers will only be responsible for the scholarship published since the last "review essay," Showalter has to account for all feminist literary scholarship extant, thus covering approximately the same ground as Register's "Bibliographical Introduction."

The two accounts differ widely: for example, Register treats Koppelman Cornillon's anthology as central while Showalter does not even allot it a paragraph of its own in her twenty-five page essay, dismissing it as "very uneven."[3] Yet on one point the two concur. "At this point," writes Showalter, "the study of female stereotypes in literature seems to promise more for the classroom . . . than for criticism, where it has lost much of its power to surprise, disturb, or rearrange our ideas. . . . Many essays of this type now have a tired air; they are only beating a dead pig" (p. 452). "At this point," writes Register, "feminist critics and teachers take for granted the existence of female stereotypes in literature; the process of discovery is complete. . . . Feminist criticism can now go on" (p. 3). The tone of the two judgments is very different: Register is affirmative ("at this point . . . the process of discovery is complete"); Showalter is disdainful ("at this point . . . it has lost much of its power"). But both historians of feminist criticism agree that "at this point," by 1975, the study of images of women is passé; "feminist criticism can now go on."

101

In 1972, *Images of Women in Fiction* culminates in Feminist Aesthetics; its final text is written by Josephine Donovan. In the Afterword to her 1975 anthology which begins with Register's assertion that we "can now go on" from the study of images of women, Donovan imagines that "[o]ut of these . . . tendencies may emerge a feminist, or feminine, aesthetic" (p. 77).

When first broached, this speculative future is primarily named as "feminist," and then, in a sort of parenthetic afterthought, as perhaps "feminine." A note distinguishes between "feminist" and "feminine": "The former derives judgments from ideological assumptions; the latter would derive from a sense of female epistemology as rooted in authentic female culture" (p. 81 n. 9). The "feminist aesthetic" is described in the present tense ("derives"); the "feminine aesthetic" is described in the conditional mode ("would derive"). After this first appearance, the Afterword names the future aesthetic on five more occasions: four times it is referred to as a "feminine aesthetic," once as a "female aesthetic." Never again does the Afterword modify "aesthetic" by "feminist."

The first characterization of the aesthetic as unhesitatingly "feminine" corresponds to a shift in the Afterword from the objectivity of an editor representing the diverse entirety of "feminist literary criticism" to a first-person-singular stance: "My own feeling is that the immediate work in feminist criticism must be to develop more fully our understanding of what a female perspective . . . includes. . . . I see a gradual falling together of truths and probabilities about women . . . and this constellation will provide the basis for a feminine aesthetic" (p. 77).

From the present to the conditional, from objective account to subjective speculation. "I have postscripted my own speculations about feminist criticism and its future," Donovan writes in the Preface (p. ix). Post-script, After-word, beyond writing, beyond *Feminist Literary Criticism*, beyond the present, beyond "feminist," Donovan's ending is visionary: "I see." Her vision moves her beyond the conditional—a feminine aesthetic *would* derive from a sense of female epistemology— into the future: "this constellation *will* provide the basis for a feminine aesthetic." As she moves into the future tense, the figure of a "constellation" appears.

The editor is not the only one in this anthology to foretell the future. At the beginning of the volume, Register states: "Feminist criticism has three distinct subdivisions. . . . The first two are well defined and frequently practiced. . . . The third type still needs formulating, but it may become the crux of feminist criticism in the future. It is a 'prescriptive' criticism that attempts to set standards for literature that is 'good' from a feminist viewpoint" (p. 2).

Register would seem to be a much less gifted seer than Donovan. In the 1980 *Signs* Review Essay, covering literary criticism published since 1978, by far the largest of the seven sections, comprising fully a third of the text, is entitled "Is There a Female Aesthetics?" Prescriptive criticism does not appear at all. And this 1980 Review Essay was written by Cheri Register herself.

In 1984, I read *Feminist Literary Criticism* for the first time, in a graduate seminar which was a first version of the present book. It was the first anthology we read and thus for us represented "early"—i.e., "primitive"—criticism. The specific target of our "sophisticated" contempt was Register and her prescriptive criticism: what a ridiculous, crude idea. By the end of 1985 I had taught the Donovan anthology three times, in variations of the same seminar at three different universities. I remember mocking the same sentence each time: "Of course, feminist criticism does not require fiction to be autobiographical; however, an author should combine personal recollection and subjective feelings with imagination and structural detail to create her female characters" (Register, p. 12).

"Of course," I would read aloud, my tone priming the students for group contempt, "feminist criticism does not *require* fiction to be autobiographical." Very generous, not to make this an absolute requirement. Then the second clause comes in with its recipe: "an author should combine," mix one part personal recollection with structural detail and stir. I did not need to comment in order to make the class laugh, only to read the sentence slowly, emphasizing the "of course," the "does not require," the "author should combine." Prescriptive criticism was so self-evidently ludicrous that simply to find someone doing it in earnest struck us academic feminist critics in the mid-eighties as tremendously funny.

In 1987, I was teaching *Feminist Literary Criticism* for the fourth time, in yet another version of the seminar. I could not bring myself to do the gag again: it was too easy. I became suspicious of a reading that met so little resistance. Why were we so unanimous in our contempt? That year I attempted to mount a defense of prescriptive criticism, convincing few if any of my students. Was I just being perverse? Hypersophisticated?

In 1989, a second edition of *Feminist Literary Criticism* came out. Trying to reinsert the book into the late 1980s, the "Introduction to the

Second Edition" begins by referring to a contemporary text: "In her recent book on feminist criticism, *Crossing the Double-Cross* (1986), Elizabeth A. Meese remarks that the 'prescriptive criticism' identified by Cheri Register in this book represented 'the first assertion of feminist critical authority.' 'An idea presented before its time, prescriptive criticism was effectively silenced by a feminist community bent on coexistence and gradual reform.'"[4] "Prescriptive criticism" provides the claim for the anthology's relevance in the contemporary situation.

"As Meese correctly notes, [the] radicalism [projected in this anthology] has since been effectively silenced and obscured by reformist and other tendencies—notably, in my opinion, by pluralism and deconstructionism" (ibid.). Donovan goes on especially to attack deconstructionism. Meese's discussion of prescriptive criticism is part of her critique of pluralism but is also part of her book's general attempt to promote an alliance between feminist criticism and deconstruction. In a sentence that falls between the two quoted by Donovan, Meese states: "prescriptive criticism merely makes explicit a feminist version of the prescription implicit in most critical discourse; in a sense, it represents the deconstructive reversal" (p. 141). Meese's rehabilitation of prescriptive criticism is itself dependent upon deconstruction.

Donovan sees the rise of deconstructionism in American literary criticism as part of the "silencing" of radical feminist criticism. Ironically, deconstruction may also offer us the opportunity to hear anew Register's prescriptive criticism. I would like here to take up Meese's suggestion and to further consider prescriptive criticism by lingering upon what may be Meese's most deconstructive proposition: "an idea presented before its time."

"Prescriptive criticism" was literally "presented before its time," proffered as a possibility for the future. Yet it is not just that the idea wasn't, in 1975, prevalent. Prescriptive criticism was in fact "presented" before it was even formulated: "The third type still needs formulating, but it may become the crux of feminist criticism in the future" (Register, p. 2).

In 1989, Donovan writes: "In reintroducing this collection of essays . . . I hope to revive the radical potential of feminist criticism projected in its pages" (p. xi). Donovan is trying to revive not something that was actual or present back in 1975, but rather "the radical potential projected." In her 1975 Afterword, Donovan says that "[p]rescriptive criticism exists in . . . the 'prophetic' mode" (p. 75). She wants to go back to a future.

The Afterword quotes from Register to present prescriptive criticism: "Register . . . uses the term 'prescriptive criticism' to describe what she believes may become the defining attribute of feminist criticism in the future, that is, 'criticism [which] attempts to set standards for literature . . . from a feminist viewpoint. It is prescriptive in that it implies a need for new literature that meets its standards' (see p. 2 above)" (p. 74). Donovan then continues: "If I may expand slightly on this definition to clarify my own thesis, criticism is here viewed as a vehicle through which literature is prescriptively related to its social, cultural, and moral environment" (p. 75). After repeated reading, I remain puzzled by the phrase "prescriptively related." Indeed, I find that, both in the 1975 Afterword and in the 1989 Introduction, when Donovan speaks about prescriptive criticism, she becomes somewhat obscure. In all fairness, it must be said that the definition of prescriptive criticism is not simply to be found.

Donovan asks the reader's permission to "expand slightly on this definition": the request implies that what has just been quoted is a definition. Yet turning back to page two, we find that the paragraph from which she is quoting ends with the following statement: "Before defining this third type of criticism it is necessary to elaborate on the other two." "This third type of criticism" refers to prescriptive criticism; Register clearly believes that she has *not yet* "defined this third type."

Donovan is not the only of Register's readers to take this paragraph for a definition of prescriptive criticism. In 1976 Annette Kolodny quotes from this same paragraph, comments that "Register's definition looks innocent enough," and goes on to question "what this new 'prescriptive criticism'" really entails.[5] Challenging the innocent appearance of Register's "definition," Kolodny does not, however, seem to suspect that what she has quoted might be something other than a definition.

"Before defining this third type of criticism it is necessary to elaborate on the other two." This is the last sentence of the untitled introductory section of Register's essay. What follows is divided into three titled sections, each devoted to one of the three types of feminist criticism. This sentence seems to reflect the structure of the essay, casting it as if the aim were "defining this third type," a goal which it is (unfortunately) "necessary" to put off. Enticing the reader with her prophecy of the crux, Register defers its coming: she will define prescriptive criticism, but not now, not yet; first we must discuss the other two. Although it is introduced on page two, we are not yet ready for prescriptive criticism: "an idea presented before its time."

We dutifully read the discussion of the other two types. Of course we must understand the past to prepare the future. However patiently we review these past achievements, our desire is to learn not what we have done but where we are going. Finally, halfway through the text, we reach the final section heading: "Prescriptive Feminist Criticism."

The section begins: "As a preface to the definition of Prescriptive Feminist Criticism, it would perhaps be helpful to take up some of the questions that have been left dangling in the summaries of the first two categories of feminist criticism" (p. 11). Once again Register speaks of the coming "definition." Again we are informed that she will do something else first. On page two, it was "necessary" to wait; here on page eleven, the deferral seems more arbitrary: "it would perhaps be helpful." We nonetheless must wait. It is not yet time to define prescriptive criticism.

Register goes through seven questions, listing the question and then discussing it for a few paragraphs. Two-thirds of the way through the essay we reach the last question and response. Then we read the following paragraph:

> Because of its origin in the women's liberation movement, feminist criticism values literature that is of some use to the movement. Prescriptive Criticism, then, is best defined in terms of the ways in which literature can serve the cause of liberation. To earn feminist approval, literature must perform one or more of the following functions: (1) serve as a forum for women; (2) help to achieve cultural androgyny; (3) provide role models; (4) promote sisterhood; and (5) augment consciousness-raising. I would like to discuss these functions one by one.[6]

The remainder of the essay is comprised of five short sections, each devoted to one of the "functions." Nowhere in the remaining pages does Register so much as use the phrase "prescriptive criticism," much less define it. If there is a definition then it ought to be in the paragraph just quoted in its entirety, after the elaboration of the other two types of criticism, after the prefatory seven questions, and before the discussion of the five functions. This must have been the moment we were waiting for: "Prescriptive Criticism, *then*, is best defined in terms of the ways in which literature can serve the cause of liberation." This is not a definition. It says in what "terms" the definition should be made, but it does not define what prescriptive criticism would be, what the prescriptive critic would do or say.

Not that a definition of prescriptive criticism cannot be distilled from the various things Register says and implies. In fact the statements found on page two work rather well as a definition, which is certainly why readers as perspicacious as Donovan and Kolodny have taken them as such, despite Register's disclaimer. But that means the definition is, in fact and extremely, "presented before its time."

Kolodny focuses on the temporality of prescriptive criticism:

> Donovan applauds prescriptive criticism as existing "in . . . the prophetic mode," a mode which "seeks to influence the future." . . . [W]hile it is wholly legitimate to want to influence the future of . . . critical inquiry on ideological grounds, I am suspicious of wanting to influence the future of creative expression. . . . [I]n feminist criticism, as in all literary critical endeavor, I would rather have the literature give rise to the critical rules than have the critical rules formulate the literature. (p. 828)

What is offensive about prescriptive criticism is the idea that criticism would come *before* literature. Pre-scriptive criticism would literally be *pre script*, criticism that comes "before writing," intrinsically and inevitably, "an idea presented before its time." The prescriptive critic speaks out of turn: she ought to speak after the writer; she presumes to speak first.

Kolodny would rather that feminist criticism, like "all literary critical endeavor," follow literature. In refusing to give literature priority, Register is not, however, proposing the critic's autonomy. In the place where she leads us to expect the definition of prescriptive criticism, we read that "feminist criticism values literature that is of some use to the movement. Prescriptive Criticism, then, is best defined in terms of the ways in which literature can serve the cause of liberation" (p. 18). This criticism will not serve literature; literature will be viewed according to its ability to serve women's liberation. Prescriptive feminist criticism, unlike "all literary critical endeavor," gives ultimate value not to literature, but to women.

Kolodny, however, does not speak here on behalf of literature, but rather on behalf of a group of women. She worries that a prescriptive criticism would oppress women writers: "We would, in effect, be placing our emerging women writers back in the same situation they were in when 'male writers, critics, and editors [with their] . . . authoritative convictions of aesthetic appropriateness, [and] access to channels of power' determined what poet Kathleen Fraser called 'our language of standards."[7] A decade later, Meese praises prescriptive criticism as "the first assertion of feminist critical authority" (p. 141). Kolodny worries over precisely such authority: the authority to judge and disapprove of literature. Kolodny's concern suggests that what oppresses women writers may be not the gender of critical authorities but the fact of critical authority. Feminist thought on authority and power has consistently been accompanied by a fear that if some women gain power, we will be in a position to oppress other women.

The question of the relation between feminist critical authority and the woman writer is absolutely central to Register's exposition of prescriptive criticism. I would like to trace in detail the pieces of her encounter with the question because, as she confronts it and when she confronts it, it is, in fact, the never-quite-articulated-as-such-but-nonetheless-central question for feminist literary criticism.

On page two, when Register first introduces the notion of prescriptive criticism, her typology is tacked to authorial gender. "Feminist criticism has three distinct subdivisions. . . . (1) the analysis of the 'image of women,' nearly always as it appears in works by male authors; and (2) the examination of existing criticism of female authors. The third type still needs formulating. . . . Thus far it is directed almost exclusively toward female writers." The first type has been "nearly always" concerned with male authors. The second mentions "female authors" but, in fact, considers not those authors or their texts, but the criticism written about them, criticism largely written by men. The second type thus actually examines another group of male writers, literary critics. It is only the third type that has primarily directed itself to female writers.

"The analysis of the 'image of women,' nearly always as it appears in works by male authors": "nearly always" is not always; Register's adverb allows that there have been analyses of the "image of women" in works by female authors. The first question that "would perhaps be helpful as a preface to the definition of Prescriptive Feminist Criticism" is: "How do feminist critics deal with female writers who employ female stereotypes in their works?" (p. 11).

Register's answer seems, at first, evasive. "Feminist critics," she begins, "themselves have not completely abandoned the serious/popular dichotomy" (p. 11). Interesting and important as this issue might be, it initially appears to have no relation to the question. Soon, however, it becomes clear that she needs this distinction to frame her answer to the question.

The complete response comprises three paragraphs. The first paragraph considers the possibility of studying stereotypes in serious literature by women.

> Those critics who direct their attention to the deleterious images of women in "serious" literature can easily ignore the stereotypes created by female writers. Since female writers are seldom reviewed in major literary publications, included in literary histories, or read in college English classes, their readership is restricted from the outset; stereotypes in their works have little opportunity to affect social conditions or the self-images of individual females. The male literary paragons who are credited with capturing the essence of the human condition . . . pose a greater threat. (pp. 11–12)

Register does not deny that female writers of serious literature employ stereotypes. This paragraph, however, reminds us that we do not study stereotypes just because they are there. What she details as seldom happening to female writers—"reviewed in major publications, included in histories, read in classes"—adds up to canonization. Canonical literature has authority; taken as wisdom or truth, it affects how others perceive themselves and the world. The second subdivision of feminist criticism has demonstrated how female authors are excluded from such authority; there is no need for the first subdivision to study them. It is not that women writers aren't sexist, it is that they have no authority and thus do not propagate sexism. We study stereotypes in powerful texts so as to expose their shortcomings and diminish their power. There is no reason to expose the shortcomings of powerless texts.[8]

Yet it is not only serious literature that influences people. The literary academy and other high literary institutions represent only one kind of cultural power. The second paragraph of the response takes up the issue of popular literature: "There are feminists, though, who do study and criticize the effects of 'popular' literature, evaluating . . . areas in which women have achieved commercial success. The stereotyping of women and the idealization of the traditional female role in popular culture were among the very first concerns of the new women's movement of the 1960s" (p. 12). There are women writers who have influence; their works arguably reach many more readers than does any "serious" literature and thus do "pose a threat." Given their broad effect, there would appear to be good reason to critique the stereotypes in the works of these women.

A note is appended to the end of the first sentence of this second paragraph. Turning to the end of the article, we read: "Susan Koppelman Cornillon of the Center for the Study of Popular Culture at Bowling Green University in Bowling Green, Ohio, has done much work in this area" (p. 26, n. 32). Register's "Bibliographical Introduction" naturally has a lot of notes, referring the reader to work that exemplifies whatever trend she is discussing. This is the only one of eighty-two notes that does not refer to a specific text or utterance.

Later in the notes we repeatedly encounter Koppelman Cornillon as the editor of *Images of Women in Fiction*. And the section on how literature can serve to "promote sisterhood" (fourth of the five functions) has a long quotation from Koppelman Cornillon's own essay in that 1972 anthology. No other text by Koppelman Cornillon is mentioned. As we saw in the previous chapter, Koppelman Cornillon's essay is an exposé of contemporary novels written by women and the anthology as a whole has such an emphasis on stereotypes in the works of women writers that it may, by itself, challenge Register's "nearly always in works by male authors." The non-textual note to Koppelman Cornillon does and does not point to *Images of Women in Fiction* in response to the question: "How do feminist critics deal with female writers who employ female stereotypes in their works?"

Register is not happy with the 1972 anthology's response to the question. Although she comes up with a persuasive reason why we need not criticize female authors of *serious* literature, the argument about influence points to the necessity for critiquing women's *popular* writing. Faced with that necessity, she would nonetheless like to avoid criticizing women writers. The third paragraph of the response begins: "Rather than emphasize existing political transgressions, feminist critics prefer to concentrate on what female writers can do in their future works, urging them to forget literary convention when they create their female characters and to rely on their own subjective experience" (p. 12).

The generalization "feminist critics prefer" covers over the fact that not all feminist critics have shared Register's preference. Some critics in Koppelman Cornillon's anthology do indeed "emphasize existing political transgressions" by women writers; Register "prefers to" discuss the future, to replace *Images of Women* with prescriptive criticism.

Kolodny worries that prescriptive criticism would harm women writers. Yet Register, in fact, opts for prescriptive criticism precisely as a way to avoid hurting those women. When feminist criticism follows women's writing, it must judge, but if it only refers to future writing, if it remains pre-script, then it can avoid criticizing women writers.

The first type of criticism in Register's typology exposes sexism in images of women penned by men; the second type exposes the sexism in images of women authors constructed by male critics. According to Register's 1975 account, these are the "frequently practiced" types of feminist criticism (p. 2). They are both negative, critical in the sense of fault-finding. Directed to texts endowed with cultural authority, they are forms of critique which, by unveiling ideology at work in a text, strive to undermine the writer's authority and the text's power. What can an ideological criticism do with writers whose authority it would like to enhance or, at least, not to undermine? "Can they be read in the same splendidly anti-authoritarian fashion?"[9] The notion of prescriptive criticism arises at the moment when a criticism that has largely been engaged in diminishing the authority of male writers faces the necessity and the desire to talk about women writers.

Standard academic literary criticism has been not critique but descriptive study. However "objective" such study may strive to be, it can never be neutral, not only because scholars have their prejudices, but for the more fundamental reason that any study adds to the prestige of the work and author studied. The long lists of secondary material about certain texts demonstrate a major aspect of their cultural authority. These texts are worthy of commentary; these are the worthy texts.[10]

By critiquing, on the one hand, these canonical texts and, on the other, the critical apparatus underpinning their status, feminist criticism works to diminish that authority. Writing about the same texts as other literary critics, however, feminists nonetheless add to those lists of secondary material. Even diminished through ideological critique, those texts still have the prestige of the only texts worthy of study. Recognizing that criticism in itself, whatever its content, supports a writer's and a text's authority, feminist criticism had to devote itself to women writers and their work.

Around 1975, feminist literary criticism underwent a major transformation. What had primarily denoted an ideological critique of male literature and criticism came to mean primarily the study of women writers and their writing.[11] The move from male to female writers has been repeatedly theorized and celebrated in feminist literary theory. The concurrent switch from ideological critique to scholarly study has never been theorized or justified.[12] Trying to imagine an ideological feminist criticism whose main focus is women's writing, Register calls into question that aspect of the transformation that went without saying. Located in the moment of transformation, prescriptive criticism bears witness to the double aspect of this shift.

Elizabeth Meese writes the history of prescriptive criticism: "First advanced by Cheri Register [the reference is to the essay in the Donovan anthology] . . . prescriptive criticism was summarily dismissed by feminists [a note here refers to two 1976 articles by Kolodny]" (p. 140). "Summarily: in a summary manner or form. Summary (adjective): accomplished or performed too quickly with inadequate consideration, preparation, or space allowed."[13] "Summarily dismissed": in the mid-seventies, prescriptive criticism was not allowed its time, barely had any time at all.

"In the mid-seventies, the notion of 'prescriptive' criticism gained brief but limited popularity among some feminists" (Meese, p. 140). The phrase "brief but limited" is odd: the two adjectives do not contrast; they are nearly synonymous. Meese's apparently gratuitous "but" expresses an awareness of something contradictory about the impact of prescriptive criticism. The opposition in the sentence should probably be located between the word "popularity," implying broad impact, and the three minimizing adjectives: "brief," "limited," and "some." It is as if Meese were presenting a sort of non-empirical "popularity," correlative neither to expanse in time nor to numbers of proponents.

Continuing to read Meese's account of prescriptive criticism, we discover the actual location of that "popularity." "Although prescriptive criticism was summarily dismissed by feminists, it still characterizes our approach in the minds of the uninformed" (p. 140). Never actually popular among feminists, prescriptive criticism might be considered the most "popular" mode of feminist criticism since "the uninformed" surely outnumber us.

When the uninformed take all feminist criticism as prescriptive, are they simply wrong? According to Meese, "prescriptive criticism merely makes explicit a feminist version of the prescription implicit in most critical discourse" (p. 141). The scandal of prescriptive criticism is that it brings into the open what usually remains covert. "Criticism gives up its pretence to describing the way things are and becomes unashamedly prescriptive."[14] Although feminist critics may want to keep our prescriptions implicit, in keeping with "most critical discourse," Meese's formulations suggest that when "the uninformed" misunderstand us, they understand what is implicit.

Practically over before it began, prescriptive criticism had almost no temporal existence. On the other hand, ten years later, it "still characterizes our approach." As Meese goes on to say, "it was just what every writer and critic feared" (p. 140). Although it only ever appeared as the most tentative, not-yet-formulated notion, as soon as prescriptive criticism was presented, it already corresponded to some image in the mind of "every writer and critic." Familiar before it was ever advanced, lasting long after it was dismissed, prescriptive criticism is arguably the most enduring mode of feminist criticism. Feminist criticism has (practically) never been and yet has always been prescriptive.

This odd temporality of the never and yet always might represent the contrast between intention and reception. Intention can project or be interpreted retrospectively, but intention never simply occurs. On the other hand, reception occurs continually and over a long expanse of time. Looking closely at the actual annunciation of prescriptive criticism, we see that it was never formulated. The more carefully and completely a notion is formulated, the more likely it is that reception will approximate to intention. Without formulation, there is likely to be little communication between intention and reception. Never formulated and continually perceived, prescriptive criticism might well embody the gap between criticism as intended and as received.

Prescription arises in the reception of discourse that is not intended as prescriptive. Carole S. Vance suggests that "even mere statements of individual, personal preference are often heard as statements of superiority, criticisms of the listener's practice, or an exhortation to try something new. Women's insecurity, deprivation, and guilt make it difficult to hear a description of personal practice as anything but a prescription."[15] Vance is not talking about feminist literary criticism; she is discussing feminist discourse on sexuality. She has an unusually acute sense of the complex and subtle ways that "prescriptivism" can arise.

"Prescriptivism" is the "tendency" for other sorts of discourse to turn into prescription, a tendency surprisingly hard to resist. According to Vance, "[t]here is a very fine line between talking about sex and setting norms; we err very easily." Vance implicitly confesses to this error through her use of the pronoun "we." "We are *especially vulnerable* to transforming statements of personal preference . . . ('I like oral sex') into statements that may be probabilistically true ('Women like clitoral stimulation more than penetration') into statements that are truly prescriptive ('Women should avoid penetration')" (emphasis added). Our explicitly prescriptive statements arise not from choice, but from an "especial vulnerability." In talking about sex, of course.

"Certainly, there are intentional efforts at chauvinism." Vance refers to intentional prescription as "chauvinism," which the dictionary defines as "undue especially invidious attachment or partiality for a group to which one belongs,"[16] but which has had a special feminist meaning of "male chauvinism," sexism. In a feminist context, the word "chauvinism" cannot help but connote the enemy. Despite the aggressive vocabulary, Vance is not primarily concerned with intentional prescription. The sentence recognizes the intentional variety only to dismiss it, as the minor mode of the problem. Most feminist sexual prescription is unintentional.

We could and should try to resist unintentionally sliding into prescriptive statements. But beyond this unpremeditated prescriptivism is the more radical case where prescription originates with the listener. "Certainly, there are intentional efforts at chauvinism. But *even mere statements of* individual, personal *preference* are *often heard as* statements of superiority, criticisms of the listener's practice, or an exhortation to try something new. Women's insecurity, deprivation, and guilt make it *difficult to hear a description* of personal practice *as anything but a prescription*" (emphasis added).

It is not just the odd woman who mistakes description as prescription; it is difficult to hear a description *as anything but* a prescription. Why do we misunderstand in this way? Vance, of course, is talking about sex. Women are insecure about sex; women are deprived of sexual satisfaction; women are guilty about sex.

Feminist *literary* history has also and repeatedly portrayed women's deprivation and guilt. Virginia Woolf's *A Room of One's Own* and Tillie Olsen's *Silences*, two of the most popular books of feminist literary theory, tell how women have been deprived of the opportunity to write as they wished or even to write at all. Sandra Gilbert and Susan Gubar's *The Madwoman in the Attic*, arguably the most influential book of academic feminist literary history, shows that women who did manage to write felt guilty about it. And as for "insecurity," however afraid we may be of having our sexual inadequacy exposed, are we less insecure about our writing?

Meese says that prescriptive criticism "was just what every writer . . . feared." Kolodny, speaking on behalf of the woman poet, makes it clear that the writer as writer suffers from prescription, whatever its gender or ideology. Kolodny believes we can dismiss prescriptive criticism and thus protect the vulnerable, emerging woman writer. Following Meese and Vance however, we can imagine that the woman writer would hear prescription even in the most objective, scholarly descriptions, even in the sort of feminist criticism that rose to prominence around 1975 so as to support women writers. Prescription lies "implicit in most critical discourse," not just because critics are covert tyrants, but because most any critical discourse is likely to be heard as prescriptive by a writer worrying if she is doing it right.

Vance's sensitive exploration of "prescriptivism" is based on an article by Alice Echols. According to Echols, writing in the early 1980s, "today's radical feminists have developed a more highly prescriptive understanding of sexuality."[17] Echols "refer[s] to this more recent strain of feminism as cultural feminism, because it equates women's liberation with the nurturance of a female counter culture which it is hoped will supersede the dominant culture" (p. 51). Whereas the radical feminism of the late sixties and early seventies promoted the ideal of androgyny, cultural feminism celebrates women's difference, female culture and ethos often seen as diametrically opposed to a destructive masculinity. According to Echols "this theoretical tendency" is "first termed 'cultural feminism' in 1975."[18] Although not named as such, cultural feminism makes a crucial appearance in *Feminist Literary Criticism*.

Donovan's Afterword has one break, dividing the short text into two sections. The second section begins:

> Many of the contributors to this volume see the concept of androgyny as an important paradigm that feminist and humanist critics will be assuming in future work. Another series of concepts likely to be developed in the next several years revolves around the concept of a female culture. Radical feminists and lesbians have been in the forefront of the women's movement in seeking the patterns that identify women as a separate cultural group. Out of these as yet embryonic tendencies may emerge a feminist, or feminine, aesthetic. (pp. 76–77)

The rest of the second and longer section of the text discusses the proposed feminine aesthetic, not mentioned in the first part of the Afterword. Whereas "many" of the contributors to the anthology see androgyny as a paradigm for the future, Donovan places those who are seeking a separate women's culture "in the forefront of the women's movement." And indeed, in the mid-seventies, while androgyny was becoming passé, cultural feminism was rising.[19]

In 1975 Cheri Register saw feminist literary criticism moving toward prescription. In fact, feminist literary criticism or, rather, academic feminist criticism moved toward theory and description. But at the moment Register is speaking, feminism, or at least radical feminism, is transforming itself into cultural feminism, into a more highly prescriptive set of assumptions about women's practice. Radical, or explicitly prescriptive, cultural feminism, does not appear to be a major voice in academic literary criticism. At the same time, however, academic feminist criticism does turn to the description of women's writing and the theorizing of a feminine aesthetic.[20] This turn, occurring around 1975, can also be understood as part of the movement termed cultural feminism.

Where Register saw prescriptive criticism in our future, Josephine Donovan predicted the formulation of a feminine aesthetic. The feminine aesthetic turned out in fact to be not only "the crux of the future" but the prescriptive criticism of the future. Every description of women's writing is, somewhere and often, received as a judgment about what women's writing ought to be.

At first, Donovan uses feminist and feminine aesthetic interchangeably, but then she notes: "I think one may distinguish between a *feminist* aesthetic and a *feminine* one" (p. 81, n. 9). From that note on, Donovan chooses to name the future "feminine" or, once, "female." Five years later Register remarks that "there appears to be some confusion about whether 'female aesthetics' means the same as 'feminist aesthetics.'"[21] She sets out to dissipate this confusion.

"The existence of our hypothetical female aesthetics must be documented, but we can construct a feminist aesthetics by testing new forms that we believe convey the necessity of change or inspire readers to pursue it" (Ibid.). Both female and feminist aesthetics are, as of 1980, hypothetical. But female aesthetics, if it exists, must be proven already to exist, "must be documented." Its formulation may be future, but its existence must be historical. "Female aesthetics" must be rooted in actual accomplishment, and so to the extent that it also functions prescriptively, it prescribes that the future be like the present or the past.

The study of past or present female culture is, surprisingly enough, appropriate both to cultural feminism and to standard academic procedure. The description of what has been satisfies both the demand for documentation and the demand that we respect what women have been and done. "Female aesthetics" became the predominant mode of feminist literary criticism in the late seventies. This transformation prepared the way for feminist criticism's installation in the literary academy as a respectable, or "authentic," mode of study.

A feminist, as opposed to a female, aesthetic "conveys the necessity of change" and thus must refer to future practice. Hence its scandal. If it is to be of service to women's liberation, feminist criticism cannot be just a celebration of what women have been or even what we are. It must advocate what has never been.[22] Feminism itself is, necessarily, "an idea presented before its time."

In 1987, I presented my work on the present book in a three-day series of seminars at Duke University. On Monday I read my chapter on *The New Feminist Criticism*; on Tuesday I presented my reading of *Feminist Literary Criticism*. After the presentation of 1975, Alice Kaplan asked why, in listening to me, she found herself opposed to definition one day and in favor of prescription the next.

Showalter's "definition" was received as prescriptive; its effect was exclusionary. Register's "prescriptive criticism" was received as definition and dismissed. The difference is not intrinsic to the concepts but refers to the relative authority of their enunciation, to history and speaking position.

By the time Showalter announced her definition and institutionalized it in her anthology, both she and feminist criticism had the authority within the literary academy to prescribe. That authority, both hers individually and that of feminist criticism, had in fact been gained by way of this definition, by way of construing feminist criticism as the descriptive study of women's writing and female aesthetics. By the time she articulates it (1981–85), it is already functioning as a definition. It is, thus, an idea presented during its time.

When Register announced her prescription, neither she nor feminist literary criticism had authority. To prescribe was to presume authority. Even descriptive statements by authorities have prescriptive weight, but without authority there can be no effective prescription.

In 1975 both Elaine Showalter and Cheri Register published accounts of the entirety of feminist literary criticism. Showalter's account judges the quality of specific texts but does not organize the various sorts of criticism into narrative sequence. Register, on the other hand, shapes her essay into a progress culminating in prescriptive criticism.

Register wrote the 1980 Literary Criticism Review Essay in *Signs*; in 1981 Showalter published an account of feminist criticism in the feminist issue of *Critical Inquiry*. Register's 1980 account is more pluralistic; Showalter in 1981 artfully arranges all feminist criticism into five sorts, each category presented as an advance over the preceding ones. Showalter is arguably the most recognized and influential feminist literary critic in the academy today. Register is no longer an academic nor, as far as I know, a feminist literary critic.

I do not wish to demonize Showalter for her enviable success nor do I mean to idealize Register for her marginality. Register spoke out of turn and was dismissed; Showalter has an exquisite sense of timing.

Feminist criticism, from the beginning, has tried to expose ideology at work in authoritative texts and, on the other hand, bring less recognized texts to our attention. The point is not to equalize authors for the sake of equality, but to produce an alteration in knowledge. Our hope is that we will thus hear some of what has been silenced in the triumphant march of canonical ideas. It is in keeping with this agenda, this endless quest for a broader and different picture, that my reading would seem to critique Showalter's definition and promote Register's prescription. Not because one idea is intrinsically or abstractly better, but because one idea has had the authority to prescribe and exclude whereas the other has been summarily dismissed. In the triumph of the one and the defeat of the other, complications, contradictions, experience, and the fuller understanding that arises from these have been covered over.

Let me applaud Josephine Donovan and the University Press of Kentucky for bringing prescriptive criticism to us, again, in 1989. It may not yet or ever be time for such presumption but perhaps, this time, our dismissal can be less summary.

9
A Contradiction in Terms

Feminist Criticism: Essays on Theory, Poetry and Prose, edited by Cheryl L. Brown and Karen Olson, was photo-offset and published by The Scarecrow Press in 1978. I have chosen it over two much better known, and more expensively produced, anthologies to represent feminist criticism in the late seventies. The other texts considered for this chapter were: *The Authority of Experience*, edited by Arlyn Diamond and Lee R. Edwards (1977), and *Shakespeare's Sisters*, edited by Sandra M. Gilbert and Susan Gubar (1979).[1] This selection bespeaks no abstract superiority of the volume chosen—on the contrary—but does disclose some of the assumptions shaping the narrative I am constructing. This account of feminist literary theory in the seventies looks back from the point of view of that moment I call "around 1981." Trying to tell the story of how we got from *Images of Women in Fiction* in the early seventies to notions of feminist criticism widely accepted in the early eighties, I find this 1978 anthology most useful.

First off, I am, to be sure, attracted by its absolutely generic title. Its subtitle is the next and possibly even stronger draw; the book is divided into three sections. The first reprints four widely influential essays in theory: two from 1971, two from 1975. Since my project is to study feminist literary *theory*, this anthology immediately claims a place in that history.

Shakespeare's Sisters, on the other hand, "emphasized practical criticism because [the editors] believe that a general theory can emerge only after a full comprehension of the range and richness of women's poetic voices, many of which have so far barely been heard."[2] As the first feminist anthology devoted to poetry, *Shakespeare's Sisters* feels it is premature to theorize. As Gilbert and Gubar point out, all the major feminist literary theory had been based upon consideration of prose. They list only two exceptions, both recent feminist books on poetry: Suzanne Juhasz's *Naked and Fiery Forms* (1976) and Emily Stipes Watts's *The Poetry of American Women* (1977). One of the changes between the early and the late seventies is this expansion of feminist criticism to poetry. Whereas Koppelman Cornillon's anthology restricts itself to "fiction," Brown and Olson's 1978 anthology divides its "practical criticism" between a section on prose and one on poetry. Feminist criticism, to be sure, continued its major emphasis on prose fiction. To consider the turn to poetry, it seems more appropriate to look at a collection that does both poetry and prose. *The Authority of Experience*, on the other hand, contains no essays on poetry by women.

"In the spring of 1975," we read in the preface to *Feminist Criticism*, Brown and Olson were surprised to find "that what women critics were writing about women's literature was not being published in respectable numbers and not readily accessible to concerned students and teachers. As a consequence, [they] decided to collect feminist criticism already in print and to supplement those articles with others that had not yet been published. [Their] work resulted in this anthology."[3] This tale of the anthology's conception makes explicit what is implicit in the table of contents: that the editors understand "feminist criticism" to be synonymous with "what women critics write about women's literature."

In contrast to this, about half of the articles in *The Authority of Experience* treat literature written by men. *Shakespeare's Sister's*, although completely devoted to women's writing, includes two articles by male critics on Emily Dickinson. This strict linking of feminist criticism to gender identity has never gone uncontested in theory, but its treatment as an unproblematic given in the first paragraph of this anthology bespeaks an assumption which became predominant during the late 1970s. To the extent that feminist criticism's coming to full voice in the literary academy around 1981 is based in this late seventies conception, it is telling to look at the first collection born of the conception. A number of the articles in *Feminist Criticism* are not feminist by any definition except that based in the gender of critic and author studied. There are articles signed by women who study the writing of women authors in a traditional, objective, "scholarly" way, with no attention paid to any gender issues.

In the theoretical section of the volume, Annette Kolodny explicitly takes up the question of defining feminist criticism:

As yet, no one has formulated any exacting definition of the term "feminist criticism." When applied to the study of literature, it is used in a variety of contexts to cover a variety of activities, including (1) any criticism written by a woman, no matter what the subject; (2) any criticism written by a woman about a man's book which treats that book from a "political" or "feminist" perspective; and (3) any criticism written by a woman about a woman's book or about female authors in general.[4]

The first definition has never, to my knowledge, been endorsed by feminists but represents a general misconception. Kolodny's article was first published in 1975, at a moment when the mainstream of feminist criticism was shifting from the second to the third definition. This formulation implies that the "'political' or 'feminist' perspective" drops away as feminist criticism turns from men's to women's books. We recognize the third definition as the working assumption of Brown and Olson's anthology. Although the first definition seems outrageous in its assumption that anything at all penned by a woman (critic) is feminist, the third definition resembles the first but doubles the woman's pen: anything written by a woman on anything written by a woman. I would not want to belittle the feminist effect of that redoubling: it often is a feminist gesture for women to choose to write about women.

In fact, for Brown and Olson, the gesture seems so feminist that they feel the need to play it down. Immediately after the first paragraph explaining why they put this collection together, the second paragraph of the preface reads:

When we discussed how to introduce the anthology, we wanted to avoid arguing its worth solely as a book by and about women writers. Certainly, giving exposure to women writers is important, and the writers we expose are good; however, they are good not because of or in spite of the fact they are women. They all can hold their own in academic circles. We prefer to offer the book simply as a valuable collection of literary essays regardless of who contributed to it and what those contributors chose to write on. (p. xiii)

Given the explicit redoubling of "women writers"—"by and about"— the "they" who can "hold their own in academic circles" refers to both. Brown and Olson want to claim a place for these authors within the academic institution of "literature" and for these critics within the academy. Trying to play by academic rules, they "prefer to offer the book simply as a valuable collection of literary essays." This position would seem to represent the conservative edge of feminist criticism, at the other extreme from Lillian Robinson's statement: "I am not terribly interested in whether feminism becomes a respectable part of academic criticism."[5]

But having assigned Brown and Olson to the opposite end of the spectrum from Robinson, I am obliged to note that they include the article in which this statement appears—Robinson's 1971 landmark essay "Dwelling in Decencies"—in their anthology. And even beyond a gesture that might be construed as a form of tokenism, I would contend that the editors' position remains contradictory. If they "prefer to offer the book simply as a valuable collection of literary essays," why entitle it "Feminist Criticism"?

Here stands the academic feminist, in contradiction. In painful contradiction. "Indeed it is sometimes quite painful to be a feminist," writes Margret Andersen in the theoretical piece that opens the collection.

> When I could not see Hamlet anymore without giving most of my attention to . . . the cavalier way in which [Ophelia] is treated . . ., when Camus suddenly was no longer flawless in my eyes because of his failure to see woman other than in her relationship to man . . . it became evident that a new way of thinking had invaded me totally. . . . [T]he *musée imaginaire*, which used to be my ultimate refuge, was not safe anymore, was in need of renovation, as everything it housed became subject to my feminist critique.[6]

Andersen took refuge from worldly imperfection in the imaginary world of great literature. She shared the values central to the literary academy, until feminism hit her. Hers is the tale of that generation of women who became literary critics before they became feminists. Awakened to feminist consciousness, she can no more give up her concern for women than she can her concern for literature. Torn by a conflict between literature and feminism, Andersen's one hope is that "renovation" is possible. She has not relinquished her belief that there should be some "flawless" realm, some better, imaginary place; literature must be cleansed of gender discrimination so that we can once again find refuge in it.

Following Andersen's opening essay, the anthology prints a pair of papers, delivered by Annis Pratt and Lillian S. Robinson at the 1970 MLA Convention, which constitute the first official debate *within* feminist literary theory. Brown and Olson's decision to reprint this debate reflects a sense that the issues discussed are, in the late seventies, still primary and not yet resolved.

Pratt entitles her essay "The New Feminist Criticism." A sentence on the second page glosses the title: "The new feminist critic should be a 'new critic' (in the aesthetic rather than the political sense) in judging the formal aspects of individual texts; she should be 'feminist' in going beyond formalism to consider literature as it reveals men and women in relationship to each other within a socio-economic context" (p. 12). In 1970, New Criticism was still the reigning mode in the literary academy; feminist criticism was considered, by both practitioners and detractors, as at odds with New Criticism. Pratt sees no need for conflict. Her "new feminist critic" would be both: new critic for the text, feminist for the context. I'm not sure what the parenthetic remark means, what "the political sense" of "new critic" would be, but the opposed pair reinforce a general binarization of the aesthetic and the political in the passage where this sentence occurs. The new feminist critic will be a new critic for aesthetic judgments and a feminist for political matters. With the assignment of separate spheres, peaceful coexistence can be assured.

Toward the end of her essay, Pratt demonstrates her ability to separate the spheres, remarking of Joyce's *Ulysses* that it is "resonant and craftsmanlike even if it is chauvinistic" (p. 17). In her response to "The New Feminist Criticism" Robinson remarks: "*Ulysses* . . . makes Annis Pratt flinch as a feminist while, as a critic, she acknowledges its literary worth. . . . [L]et us think of how to approach the novel not as a feminist one moment and as a critic the next, but as a feminist critic."[7] Pratt confidently proposes a synthesis of feminism and (new) criticism, but Robinson perceives Pratt's "new feminist critic" as split, at odds with herself, and hopes for a feminist criticism that would be truly whole, without the separation between aesthetic and political judgments.

Pratt writes: "It is difficult not to feel about Molly Bloom on her chamberpot what Eldridge Cleaver must feel about Jack Benny's Rochester, but a good critic will not withdraw her attention from a work which is resonant and craftsmanlike even if it is chauvinistic" (p. 17). Here is Robinson's account of the sentence: "Annis Pratt says she responds to Molly Bloom on the chamberpot as a black militant must to stereotypes of Negro servants. The solution is not to ignore it and go on to something else" (p. 32). In the complete context of Robinson's paragraph it is clear that she thinks Pratt recommends that the feminist critic "ignore *Ulysses* and go on to something else." When Pratt tells us *not* to withdraw our attention, why does Robinson understand her to be telling us to withdraw our attention?

Here is Pratt's next sentence: "If the critical palate is soured by the evaluation of the works of Durrell, Burgess, Faulkner, Nabokov, Bellow, etc., it would seem better to turn one's attention from attack to defense, from examples of distorted images of women to examples of healthier representations" (p. 17). Durrell, Burgess, et al. presumably join Joyce as authors of works that are "resonant and craftsmanlike even if chauvinistic." Pratt does not seem to be making any distinction between the author of *Ulysses* and these other male novelists. Yet her advice to feminist critics seems to reverse itself from one sentence to the next. Repeating the word "attention," first she tells us not to withdraw our attention, then she suggests we *turn* our *attention* "to examples of healthier representations," that is to other works.

Robinson is both wrong and right in her reading of Pratt. She is literally wrong when she implies that Pratt tells us to turn away from *Ulysses*. Robinson has it that she and Pratt disagree, that Pratt would have us ignore *Ulysses* whereas she would have us attend to it. In fact Pratt already disagrees with herself as to what we should do with such great sexist books. Finally, Robinson is right when she says that Pratt is "a feminist one moment and a critic the next." What we see in Pratt's successive sentences is the conflict between these two moments manifesting itself as literal contradiction.

Robinson's "Dwelling in Decencies" wants to take the feminist critic beyond this self-contradiction. Originally published in *College English* in 1971, "Dwelling in Decencies" is reprinted twice in 1978: in Brown and Olson's anthology, and in a collection of Robinson's essays entitled *Sex, Class, and Culture*. In both books, we read, unchanged, the sentence: "let us think of how to approach the novel not as a feminist one moment and as a critic the next, but as a feminist critic." In *Sex, Class, and Culture*, in an essay written especially for that 1978 volume, we also read: "despite my continuing concern with elaborating a feminist criticism that would in fact be feminist, I don't think it occurred to me until quite recently that there might really be a contradiction between the two terms."[8]

Pratt believes she can be both feminist and (academic) critic. Robinson helps us see that Pratt is not as successful in synthesizing the two as she thinks, but suffers, if unwittingly, from their contradiction. Aware of the price of Pratt's compromise, Robinson proposes truly to synthesize feminism and criticism, only to realize, some years later, that "there might really be a contradiction between the two." By 1978 Robinson suspects that feminist criticism is a contradiction in terms.

Both Pratt and Robinson believe they see a remedy to the pain expressed by Margret Andersen. Yet neither of them succeed in resolving the conflict. I do not wish to minimize the difference between Pratt's and Robinson's solutions. Pratt would alter feminism to fit literary criticism; Robinson would alter literary criticism to fit feminism. That difference is enormous, reflecting which value is primary for the feminist critic. But despite their differences, neither manage to resolve the contradiction between feminism and literary criticism, and both earnestly try. Here stands the feminist critic, whether she cares more for literature or for women, privileges art or prefers politics, to the extent that she cares deeply for both she will suffer, at least implicitly, manifesting itself symptomatically when not explicitly declared, an internal struggle between her feminist critique and her imaginary museum.

After the Pratt-Robinson debate, the theoretical section of *Feminist Criticism* closes with Kolodny's 1975 article. Toward the end of that essay, Kolodny turns to the very problem which pains Andersen and drives Pratt into contradiction:

> this . . . raised consciousness . . . will . . . pose the most difficult task for the feminist critic, challenging her to find better ways of appraising and talking about authors whose attitudes . . . she finds repugnant. Norman Mailer's name, of course, comes first to mind. . . . I'm not certain that we . . . want to stop teaching or reading *The Naked and the Dead*, which, however little attention it pays to its female characters, is still probably the finest novel to come out of World War II. Disappointing though it is, art and politics may not always coincide in ways we would like. (p. 53)

A realist, Kolodny accepts the fact that "art and politics may not always coincide." She does recognize that "we would like" them to coincide. We gather that the feminist critic's desire for art and politics to coincide must be very strong for even a mere "not always coinciding"—which leaves open the possibility of a most-of-the-time coinciding—to be "disappointing." But the understatement can also be read as irony, mocking the impossibly idealistic assumption that art and politics always coincide. Andersen's idealism, her belief that great writers should be "flawless," causes her pain. The mature thing to do is accept that the world is not always as we would have it be, swallow our disappointment, and go on with our tasks of teaching and reading. This is "the most difficult task for the feminist critic."

The year after Kolodny's article was published in *Critical Inquiry*, William W. Morgan takes it to task in the pages of the same journal for "separating political and aesthetic judgments," quoting the remark about *The Naked and the Dead* along with the following sentence about "art and politics" not coinciding.[9] In the same 1976 issue of the journal, Kolodny responds:

> Morgan takes out of context my phrase about the necessity for feminist critics to "separate political ideologies from aesthetic judgments" and attaches it to my passing reference to Norman Mailer. In the original article, the Mailer reference appears in a paragraph which simply lists some of the difficulties which her "raised consciousness . . . will . . . pose . . . for the feminist critic, [among them] challenging her to find better ways of appraising and talking about authors whose attitudes . . . she finds repugnant." (p. 826, ellipses and additions Kolodny's)

Kolodny literally misrepresents her own paragraph. The first sentence from the paragraph in question reads: "it is precisely this same raised consciousness which will also pose the most difficult task for the feminist critic, challenging her to find better ways of appraising and talking about authors whose attitudes . . . she finds repugnant" (p. 53). Kolodny makes it look as if the Mailer/sexist author thing were mentioned in passing as one "among" several difficulties, whereas in fact it is the unique difficulty discussed in this paragraph, and is there termed "the most difficult task for the feminist critic."

Unlike Andersen and Pratt, Kolodny, in her 1975 text reprinted in *Feminist Criticism*, seems untroubled by the prospect of great sexist literature. Her treatment of the dilemma is level-headed, reasonable, and even jocular. Yet a year later this "passing reference" seems to give her some trouble, enough so that she feels impelled to change her tune, through a process we might want to call secondary revision.[10]

After dismissing her passing reference to Mailer, Kolodny continues: "My insistence on the separation of 'political ideologies from aesthetic judgments' comes from the previous paragraph, in which the topic under discussion was the danger of 'prescriptive' criticism" (pp. 826–27). As we saw in the last chapter, Kolodny worries about the oppressive effect of prescriptive criticism on women writers. Kolodny would like to withdraw our attention from the problem of great sexist literature and turn to the issue of feminist critical support for women writers.

When Pratt writes "it would seem better to turn one's attention . . . from examples of distorted images of women to examples of healthier representations" (p. 17), she appends a note: "The editors of the Fall 1970 issue of *Women: A Journal of Liberation*, for example, carefully juxtapose a section on 'The Men Who Wrote About Us' (stereotypical criticism) with one on 'Discovering Our Sister Authors'" (pp. 19–20 n. 11). Pratt's adverb "carefully" implies that there is some danger for feminists in considering "The Men Who Wrote About Us," a danger we should counter by turning to women writers.

Five years later, Margret Andersen is similarly "careful" in her presentation of feminist criticism. "There is quite definitely a destructive element in feminist criticism," she writes, proceeding to tell of the attack on her love for *Hamlet* and Camus, the invasion of her imaginary museum. Following her war report, she announces: "This then is the constructive side of feminist criticism," and proceeds to tell of her new appreciation for Colette (pp. 5–6).

All the articles in the theoretical section of *Feminist Criticism* confront the problem of the great sexist author; all are written by 1975. Around 1975, the contradiction between feminist critique and love for literature become unbearable, academic feminist criticism turns to women's writing. The practical criticism in this anthology bears out this post-1975 direction: looking only at literature by women should allow the feminist critic to move beyond contradiction.

The first writer studied is Emily Dickinson, in an article by Barbara J. Williams published for the first time in this 1978 collection. The "modernist" literary tastes of the New Criticism which ousted most of the women previously included in the American literary curriculum, in fact, actually "focused serious attention on Emily Dickinson."[11] Harold Bloom, in the 1970s defining who was and what made a "strong poet" in terms that seemed to exclude women, as they were excluded from his examples, includes Dickinson.[12] In her study of Dickinson, Williams can quote Archibald MacLeish's pronouncement: "she is poet."[13] Emily Dickinson, first and foremost, can "hold her own in academic circles."

Williams entitles her article "A Room of Her Own." The title refers to Virginia Woolf's founding text of feminist literary criticism. Both a feminist and a high literary modernist, Woolf holds out the hope that we could serve both value systems, could combine our allegiance to feminism with an allegiance to reigning standards for literature. Gilbert and Gubar's anthology of poetry criticism likewise takes its title from *A Room of One's Own*. "Shakespeare's Sister" is Woolf's fantasy of a woman who would be as transcendent a poet as the recognized master of English literature. Although Woolf was still waiting for that woman poet to be born, Gilbert and Gubar's 1979 anthology might almost bestow the title on Emily Dickinson. Even though they must apologize in their Introduction for how many major women poets are missing (p. xxiv), they include three essays on Dickinson; the only essays penned by men in the collection are both devoted to Dickinson. Each of the book's four sections gets its title from a Dickinson quotation and is preceded by a Dickinson poem. Gilbert and Gubar's *Madwoman in the Attic*, published in the same year as their anthology, asks: "How did this apparently 'gentle spinster' . . . come so close to being 'Judith Shakespeare'?"[14]

A study of nineteenth century British novelists, *The Madwoman in the Attic* ends with a chapter on Dickinson. Suzanne Juhasz's 1976 *Naked and Fiery Forms*, the first feminist book on poetry, considers twentieth-century American poets but begins with a chapter on Dickinson. These two crucial feminist studies overlap here, and only here, straining the boundaries of their chosen subjects. In the late 1970s, the academic feminist critic needs Dickinson, needs a woman who is beyond question a great poet, who can hold her own in academic circles, which, under the sway of modernism and New Criticism, value the poet much more than the novelist, value the poet not as a writer but as artist.

In her essay on Dickinson, Williams writes: "she was born a woman, and a poet, and she perceived that the two distinctions represented a conflict of interests" (p. 72). The article concludes with the triumphant resolution of that conflict: "In the final analysis, Emily Dickinson wrote . . . *as* a woman. . . . The Promethian voice of the woman artist can speak for all . . . . As an artist, she no longer needs to apologize for the 'femaleness' of her work. Woman as Artist has come of age" (pp. 87–88). This final paragraph moves from Dickinson in the past tense ("wrote") into an indefinite present ("the woman artist no longer needs"). When Dickinson resolves the contradiction, she resolves it not just for herself but for today.

The contradiction Williams locates in Dickinson is absolutely central to Juhasz's study of modern women poets. On the first page of *Naked and Fiery Forms*, we read: "To be a woman poet in our society is a double-bind situation, one of conflict and strain. For the words 'woman' and 'poet' denote opposite and contradictory qualities and roles." Two chapters from Juhasz's book are reprinted in the Brown and Olson anthology. The first begins: "Sylvia Plath is the woman poet of our century who sees the double bind inherent in trying to be both woman and poet with the coldest, most unredeeming clarity: her life and her art embody her attempts to find a solution. She never finds one."[15] Although Juhasz's Plath is not as successful as Williams's Dickinson, this article does end with an upbeat sense of the present. Juhasz, herself a poet, concludes: "When I read Plath's poetry . . . [i]t makes me want more than ever . . . to fight to be able to live as both woman and poet; to make it possible for these to be harmonious facets of one person. Because Plath lived, and died, and wrote as she did, this goal has become more possible" (p. 130).

Williams and Juhasz agree that things are getting better, that we are moving toward a historic synthesis of the contradiction between woman and poet. The last poet studied in *Naked and Fiery Forms* is the contemporary feminist, Adrienne Rich. Rich's individual trajectory recapitulates the book's overall progress. Like Plath, Rich begins as an extremely competent craftswoman alienated from her own voice. By the end she achieves integration and great poetry and becomes a feminist poet. Her poetry of the seventies pleases Juhasz as a poet *and* as a feminist; art and politics coincide.

The last chapter of *Naked and Fiery Forms*, entitled "The Feminist Poet," reprinted in Brown and Olson's collection, is not just about Rich but also considers another contemporary poet, Alta. At the beginning of her discussion of Alta, Juhasz tells us that "the most common negative response to her poetry is: 'It isn't poetry'" (p. 165). Juhasz's use of the word "poetry" in this sentence in itself mocks the "common response." The last paragraph of her chapter cites the dictionary definitions of "poem," "poetry," and "poet" and concludes: "These broad definitions do not exclude Alta; it is . . . culture-bound criteria that exclude her" (p. 185). Whereas Rich, like Plath and Dickinson, satisfies existing critical standards, and feminist criticism need only demand that we do not discriminate against them as women and/or feminists, to make Alta's case the feminist critic must call our cultural criteria themselves into question.

"There is . . . an important difference between the poetry of Rich and Alta. . . . [Rich's] forms are neither shocking nor threatening although her ideas may be. . . . Alta's very forms . . . are radical and shocking and threatening. How does one evaluate such poetry? But is it good?" (p. 184). The striking form of the last question echoes another that recurs as a sort of refrain in this chapter: "But is it poetry?".[16] Referring to Alta's writing as "such poetry," however, would seem at least to dispose of that question.

In response to these questions Juhasz first attempts to establish what she means by "good" and then closes the paragraph with her evaluation of Alta's poetry:

> when her poems are tight as a fist, when every word works not only better than any other word in its place could work but also with excitement and power, then Alta is very good. Yet Alta will print poems that do not work this well simply because of their message, their theme or statement. At this point, I think, politics and art part company. And I can continue to respect the political philosophy that tells Alta to print the lines, even if I do not want to call the lines poetry. (pp. 184–85)

The explicit question here: "But is it good?" The answer turns out to be "the most common negative response to her poetry: 'It isn't poetry.'" Twenty pages earlier Juhasz seemed to mock those who responded thus. A half page later she cites Webster's "broad definition" of poetry to show that it does "not exclude Alta; it is culture-bound criteria that exclude her." The critic who defends Alta against exclusion from the realm of poetry herself says "I do not want to call the lines poetry."

"At this point, I think, politics and art part company." Alta brings Juhasz to the same pass where we left Mailer with Kolodny. *The Naked and the Dead* offends us politically but suits our aesthetics; Alta may suit our politics but can offend our aesthetic sense. Although it may reverse the terms, the turn to women writers will not necessarily spare us this conflict. And once again, at the point where politics and art part company, the feminist critic seems to contradict herself.

Like Suzanne Juhasz, Ellen Morgan also has two essays in *Feminist Criticism*. Like Juhasz's chapter "The Feminist Poet," Morgan's "Human-becoming: Form and Focus in the Neo-Feminist Novel" considers explicitly feminist writing of the seventies. Morgan divides the neo-feminist novel into three sorts. She devotes four paragraphs to the *bildungsroman* and four to the historical novel, but the third type rates only two paragraphs. Whereas the first two are presented straightforwardly, the third is introduced apologetically: "A few words need to be said about the third form in which neo-feminist influence on the novel has been surfacing. The propaganda novel seems to be an unavoidable corollary of social movements of any scope" (p. 275). The other two forms, she chooses freely to discuss, and with relish, but "a few words need to be said" about this third. It is an obligation, not necessarily pleasant, but "unavoidable." She then characterizes this sort of writing: "Neo-feminist journals contain some writing . . . which is propagandistic: that is, writing in which message is more important than, and emphasized to the detriment of, form and/or language. . . . [S]uch works may be primarily valuable as message." The terms recall Juhasz's description of the poems she does not like: "Yet Alta will print poems that do not work well simply because of their message."

For Juhasz, this is where politics and art part company, but Morgan tries to reunite the two. "Propagandistic writing can share with art what is perhaps the most important characteristic of art—magnitude of conception—even if it lacks magnitude of form and language. The capacity to teach and to delight which some neo-feminist work of this kind has would suggest that critical standards which deny literary legitimacy and value to propagandistic writing are inadequate tools for its evaluation" (p. 276). Joining propaganda to art, or at least to "the most important characteristic of art," may lead Morgan into some pretty murky formulation ("magnitude of form and language"), but she certainly attempts to mount a serious defense of this writing.

At the beginning of this same paragraph, Morgan calls the propaganda novel "an unavoidable corollary of social movements," implying an evil, although one necessary if we would have social movements. Since it, regrettably, exists, she must do her duty and discuss it. Yet by the end of the paragraph, she has done her job so earnestly that not only has her reluctant tone disappeared, she is positively praising propagandistic writing and challenging "critical standards" that deny its value.

Morgan echoes Horace—"to teach and to delight"—when she questions critical standards. At a similar moment Juhasz invokes the dictionary ("Webster defines a poem as . . .", p. 185) against the criteria that would exclude Alta. In both cases, when the feminist critic wishes to challenge reigning cultural authorities, she, in fact but not explicitly, invokes a higher cultural authority. Morgan echoes but does not name Horace. Juhasz uses the dictionary against "culture-bound definitions," neglecting the fact, all too well-known to feminists, that the dictionary reflects a culture's definitions. The feminist needs cultural authority in order effectively to dispute cultural authority. This same gesture is writ large in the 1977 anthology *The Authority of Experience*. The title would seem to claim experience as an alternative to traditional literary authority, but the phrase is in fact taken from Chaucer's *The Canterbury Tales*, as the volume's epigraph shows.

After boldly challenging our critical standards, Morgan begins a new paragraph, the last of the two devoted to propagandistic writing: "While on the subject of the propaganda novel, I should explain that I do not think neo-feminist writing is, or will be, chiefly propagandistic." The rest of this paragraph sets out to prove that feminists need not write this way. The attempt to persuade us that feminists will produce art not propaganda would seem to undercut the defense of propagandistic writing immediately preceding. Morgan would have it both ways: challenge the standards that devalue feminist writing and argue that feminist writing can satisfy those same standards.

The paragraph continues: "Where there is passion for reform, there is the desperate need for form," eloquently suggesting that the feminist commitment in itself will impel the writer to art. "Humanbecoming" was originally published in Koppelman Cornillon's anthology. Although no mention is made of the fact, it has been substantially revised. The original version of this sentence reads: "Where there is passion, there is the need for form, for containment and refining."[17] The later version of the sentence is more artful in making its point. In particular, the rhetorical find of "reform/form" implicitly argues for a necessary relation between social movement and art. Note also that between 1972 and 1978 the "need for form" has become "desperate."

In 1972, the paragraph concludes with one last sentence: "Obviously, to use Ellison's *Invisible Man* as just one case in point, passionate consciousness of oppression does not preclude the creation of art." In the 1978 version four sentences, demonstrating that feminists actually need to make art, are inserted between "the need for form" and the Ellison analogy. And then the paragraph concludes: "To use Ellison's *Invisible Man* as just one case in point, passionate consciousness of oppression not only does not preclude, but can well call forth the creation of art" (p. 276). In 1972 it was sufficient that political consciousness not get in the way of art; by 1978 a more desperate need for form makes the feminist critic argue that politics "can well call forth art." Morgan attempts to prove not only that politics and art need not part company but that they are made for each other.

Morgan argues first that we are wrong to deny propaganda status as art. Then she argues that political passion will inevitably produce art, as traditionally defined, in opposition to propaganda. Either gesture would help close the gap between politics and art, except that they contradict each other.

Writing about contemporary feminist literature, Juhasz and Morgan both get tangled in contradiction. Contemporary feminist literature is not the only sort of women's writing that leads to this problem. Myra Jehlen has found essentially the same contradiction at work in Nina Baym's 1978 book on American women's novels of the mid-nineteenth century. Confronting the problem of why these immensely popular domestic novels were not great literature, Baym, according to Jehlen, comes up with two analyses. Since Jehlen's delineation of the feminist critic's contradiction accords so well with my analysis of Juhasz and Morgan, I will quote it in extenso:

> In the first place, [Baym] says, the women novelists never claimed to be writing great literature. They thought of "authorship as a profession rather than a calling, as work and not art. Often the women deliberately and even proudly disavowed membership in an artistic fraternity." . . . "yet," she adds (and here she is worth quoting at length because she has articulated clearly and forcefully a view that is important in feminist criticism), "I cannot avoid the belief that 'purely' literary criteria, as they have been employed to identify the best American works, have inevitably had a bias in favor of things male— in favor, say, of whaling ships rather than the sewing circle as a symbol of the human community. . . . While not claiming literary greatness for any of the novels introduced in this study, I would like at least to begin to correct such a bias by taking their content seriously. And it is time, perhaps—though this task lies outside my scope here—to reexamine the ground upon which certain hallowed American classics have been called great." . . . She is having it both ways, admitting the artistic limitations of the women's fiction ("I have not unearthed a forgotten Jane Austen or George Eliot, or hit upon even one novel that I would propose to set alongside *The Scarlet Letter*") and at the same time denying the validity of the criteria that measure those limitations; disclaiming any ambition to reorder the literary canon, and on second thought, challenging . . . the grounds for its selection.[18]

Baym feels about these domestic novels what Juhasz feels about Alta: "admitting the artistic limitations and at the same time denying the validity of the criteria that measure those limitations." Both critics point out that the writers are in fact intentionally trying to do something different than making art. Baym: "Often the women deliberately and even proudly disavowed membership in an artistic fraternity." Juhasz asks "But is it poetry?" and replies by quoting Alta: "this ain't a poem, it's just something i have to say."[19]

"Alta is making a distinction . . . between time-bound and timeless art. She is writing, not for eternity, but for now. Yet when Alta is very good, and often she is, her poems express the human spirit on a level that might very well be timeless— who can know?" (p. 168). Trying to appreciate a writer who challenges academic literary beliefs, the critic ends up praising her in terms from the very ideology being challenged. The academic critic can and cannot recognize an alternative (anti-) aesthetic.

Baym is writing about popular novelists. "Alta's art is not elitist but popular" (p. 184). The literary academy takes as its central purpose the transmission of a culture superior to "popular" culture. Literary criticism has traditionally tried to determine what is superior and to help the general reader, the student, appreciate those higher things to be found in literature. When the academic critic turns to the appreciation of popular literature, even of intentionally-popular-as-opposed-to-high art, she gets caught in contradiction.

Feminist criticism can avoid this contradiction by sticking to women writers who, if not already canonical, can satisfy the criteria that underpin the literary curriculum. And that indeed has, by and large, since 1975, been the path of feminist criticism: dodging, on the one hand, the great sexist writer and, on the other, the popular woman writer. While the mainstream of feminist criticism studies the great women writers, at the more contentious edges of that mainstream, feminist critics either demonstrate that a certain great male writer is not sexist or establish that a certain woman writer relegated to "popular" status is in fact an artist. All this activity allows the feminist critic to avoid contradiction between her feminism and her belief in literature.

Avoiding this contradiction leaves intact a central piece of the ideology of the literary academy, the belief that the artist is not only a craftswoman but wise, a superior human being. If feminism and literature split, then beauty and truth come unglued. That is the threat posed by Norman Mailer and Alta. Where traditional criticism loves to show that the well-wrought verse or sentence or plot also contains fundamental humanist understandings, feminist criticism is enamored of the writer whose exquisite sentences can be shown to express whatever feminist theory the critic espouses.

Behind this belief is the notion of an artistic elite, an aristocracy of talent, who not only write well, but are simply superior. Through the appreciation of great literature, which all of us who teach literature foster unless we actually contest it, we further the appreciation of great individuals. This is what for Robinson creates the contradiction between literary criticism and feminism.[20]

"It is time for us to confront the fact that the main problem in Anglo-American feminist criticism lies in the radical contradiction it presents between feminist politics and patriarchal aesthetics." Thus Toril Moi concludes her chapter on American feminist criticism from the late 1970s, "Women writing and writing about women."[21]

Although I share Moi's sense that some contradiction between aesthetics and politics is at the very heart of feminist criticism, I am not confident I know how to resolve that contradiction either through better aesthetics (Moi proposes modernism rather than realism) or better politics.

"This analysis . . . has . . . been an exercise in joining rather than avoiding the contradiction between ideological and appreciative criticism on the supposition that the crucial issues manifest themselves precisely at the points of contradiction." Thus Myra Jehlen concludes her 1981 consideration of the same body of feminist criticism.[22] Jehlen feels the contradiction is something to explore rather than be ashamed of: "contradictions just such as that between ethical and aesthetic that we have tried to resolve away lest they belie our argument frequently are our firmest and most fruitful grounds" (pp. 200–201).

Moi's 1985 account of American feminist criticism ends with a discussion of this 1981 article by Jehlen: "Jehlen argues for the separation of politics and aesthetics in an attempt to solve a perennial problem for radical critics: the problem of how to evaluate a work of art that one finds aesthetically valuable but politically distasteful" (pp. 84–85). Jehlen's argument is extremely complex and I cannot share Moi's relegation of it to any simple separation of politics and aesthetics. I am sure Jehlen would agree with Moi's assertion that "to require a simple and uncomplicated answer to the highly complex problem of the relationship between politics and aesthetics is surely the most reductive approach of all" (p. 85).

Moi concludes her discussion of Jehlen: "It should be clear by now that one of the chief contentions of this book is that feminist criticism is about deconstructing such an opposition between the political and the aesthetic. . . . This is why Jehlen's views seem to me to undermine some of the basic tenets of feminist criticism" (p. 86). Immediately after her consideration of Jehlen, Moi writes:

Some feminists might wonder why I have said nothing about black or lesbian
. . . feminist criticism in America in this survey. The answer is simple: this
book purports to deal with the theoretical aspects of feminist criticism. . . .
[*in*] *so far as textual theory is concerned* there is no discernable difference
between these three fields [black, lesbian, and the rest of feminist criticism].
This is not to say that black and lesbian criticism have no *political* importance; on the contrary. (p. 86, emphasis Moi's)

Then she concludes her consideration of American criticism: "The
radically new impact of feminist criticism is to be found not at the level
of theory or methodology, but at the level of politics" (p. 87). Moi
decries the separation between aesthetics and politics but the opposition between theory and politics is absolutely central to her book.

When New Criticism held sway in the literary academy, the reigning
values were aesthetic. The academic feminist critic was torn between
those values and her feminism. By the mid-1980s the dominant discourse in the literary academy is poststructuralist and the reigning
values are theoretical. Now the academic feminist is torn between
theory and politics. Where once she looked to Emily Dickinson to
resolve the split, now she pins her hopes on Julia Kristeva, "for in her
can truly be found the female intellectual, demanding comparison with
Derrida and Lacan."[23]

Early in 1990 I delivered a version of this chapter as a lecture at a
few universities. I was puzzled by the response I got. Finally it dawned
on me that in our post-poststructuralist certitudes, my audience assumed that I was describing an error of earlier days, a foolish aesthet-
icist stance, that we were comfortably beyond, thanks to the poststructuralist critique of transcendental aesthetics. But that is not my
supposition. I find the academic feminist of today equally in contradiction: only the terms have shifted from art to theory. If we understand
the conflict as that between feminism and the reigning values of the
literary academy, when we factor in the shift that took place in the
literary academy in the early 1980s, we see we are not beyond the
contradiction at work in the 1978 anthology.

There are nine essays in the poetry section of *Feminist Criticism*.
There are likewise nine essays on the novel, but the prose section does
not end there; it includes three additional essays, unbalancing the
volume in the direction of prose. The last two essays in the prose
section extend beyond fiction, beyond literature as "poetry in the broad

sense,"[24] to treat autobiographical writing. Lynn Z. Bloom treats writing by such non-literary figures as Margaret Sanger and Margaret Mead right along with works by literary women such as Gertrude Stein and Nikki Giovanni. The final essay, on writing by feminists of the first and second wave, considers Emmeline Pankhurst and Elizabeth Cady Stanton along with more literary, but certainly not nearly canonical, figures like Kate Millett and Rita Mae Brown.

The author of this last essay, Kathleen Dehler, according to the Biographical Sketches which immediately follow, "teaches English and women's studies on both the college and secondary school levels." At the other extreme of *Feminist Criticism*, the author of the first essay, Margret Andersen, is a (full) professor and department "chairman" (p. 353). Whereas Andersen clearly "holds her own in academic circles," Dehler is located on the perimeter. The prose section runs not only to the edge of literature, but also to the border of the academy.

Between the two essays on autobiography and the nine on fiction is a piece by Estelle Jelinek on Anaïs Nin. Jelinek works on women's autobiography; Nin has published novels but is better known for her diaries. Jelinek's essay is not, however, a study of Nin's writing but rather examines the relation between Nin as a public figure and feminism.

"[W]omen who call themselves feminists or Marxists swoon at [Nin's] words. . . . These women seem incapable of discerning the inherent contradictions between their sexual and/or radical politics and her views" (p. 318). Jelinek compares Nin to another charismatic female literary figure: "One could see Nin's individualism carried to the fascistic extremes that Ayn Rand articulated. . . . How can feminists and radicals of all types accept uncritically this elitism and miss the incompatibility with the rest of their lives?" (p. 317). "Fascistic" by association, Nin's incompatibility with leftist politics is heightened.

The "contradictions" involve Nin's individualism and its corollary, elitism. Consistently linking feminists with Marxists and other "radicals," Jelinek ascribes to feminism the leftist belief in collectivity as against individualism. We might be tempted here to separate out the socialist feminists from the liberal feminists as a way of resolving the contradictions. Liberal feminism embraces individualism, attempting to cleanse it of the sexist discrimination which only allows men individuality. Nin, the great woman, would then be the darling of liberal feminism. But Jelinek's analysis does not allow us to dissolve the contradiction through polarizing feminisms. She continually insists that it is not just feminists but "Marxists," "radicals of all sorts," who adore Nin. The contradiction is not between differing feminisms but within feminists.

Nin's elitism centers around the concept of the artist: "She doesn't really care about anyone but artists" (p.317). This recalls the author of *The Fountainhead*: "Ayn Rand upheld this . . . vision of the creative-artist as a superior human being and, concomitantly, the inferiority of the masses" (p.317). This is, literally, the ideology of the literary academy. Yet the feminists who are compromised by their attraction to Nin's aesthetic elitism are not just literary academics.

When feminist literary criticism devotes itself to geniuses like Emily Dickinson and Virginia Woolf, it contradicts feminism by preferring the woman who is different from and better than other women. But in that contradiction, feminist criticism participates in the general feminist embrace of great women. The contradiction between feminism and (academic) criticism can also be found as a contradiction within feminism. The feminist identifies with other women but also struggles to rise above the lot of women. Feminism both desires superior women and celebrates the common woman.

I am not claiming that Anaïs Nin is a great woman or that she should be a role model for feminists, but the contradiction Jelinek deplores in feminist feeling for Nin can also be located in feminist adoration of women with much better feminist credentials or politics. The fundamental form of the contradiction lies in the relation between feminism as a mass movement of gender consciousness and the elevation of feminist "heroes" above that mass.

In the early 1970s, feminists spoke of the need for role models. Cheri Register lists "providing role-models" as one of the five functions literature can serve for women's liberation.[25] Literature already is in the business of providing role-models, that is certainly one of the ways it most directly affects society. Noting that the ideology of "art" makes unique, special individuals of literary figures, both writers and characters, Lillian Robinson writes: "It is not role models we need so much as a mass movement, not celebration of individual struggle . . . so much as recognition that we are all heroes."[26]

Jelinek closes her essay on Nin with the statement: "hero-worshipping should be anathema to all serious radicals and feminists" (p. 323). Whether in some ideal, superior version of feminism, "serious" feminists would completely shun "hero-worshipping," in the real, "popular" form that feminism is usually found, we tend to celebrate exceptional individual women.

"Feminist critics themselves have not completely abandoned the serious/popular dichotomy."[27] In feminism, as in feminist criticism, separating the "serious" from the "popular" is a way to alleviate contradiction. This chapter has tried to resist such moves. I am as desirous of resolving contradictions as the next girl, but I find myself drawing us back to them, refusing the separations that allow us to avoid but not resolve contradiction.

IV
GOING ON (IN)

10
Tongue Work

The 1985 anthology, *Conjuring: Black Women, Fiction, and Literary Tradition*, begins with a quotation from Alice Walker. Two hundred and fifty pages later, the last article ends quoting the same author. In our approach to this anthology, we might begin by taking Alice Walker as a frame of reference.

The epigraph to *Conjuring*'s Introduction is the "closing note" to Walker's 1982 novel *The Color Purple*. The Introduction begins by elaborating on this "closing note" so we might say that this anthology takes up directly from Walker's novel. The last sentence of the Introduction, explaining the collection's title, is immediately preceded by a quotation from the same novel. " 'Whenever you trying to pray, and man plop himself on the other end of it, tell him to get lost. . . . Conjure up flowers, wind, water, a big rock.' We propose our volume's title, *Conjuring*, as a tribute to the powers of Hurston and Walker."[1] The immediate reference for the anthology's title is this use of the word "conjure" in Walker's novel.

The title is explicitly proposed as a tribute to two writers, Walker and Zora Neale Hurston. Yet that does not so much double the frame as double the reference to Walker. In 1973, posing as Hurston's niece, Walker placed a stone near Hurston's unmarked grave.[2] In 1979, she edited a volume of Hurston's writing.[3] Walker claims Hurston as her literary foremother, as the strong precursor to contemporary black women's fiction. *Conjuring*'s Introduction understands Hurston's work specifically in relation to what Walker does in *The Color Purple*: "Hurston planned the garden, but it would take Alice Walker to plant it. If Hurston could have imagined a novel in which Janie had indeed gone home to look for her mother . . . then she might have written Alice Walker's *The Color Purple*. Still, Walker has claimed about *Their Eyes Were Watching God* that '*there is no book more important to me than this one.*'"[4] Hurston's novel is here construed as a *Color Purple* manqué. "Still," Marjorie Pryse goes on in the Introduction, Walker claims *Their Eyes* as the most important book to her, and we thus claim Hurston's novel because of its value to Walker, and as a stepping-stone on the path to *Purple*.

Half a paragraph later, the Introduction states that *"The Color Purple* stands as yet another monument to Hurston" (p. 15). Walker laid a stone, inscribed "A Genius of the South," by Hurston's grave. Here, Pryse connects the 1982 novel to that stone. In this configuration Walker's Pulitzer Prize-winning novel would serve to glorify Hurston. The relationship is thus construed in two opposite ways: in one, Hurston is a first draft for Walker; in the other, Walker is a secondary reflection of Hurston. These two versions of the relationship bespeak a tension, if not a paradox, absolutely central to the literary tradition Pryse would portray, a tradition which would honor the mother, but which also surpasses the mother precisely in its ability to "go home to look for mother."

1982, the year *The Color Purple* was published, the first anthology of "Black Women's Studies" appears. *But Some of Us Are Brave* opens with a poem by Alice Walker entitled "Women" which celebrates "My mama's generation": "How they knew what we/*Must* know/Without knowing . . . it/Themselves." Five hundred pages later this landmark collection closes with Walker's 1972 syllabus for a course on Black Women Writers, the earliest of the twenty syllabi included in the volume.[5] Alice Walker was first to set the course for looking back at the black literary foremothers.

Conjuring's Introduction explicitly tells its literary history from Walker's perspective: "Once again looking backwards through the eyes of Alice Walker, Hurston's literary daughter . . . we can see that . . . the literary tradition of black women's fiction finds its . . . first real flowering in Hurston" (p. 12). "The eyes of Alice Walker" reclaim this point-of-view image from its worn familiarity, for, in fact, only Walker's left eye can see.[6] Pryse hopes the anthology "can provide students and scholars alike with a laboratory for examining the origins and patterns of development that characterize literary traditions in general" (p. 3). The combination of this singular gaze with the gesture toward the general might remind us that "literary traditions in general" are formed by looking backwards through specific and embodied eyes and often, as in this case, in order to construe the past as forerunners and precursors leading up to a privileged work or author or movement in the present.[7] And as in any search for roots, the past is seen as leading up to the present inasmuch as the present is in search of its own past.

Looking backwards through Walker's "eyes," we see a "flowering."

In 1974, Alice Walker published the article "In Search of Our Mothers' Gardens." The essay quotes from *A Room of One's Own* to echo Woolf's complaint that in the past women did not have the opportunity to make art. The founding text of Anglo-American feminist literary theory gives us the fictive Judith Shakespeare, the woman artist with no outlet who died, seduced and abandoned. Walker's African-American revision discovers that "our mothers," black women of previous generations who did not have the opportunity to make art in high cultural modes, expressed themselves and made beauty in homely modes. Where Woolf's *Room* bemoans women's past exclusion from culture, Walker's *Gardens* celebrates women's past creations not recognized by our cultural institutions. Woolf's model for future cultural production is William Shakespeare; in the inaugural text of black womanist literary theory the model is Walker's mother, a superb and impassioned gardener whose "fame as a grower of flowers spread over three counties."[8] This provides Walker with her central metaphor for the art of the foremothers. This garden metaphor is another way in which Pryse sees through "the eyes of Alice Walker": "Hurston planned the garden, but it would take Alice Walker to plant it" (p. 15).

Marjorie Pryse subtitles her "Introduction" to *Conjuring*: "Zora Neale Hurston, Alice Walker, and the 'Ancient Power' of Black Women." The phrase "ancient power" is central to Pryse's notion of the anthology: "The 'ancient power' black women writers document in their fiction and express as the intersection of black, female, and folk vision serves as a predominant and unifying concern for the writers of many of the essays in this collection, as well as for the novelists themselves" (p. 20). The "literary tradition" that Pryse and this anthology would portray is the exploration and transmission of this "ancient power," a power often synonymous with "conjuring," a power that belongs to those generally considered disempowered by race, sex, and class ("black, female, and folk").

Gloria Hull's contribution to *Conjuring* gives us Toni Cade Bambara's phrase "ancient wisdoms" for "avenues of knowing/being which are opposed to the 'rational,' 'Western,' 'scientific' mode." Lined up with the "ancient wisdoms" are "root men . . . conjure women . . . obeah folks."[9] In the last article of the anthology, Barbara Christian quotes Toni Morrison's phrase "ancient properties," which she relates to the ability "to nurture." Opposed to "the decadent Western view of woman," these "ancient properties" are represented by a female "Caribbean sage."[10]

"Whenever we find interest in folklore in novels by black women we also find stages in the tradition's emerging perception that women have the ability to reclaim their 'ancient power'" (Introduction, p. 20). The power is "ancient," belongs to the dark past, yet women's ability to reclaim it is "emerging," grows successively as we move from past to present to future. There is an implicit developmental narrative here ("stages in the emerging perception"), the suggestion of progress. The tradition is maturing, but toward a future reunion with an "ancient power." This sort of circular teleology, in which the goal is the recovery of a lost origin, might, as Pryse suggests, typify the construction of "literary traditions in general." For example, Virginia Woolf's narrative of the British women's fictional tradition portrays stages progressing from the seventeenth through the twentieth centuries and working toward a glorious future, the reclamation of the original power that was lost to us: the genius of "Judith Shakespeare," the woman artist whose talent was wasted at the beginning of Woolf's narrative.[11]

Like Woolf, Pryse constructs a tradition heading toward the recovery of lost glory. Rather than bemoan the lack of a female Shakespeare, this tradition would honor the black foremothers. But the circular teleology, at once progress and movement backward, disrupts any simple ancestor worship. Such circularity can have the local effect, at any point on the tradition's time line, of ambiguity as to whether the present represents an improvement over, or a dimmer reflection of, the past: an ambiguity we have seen in Pryse's version of the relation between Hurston and Walker.

The phrase "ancient power" is taken from Hurston's novel *Their Eyes Were Watching God*. Janie, the protagonist, is raised by her grandmother, Nanny. "Janie sees her grandmother's head and face as 'the standing roots of some old tree that had been torn away by storm. Foundation of ancient power that no longer mattered.'"[12] Pryse's "ancient power" is thus, first of all, a reference to this grandmother, who had been a slave, who raised Janie and passed on knowledge to her, black, female, folk knowledge, just as, according to Pryse, Hurston will pass on black, female, folk knowledge to generations of fiction writers that come after her.

But the "ancient power" in Janie's vision of her grandmother also belongs to the roots of a tree that is no longer there. Although these roots once could nourish and sustain a tree, the tree has not survived. The word "power" here thus appears in an ironic context; it is a trace of some former power that "no longer mattered." "Ancient" here might also suggest obsolete.

In fact, Janie hated her grandmother. The Introduction reclaims the grandmothers with the very phrase used to describe their power as outmoded and meaningless. The irony is not lost on Pryse who, on the contrary, would exploit it to effect a specific revision in order to reclaim precisely what Janie denied: "The novel that ironically presents Janie as 'hating' her grandmother actually provides a crucial link between generations of black women and established storytelling . . . as essential to passing down the 'ancient power' that will enable black women to fulfill their dreams" (p. 14). The irony for Pryse is that while Janie does not search for her mothers' gardens, will not claim those old roots, Hurston passes down the "ancient power" from her foremothers to her literary daughters.

Yet that is, for Pryse, somehow, not enough. Pryse concludes the paragraph: "Yet although she professes to 'hate' her grandmother, by coming back to Starkville . . . Janie actually does return home" (p. 14). "Yet although," Pryse doubly stresses the contrast between Janie's profession of animosity and what she "actually" does, suggesting that her acts belie the statement. Both times she mentions Janie's hatred, she puts the verb "hate" in quotation marks, suggesting it may not be true. In contrast to this questionable verb, "Janie *actually* does return home": that is presented as undisputed fact. But Starkville is not where her grandmother lived; it is not an ancestral matrilocus. Starkville is where Janie went and lived with her second husband when she ran away from the man Nanny had married her to. It is not self-evident that returning to Starkville makes her "hatred" of her grandmother ironic.

Back in Starkville, Janie recounts her adventures to her friend Pheoby. Pryse writes: "In the act of storytelling Janie has managed to . . . make her grandmother's 'ancient power' matter again. . . . The child abandoned by her mother restores the network of female connectedness in her long talk with Pheoby, who promises as Janie begins her story to report her narrative to others. One generation of storytellers bequeaths her power to the next" (pp. 14–15). Janie tells Pheoby and Pheoby will pass the story on to others. The phrase "generation of storytellers" makes the relation between friends metaphorically intergenerational. Treating Janie's story as a heritage of knowledge, the

critic translates female friendship into the relation between literal generations of women and asserts that the grandmother's power is "restored."

"If Hurston could have imagined a novel in which Janie had indeed
gone home . . . then she might have written Alice Walker's *The Color
Purple*" (p. 15). Hurston could not and did not. Pryse makes that clear
but also cannot quite keep from trying to prove that Hurston did, sort
of.

On a theoretical level, Pryse's apparent contradiction can certainly
be resolved. African-American women's fiction is progressively improv-
ing; the contemporary novels are the best that have ever been. The
"ancient powers" are not that of fiction writers but of black women in
more traditional, homely activities: nurturing their children and their
people, surviving in a racist society, practicing the arts of conjure, of
quilting and gardening. Today's novelists are putting into their literary
productions the powers black women manifested in the past, although
not in past literary endeavor. The black foremothers were magnificent,
but not as novelists. Thus there is no contradiction, simply a confusion
between realms. In the literary realm there is progress, but in the arts
of living, the black mothers could not be surpassed, only followed,
with awe and respect.

Except that Pryse presses the analogy between literary and literal
foremothers. The continual slipping back and forth between the two
realms not only makes it difficult for us to sort them out, but pushes
her to find evidence of the grandmothers' powers in the literary foremothers.

Besides writing the Introduction, Marjorie Pryse has also contributed an article, on Ann Petry's *The Street*, to the anthology. While
the standard reading of Petry's 1946 naturalist tragedy considers the
protagonist Lutie Johnson "lacking in power to substantially alter the
course of her life,"[13] Pryse believes Petry provides an alternative which
Lutie tragically refuses. "*The Street* offers its readers an alternative in
the vision of a black community which might embrace its grandmothers" (p. 129).

Pryse contrasts Lutie's mistakes with the right choices made by
another female character, Min. "Min serves as Lutie's foil for Petry. . . .
Min . . . lives by the same instincts Lutie Johnson rejects when she
refuses to listen to her Granny's voice" (pp. 125–126). Unlike Lutie who
turns to powerful white men for help, Min goes to a root doctor. Going
to a root doctor is like listening to Granny: both tap into the "ancient

power." In this article, the "ancient power" can go by the name of "motherhood—but a motherhood not of biology but of human connection in which the [root doctor] becomes the symbol of nurturing power in the black community" (p. 129). Pryse explicitly connects these metaphorical "mothers" to "roots (and root doctors)." When Hurston's Janie saw her grandmother's "ancient power," she actually saw her as a root.

Although the critic insists on Granny's voice as an alternative force, Granny is the shadowiest of absences in *The Street*:

> Granny never appears as a character in the novel but she exists as a memory in Lutie's mind. We learn that Lutie's mother died . . . and that her grandmother raised her. Perhaps if Ann Petry had been able to read recent novels by Paule Marshall, Alice Walker, Toni Morrison and Toni Cade Bambara, she might have been more aware of the fictional potential of Granny in her novel—for Lutie's Granny (like her fictional predecessor, Janie's grandmother in Zora Neale Hurston's *Their Eyes Were Watching God*) seems to have given Lutie at least some of the . . . knowledge she needs to counteract the street. (pp. 123–24)

Not only does Granny never appear, but, Pryse suggests, even the "memory" does not fulfill her "fictional potential." If Petry had read Marshall, Walker, Morrison, and Bambara, then she might have tapped Granny's "ancient power." But even this literally impossible fantasy might not be enough: "*Perhaps* Petry *might* have been more aware." Petry's Granny is a far cry from what Pryse would have her be.

"If Hurston could have imagined a novel in which Janie had indeed gone home to . . . 'tend her grandmother's grave' then she might have written *The Color Purple*." As Pryse says, Lutie's Granny is like Janie's Nanny: above all, perhaps, in not being sufficiently embraced by either their granddaughters or their authors.

"If Ann Petry had been able to read recent novels by Paule Marshall, Alice Walker, Toni Morrison and Toni Cade Bambara": a note appended to the list of contemporary writers names five novels published between 1969 and 1982, ending with Walker's *Purple*, "which portray women who understand the power of black, female traditions" (p. 131 n.9). If only Petry had been able to read them. If only Petry had succeeded her successors, then she could have truly been their predecessor. The present provides us with novelists who understand "black, female traditions"; the black female fictional tradition begins there, with that understanding, and revises its way backwards.

In the opening paragraph of the volume's final article, Barbara Christian states: "Afro-American women writers today are no longer marginal to literature in this country; some of them are its finest practitioners" (p. 234). Afro-American women writers were, up until the present, marginal. Christian, however, is not protesting some form of discrimination which, in the past, actively marginal*ized* these writers. When she asserts that some of them are, today, "its finest practitioners," she implies that contemporary novelists have earned their central status through (objectively judgeable and judged) fine writing and that writers of past generations deserved their marginal status.

From this premise Christian goes on to make her case for studying pre-contemporary writing: "But in order to really understand the remarkable achievement of a Toni Morrison, an Alice Walker, or a Paule Marshall . . . one must appreciate the tradition from which they have come." Today's novelists are so great we might think there is no reason to look to their predecessors, "but," Christian asserts, we must look back in order better to appreciate the glory of the contemporaries. She is not questioning the secondary status of earlier writers; she is giving them value as precursors: secondary, reflective value. The tradition has value precisely because it has given birth to these geniuses.[14]

Not all literary traditions work this way. The dominant European male tradition has repeatedly conceived itself as a continual falling away from ancient literary glories: all down hill after Homer, or after the classics, or after the Renaissance. English Literature is still more often than not seen as having its greatest glories in Chaucer, Shakespeare, and Milton; anything later has to measure up to those standards.

Conjuring's literary tradition runs the opposite way. Earlier writers are valued because of their relation to contemporary writers. If we are to believe Harold Bloom's accounts, this would be a Euro-American male poet's dream come true, a standpoint from which all ancestors are subordinated as necessary but not sufficient precursors.[15] Suffering no anxiety of influence, the black women poets indeed choose to search out and reclaim their mothers' art.

This specific valuation of the tradition in fact functions as a structural principle for *Conjuring*. Despite their starring roles in Pryse's Introduction as the mother-daughter dyad epitomizing the tradition, neither Hurston nor Alice Walker rate an article in the collection. Nor does Frances E. W. Harper, always cited as the first African-American woman to publish a novel. *Conjuring* chooses instead to include a piece on Harper's much less well known contemporary, Pauline Hopkins.

Claudia Tate's article on Hopkins, subtitled "Our Literary Foremother," is a typical attempt to go back and reclaim a neglected one. Tate complains: "Despite her prolific writing career, Hopkins has been omitted from the canon of American literature. We might conjecture that her race and gender are somewhat responsible for her omission."[16] Protesting that prejudice excluded Hopkins from the literary canon, the critic does not argue that the novels are literary masterpieces. Having pointed out numerous flaws and weaknesses, the article concludes: "Her excessively episodic and melodramatic techniques resulted in her failure to meet twentieth-century critical standards; nevertheless, she was a serious writer, who wrote three novels at the turn of the century. This fact, alone, demands that we retrieve her work from obscurity" (p. 65). Tate's less than glowing evaluation suggests that literary "technique" kept Hopkins from meeting critical standards for the canon. Tate does not question those standards. Her strongest claims for Hop kins call the writer "serious" and "prolific." This reclamation implies we must study "our literary foremothers," not because of their excellence but because they worked long and hard.

Deborah E. McDowell's essay on Jessie Fauset and Bernard Bell's on Ann Petry both begin, like Tate, by complaining of critical neglect of their respective novelists. The articles suggest the neglect stems from gender prejudice in African-American criticism and go on to remedy it with accounts of the authors' works. These critics treat their authors as more deserving of attention than they've gotten, but neither conveys a sense of a brilliant writer.

Hopkins is in the volume in place of Harper and Fauset is included instead of Hurston, not because they are better, or even as good, but precisely because the anthology wants to fill in the tradition around the great names. Yet *Conjuring* does not leave us with the sense that there were others at home just as glorious as the well-known reputations. Rather it communicates that the foremothers were serious, hardworking, and brave.

The first anthology devoted to "Black Women in Literature," published in 1979, was entitled *Sturdy Black Bridges*. A poem by Carolyn Rodgers, which closes the anthology, ends: "My mother . . . is very obviously/a sturdy Black bridge that I/ crossed over, on."[17] Choosing that phrase for its title, the 1979 volume places the mother in the center of its literary vision of black women. The phrase, the poem, the anthology, black women claiming the black female tradition, all celebrate the powers of the mothers. But the mother is appreciated as what the daughter "crossed over, on." It is the daughter who "crosses over," and her crossing, retrospectively, validates the mother's strength.

One of the editors of *Sturdy Black Bridges*, Bettye J. Parker, later published a critical essay on Carolyn Rodgers's poetry. According to Parker, now Parker-Smith, "It Is Deep," the poem which gives us "sturdy Black bridge," dates from a phase of Rodgers's writing which "was her frantic attempt to free herself from her mother's will. But she continues to be overwhelmed by her mother's presence, which is possibly the strongest influence in her life."[18] Perhaps the "anxiety of influence" is not unknown to the black woman writer. It might, however, precipitate ratios of revision other than Bloom could imagine.

In *Conjuring*'s literary tradition the hardworking "foremothers" are secondary to the brilliant "daughters." But these geniuses are nonetheless also, literally, daughters of powerful mothers. Toni Cade Bambara: "It does no good to write autobiographical fiction cause the minute the book hits the stand here comes your mama screamin how could you . . . it is nineteen-forty-and-something and you ain't too grown to have you ass whipped."[19]

"The relationship between a Black woman and her daughter (especially if they are poor) is perhaps the most complex relationship that exists between any two human beings. . . . These daughters are awed by their mother's ability to . . . survive within a dehumanizing system. . . . More often than not, a strain permeates the relationship. . . . They never (no matter how tall they become) grow up to their mothers" (Parker-Smith, p. 397). No matter how much the daughters "strain," they can never measure up to their mothers. Bloom's white male poets might recognize this "strain."

"It is both the *depth* of her mother's struggle and her pain that traumatized [Rodgers]. Just an ordinary woman—nondecorative—but she has what her daughter may lack: unfathomable strength" (Parker-Smith, p. 400). This loss of strength from sturdy black mother to successful daughter is, according to Renita Weems, also a theme in Toni Morrison's writing. The black woman critic is herself "traumatized" by this realization of lack: "Morrison's . . . theme shook the chains of my own enclosed reality. I was forced to ask myself, why it was that I— who supposedly have more than my mother in terms of possessions and skills—have not the sense of stability, conviction, or propriety that she has? Why is it that my life crumbles more easily than hers? . . . Through the creation of generations of women, Toni Morrison asks, '. . . What have our children lost that we were too busy making do to lose?'"[20]

Weems finds an example of this theme of degeneration down the female line in Morrison's 1981 novel *Tar Baby*: "Jadine is absolutely ignorant of the sense of responsibility that her Aunt Ondine obviously took for granted when she took in her orphaned niece and raised her like her own." At the end of *Conjuring*, Christian comments on the same inadequacy in Jadine: "In pursuing her own desire to 'make it,' Jadine forgets how to nurture those who have made it impossible [sic] for her to be successful" (p. 245). I presume that Christian means to say "possible" not "impossible."

In her reading of Morrison, Weems consciously identifies, as a weak daughter, with Jadine's inability to nurture her Aunt. Perhaps Christian is unconsciously expressing a similar identification, unconsciously echoing Jadine's refusal to recognize that her success depends on the work of the previous generation. The Aunt/Mother's suffering and strength can make success "possible" but also "impossible," can be not only enabling but also traumatizing to the "successful" woman, to the woman who has "more in terms of possessions and skills" than her mother.

I am not trying to say that Christian actually or simply means "impossible" rather than "possible." I am not trying to say that the womanist critic who celebrates the literary or the literal foremothers actually resents them, feels some sort of negative emotion that is covered over by valorization. I am trying to draw out a "strain" which, in *Conjuring*, shadows the clear and central affirmation of the foremothers' power. When we consider the possibility that Janie did not actually hate her grandmother, we might want to balance it against the possibility that today's successful black daughter does not simply appreciate the Aunts that she crossed over, on.

Janie did not go home to tend her grandmother's grave. But in 1973, Alice Walker went to Florida, posed as Zora Neale Hurston's niece, and put up a stone near her unmarked grave. This literary kinship, claiming the place of literal kinship, is the heart of the literary tradition Pryse "introduces" in *Conjuring*. It is a tradition that begins when Walker reclaims her "Aunt Zora," a tradition Pryse carries on when she looks back at Hurston's *Eyes*, reading it through Walker's "eyes."

Pryse reminds us that Hurston refers to Janie and Pheoby as "kissin'-friends." She also quotes Janie saying that when Pheoby retells the story, "mah tongue is in mah friend's mouf."[21] Three pages later, the Introduction gives new meaning to Janie's two phrases: "the connection between Celie and Shug . . . is . . . decidedly sexual. Quite literally these are 'kissin'-friends' whose tongues are in each others' mouths" (p. 18).

Hurston failed to write *The Color Purple*. Separation between women is too strong in *Their Eyes*. But Walker succeeds. The woman who went "In Search of Our Mothers' Gardens," not only teaches us to revere the bond between female generations, but gives free rein to female friendship. To the extent that *Purple* is seen as the culmination of what *Eyes* attempts, Pryse sets up an implicit teleology where "kissin'-friends" ought to go all the way.

The Introduction concludes: "'Whenever you trying to pray . . . say Shug. Conjure up flowers . . . a big rock.' We propose our volume's title, *Conjuring*, as a tribute to the powers of Hurston and Walker, and as a reminder . . . of the oath we all must take to continue the work of speaking with each others' tongues in our mouths, thereby illuminating women's lives" (p. 22). The volume's title, as presented here, is most immediately a reference to something Shug taught Celie. Shug also taught Celie about the "button" and the "wet rose" between her legs, about what Shug calls "finger and tongue work."[22] By this point, the phrase "speaking with each others' tongues in our mouths" not only means passing on the heritage of stories, but also something, if technically more difficult, a lot hotter. As the Introduction gestures out toward the actuality of the 1985 book and its readers, toward the future of a tradition, passing on the heritage conjures the reader into some sort of sexy chain. Writing and telling are also "finger and tongue work."

The Introduction centers the anthology and its literary tradition on female connectedness. It equivocates between different varieties of female bonding, from intergenerational nurture through friendship to lesbian love and, in the register of more properly literary relations, also expands outward from characters to authors, critics, and readers. Without specifically articulating the relation between, say, Janie's grandmother and Shug and Celie's sex play, it suggests an unbroken continuum between all these realms. The equation between female heritage, female friendship, storytelling, and womanist criticism is fairly representative of the main stream of critics who have been working to establish a black female literary tradition. But the glide in and out of lesbianism represents something bolder.

In her survey at the end of *Conjuring*, Christian declares that a "radical change in the fiction of the 1980s is the overt exploration of lesbian relationships among black women" (p. 246), citing four books by major writers, all published in 1982. Given the lag time between publication, reading, writing criticism, editing and then publishing a collection, this represents the approximate fictional present for the 1985 critical anthology. Nothing published later than 1983 is cited anywhere in the volume.

In the early eighties, the latest hot thing in black women's fiction is lesbianism. The anthology too could be said to belong to this moment. But more than just a moment, the teleological progression toward *The Color Purple* frames this historical movement as a progressive revealing of a truth, an ultimate female connectedness that was earlier only partial.

Christian, commenting upon one of the 1982 books: "In *Zami* ... the definition of a lesbian relationship is extended, since Lorde beautifully demonstrates how the heritage of her Grenadian mother is integrally connected to her development as a woman-identified woman" (pp. 246–47). Audre Lorde reclaims the heritage of the mother and retranslates that heritage into lesbian terms.

Thelma Shinn, in her article in *Conjuring*, says of a character by Octavia Butler: "Amber's knowledge has literally been transferred to her . . . by her friend and lesbian lover . . . Kai, suggesting an archetypal Demeter/Kore pattern of 'uniting the feminine generations.'"[23] The phrase "uniting the feminine generations" could describe the tradition *Conjuring* would establish. Shinn feels free to apply the phrase, and the mother/daughter paradigm, to an explicitly lesbian connection. Lorde and Shinn go along with the Introduction: equating the reclamation of the black mother's power with sexual love between women.

There is a precedent for *Conjuring*'s lesbianization of the literary tradition: one that is, however, not mentioned explicitly in the volume. Commenting on the subject of female friendship, Pryse writes in the Introduction that "Morrison's *Sula* stands as a major link between Hurston's Janie and Alice Walker's Celie" (p. 20). The Introduction has, by this point, read Janie and Pheoby's friendship as a precursor to Celie and Shug's. This sentence places Sula and Nel's friendship midway between them. If not yet overtly lesbian, this friendship is more intense than Janie and Pheoby's and thus represents another stage on the path to *Purple*. This placement echoes what is certainly the most famous reading of *Sula*.

In her 1977 article, "Toward a Black Feminist Criticism," Barbara Smith interprets *Sula* as a "lesbian novel," focusing on the "passionate friendship" between Sula and Nel. To support her interpretation, Smith quotes a paper by Lorraine Bethel which states: "I am not suggesting that Sula and Nel are being consciously sexual, or that their relationship has an overt lesbian nature. I am suggesting, however, that there is a certain sensuality in their interactions that is reinforced by the mirror-like nature of their relationship."[24] Bethel and Smith would unveil an unconscious or covert lesbianism in *Sula*. This interpretation corresponds to Pryse's placing Sula in line between Janie and Celie in the progression to full female connection.

In her groundbreaking article, before performing her lesbian interpretation of *Sula*, Smith sets forth a principle that is fundamental to *Conjuring*: "a Black feminist critic . . . would . . . work from the assumption that Black women writers constitute an identifiable literary tradition. . . . [N]ot only is theirs a verifiable historical tradition . . . but . . . Black women writers manifest common approaches to the act of creating literature" (pp. 163–64). Thus, in 1977, Smith both asserts the black, female tradition and proceeds to lesbianize it.

In 1982, Smith republished "Towards a Black Feminist Criticism" in the anthology she edited with Gloria Hull and Patricia Bell Scott. In that 1982 collection, Smith's essay heads off the "Black Women's Literature" section where it is immediately followed by a reading of Hurston by Lorraine Bethel, the same critic cited in the reading of *Sula*.

In her article on Hurston, Bethel stresses the idea of the literary tradition: "I have subtitled this essay 'Zora Neale Hurston and the Black Female Literary Tradition' because as a Black feminist critic I believe there is a separable and identifiable tradition of Black women writers. . . . Hurston's work forms a major part of this tradition."[25] The article seems, in many ways, typical of contemporary womanist writing on Hurston, until Bethel painstakingly makes her way toward a final surprising assertion: "Hurston's vision is not only woman-identified, but also lesbian in that it acknowledges and asserts the validity of primary love relationships between women" (p. 187). Like Pryse, Bethel would have Hurston write *The Color Purple*.

In her consideration of the novels of 1982, Christian agrees that *The Color Purple* is kin to *Their Eyes Were Watching God*. But Christian's exploration of the kinship also focuses on a difference: "in *The Color Purple* Walker does for the sexual relationship between black women what Hurston in *Their Eyes*... did for sexual relationships between black women and men" (p. 246). Whereas Pryse connects *Purple*'s lesbian love to Janie and Pheoby's friendship, Christian links it to Janie and Teacake's love. Pryse makes *Eyes* an unrequited first draft of later lesbian fruition; Christian sees the two novels as similar successes in different genres.

While Pryse's version of the history involves a gradual but continual reclamation of female connectedness, an unbroken progress, Christian considers the overt portrayal of lesbianism in 1980s fiction to be a "radical change." In response to efforts like Bethel's, Smith's, and Pryse's to press a lesbian continuum, Christian says flat out: "This exploration [of lesbian relationships] is not, I believe, to be confused with the emphasis on friendship among black women that is a major theme in earlier literature."[26] As she tells the story, this is the emergence not of something previously hidden in the fiction, but of something new.

Pryse would string black, female fiction along an unbroken continuum of female connection, running from Granny's voice through friendship to sexual contact. The Introduction deftly throws us this line to guide our reading of the anthology. But Christian, in her own reader's guide, would mark a break in the tradition before the latest move; she would draw the line before female connection goes all the way.

Immediately preceding Christian at the end of the volume is Gloria Hull's reading of Bambara's 1980 novel, *The Salt Eaters*. Hull thinks this is a great book. In the entire sixteen page article, exploring multiple dimensions of the novel, Hull has only one critical thing to say:

> The movement which is least concretely handled in the novel is lesbian and homosexual rights. . . . This scant and indirect attention—especially in such a panoramic work which so wonderfully treats everything else—is unrealistic and all the more glaring. It indicates, perhaps, that for the black community at the heart of the novel, unabashed recognition of its lesbian and homosexual members and participation in their political struggle is, in a very real sense, the final frontier. (pp. 227–28)

Both times she names the sore spot, the critic says "lesbian and homosexual," carefully placing lesbian first and keeping them grouped together. But, in fact, her examples of Bambara's "scant" attention tell a different story. Hull can cite only three examples: "'Gays' are catalogued in one or two lists; a joke of sorts is made about Ahiro 'hitting on' Obie; and there is a surreal encounter [with] . . . a group of wacky male cross-dressers whose sexuality is left in doubt" (p. 227). Whether or not the cross-dressers are homosexual, the sure thing about all these examples is their gender. However "scant and indirect" the attention to homosexuals, there is a complete absence of lesbians.

Hull's article originally appeared in Barbara Smith's 1983 anthology, *Home Girls*, a collection which places the lesbian at the center of black feminism. The circumspect formulation "lesbian and homosexual" may be an attempt to soften the criticism, devastating enough in that context. Despite this attenuation, Bambara's exclusion of lesbians cannot be ignored by Hull and provokes the sole instance of the critic finding fault with the novel. Although the *Home Girls* context may have something to do with Hull's criticism, that context might be broadened to a moment around 1983, and include *Conjuring*.

Hull's critique does not so much fault the author, but rather moves to a more general disappointment with "the black community." Dealing with lesbians is, for the black community, "the final frontier." Although Hull is talking about the failure to recognize lesbians, her notion of the "final frontier" corroborates the sense that the lesbian represents the last stage in some progress. Where Pryse reconstructs the progress as smooth, Hull's reading of the 1980 novel bears out Christian's sense of some sort of discontinuity between the overt novels of 1982 and what came before. Bambara's novel, subject of the last essay in practical criticism in the collection, is thus marked as not contemporary with the critical volume. *The Salt Eaters* remains on the other side of a "frontier." *Conjuring* has crossed over and looks back from that vantage to see Bambara's folk fall short.

A lesbian perspective also threatens to disrupt another of the collection's praisesongs. Hortense Spillers claims that her reading of Paule Marshall's 1969 novel, *Chosen Place, Timeless People* "guards against the superlative degree of praise and assertion," but if she must "guard," it is because the danger is near.[27] Spillers likes this novel as much as Hull admires *The Salt Eaters*. Where Hull is on one point forced to depart from her usual appreciation of Bambara, Spillers manages to keep her text free of criticism. But the spoiler is kept at bay with great effort. Spillers relegates consideration of the novel's lesbian relationship to a footnote, but the note is well over a page long, by far the longest note in the entire anthology.

The note begins: "Professor Judith Fetterley has discussed parts of the novel with me, and in her opinion, the work is homophobic. Although the relationship between Merle and her London patroness . . . is not, to my mind, a major thematic issue in the novel, we should pause to consider it as an illustration of the sorts of conflicts that arise among discontinuous reading and interpretive communities" (p. 172 n. 6). The suspicion of "homophobia" arises in another reader, a white feminist critic. Spillers's attempt to clear this suspicion takes three main tacks: (1) the relationship is not a major issue; (2) the important aspect of the relationship is the power inequity between the colonizer patroness and the colonized protagonist regardless of "whether 'straight' or homoerotic"; (3) there will always be multiple and divergent readings of literary texts reflecting the vested interests of reading communities, here presumably black women versus (white) lesbians. On this last, literary theoretical point, Spillers cites Fetterley's own book for support, thus gently but cleverly suggesting Fetterley's concession to her refutation.

Although Spillers herself does not consider the protagonist's past lesbian relationship "a major thematic issue," she feels "we should pause" to respond to Fetterley's charge. Presumably she does not respond in print to everything said to her about the novel. Separately and even together her three arguments are, indeed, persuasive. But the fact that she needs to respond to Fetterley and the sheer length and ingenuity of her response mark this as a troubling question. Marshall's homophobia remains a possibility that this long note cannot conjure away. In fact, it conjures it into the anthology, while trying to contain it in the margins of the text.

In the Introduction to *Conjuring*, Pryse reconstructs the tradition backwards from Alice Walker's overtly lesbian 1982 novel. In chapter 7 of the anthology, Pryse groups *The Color Purple* along with a select coterie of contemporary novels that likewise understand the black, female tradition: here Walker's novel stands with Toni Cade Bambara's *Salt Eaters* and Paule Marshall's *Chosen Place, Timeless People*. The Introduction's reading of *The Color Purple* underwrites a playful lesbianization of the tradition, but the anthology's readings of these two other novels suggest that "speaking with each other's tongues in our mouths" might make some carriers of the tradition gag.

The lesbian relationship in Marshall's 1969 novel is interracial, and viewed negatively in the novel and in the criticism. Spillers equates the affair with another destructive relation Merle has with a rich white woman, this one her rival for a man, "that powerful other who can buy affection or buy it off" (p. 173). In this reading, it is the interracial and cross-class dimension not the homoerotic that makes it a bad affair.

The lesbian connections that Pryse, Walker, and Lorde celebrate are between black women. "One question which these novels leave unanswered is whether the bond between women might be so strong that it might transcend the racial and class divisions among women" (Christian, p. 247). The double use of "might"—"might be so strong that it might transcend"—marks this possibility as extremely tenuous. In this, her last sentence about the overt lesbian exploration of 1982, Christian points beyond the "final frontier," presumably beyond *Conjuring*.

The Introduction's exploration of "the bond between women" never once mentions interracial female bonds. Pryse's emblematic novels, *Eyes* and *Purple*, are virtually devoid of nonblack characters. We are certainly led to believe that the woman-to-woman relationships that the collection explores exclusively involve black women.

We are also given to assume that every article in the anthology is about writing by black women. But, in fact, *Conjuring* includes one article which also discusses black men's and white women's writing, a chapter which violates the volume's chronological order. Between Claudia Tate's reclamation of Pauline Hopkins and Deborah McDowell's reconsideration of Jessie Fauset appears an article by Elizabeth Schultz which looks at recent fiction by black men and white and black women. Schultz's essay is subtitled "A Study of Interracial Friendships between Women in American Novels."

These interracial friendships disrupt the volume's focus and its structure, interrupt its orderly construction of a literary tradition. This radically out of place article is nonetheless included, bespeaking some not fully integrated agenda.

Pryse twice mentions Schultz's article in the Introduction. The first time is in the middle of a paragraph about "the commitment to folk life and its connection to vision for black women." After a sentence about Nella Larsen and Ann Petry missing that connection, Pryse writes: "In recent decades, Louise Meriwether's *Daddy Was a Number Runner* (1970) and Toni Morrison's *Sula* (1974), along with many other works that Elizabeth Schultz discusses in her essay in chapter 4, explore friendship between women, fully grounded in the black experience, as a means of liberation" (p. 20). The paragraph then concludes with discussion of *Daddy* and *Sula*. We assume that Schultz's essay about "friendship between women, fully grounded in the black experience" is about friendship between black women just as we assume that it is about black women's fiction.

Pryse's next paragraph begins: "The 'ancient power' black women writers document in their fiction and express as the intersection of black, female, and folk vision serves as a predominant and unifying concern for the writers of many of the essays in this collection, as well as for the novelists themselves. Essays by Thelma Shinn, Elizabeth Schultz, Minrose Gwin on *Jubilee*, and Gloria T. Hull all consider the influence of women as friends, mentors, and visionary guides for each other" (pp. 20–21). We presume that Elizabeth Schultz is writing about black women's fiction, just as we assume that the women who are "friends, mentors, and guides for each other" are all black.

This list designates three essays solely by the critic's name, but it gives Minrose Gwin's topic. Gwin has two essays in *Conjuring*, one on Margaret Walker's *Jubilee* and the other on female slave narratives. Both are taken from her book, *Black and White Women of the Old South*.[28] As this title suggests, her articles in *Conjuring* focus on relations between black and white women. Without mentioning the theme in the Introduction, the anthology, in fact, devotes three chapters to interracial female relations. These chapters occasion at least two irregularities in the volume's structure: in one case, a deviation from chronological order and the field of black women's fiction; in the other, the sole instance of a critic contributing more than one essay.

Only the second of Gwin's two essays belongs in the list of those exploring "women as friends, mentors, and guides for each other." Her first essay, "Green-eyed Monsters of the Slavocracy," explores a very different register of relations between women. Slave narratives reveal horrifying scenes of mistresses tormenting women slaves. Gwin interprets these narrative portrayals as the ex-slave's revenge: "Jacobs writes so bitterly . . . that she seems . . . to transform *Incidents* into a vehicle of rage directed toward her former mistress. . . . Jacobs flogs her powerless former mistress over and over throughout her narrative."[29] Attributing metaphorical violence to the slave narrators not only militates against construing the slave as passive victim, object rather than subject, but transforms the scene into one of mutual aggression. Rather than pitting blue-eyed devils against brown-eyed martyrs, Gwin attributes the pervasive cruelty and hatred to the green eyes of jealousy. A structure of sexual rivalry divided and conquered these women. Gwin's feminist paradigm suggests that institutionalized jealousy prevented these differently oppressed women from recognizing their sisterhood.

Gwin's second essay in *Conjuring* also considers relations between black and white women in the nineteenth-century South from the point of view of a female ex-slave. This essay is a version of the last chapter of Gwin's book where it functions as a sort of ending to the painful story of cruelty between women of different races. Chapter 8 of *Conjuring* retains this sense of *Jubilee* as culmination and resolution: "*Jubilee* . . . may . . . be seen as a natural culmination of . . . treatments . . . of the profoundly ambivalent relationships between black and white southern women during that chaotic period of history. . . . *Jubilee* may be read as a moral resolution of . . . treatments of interracial relationships among nineteenth-century southern women."[30] Vyry Ware, *Jubilee*'s protagonist, transcends interracial hatred, forgives her cruel mistress, and creates bonds of sisterhood between the races. Gwin's interpretation of *Jubilee* directs the old animosity between black and white women into the path toward female connection.

Gwin prizes interracial sisterhood and is troubled by the possibility that *Jubilee* achieves that goal too cheaply. She wants the connection between black and white women to be solid and well-grounded: "The issue is whether this is a meaningful reconciliation or whether it is a facile distortion of far deeper and more painful conflicts" (p. 138). At several points in the essay, Gwin pauses over the validity of this resolution. She never relinquishes the notion that Margaret Walker had a complex, regenerative vision, but she also admits that "Vyry's limited articulation of Walker's humanistic values does perhaps make life simpler than it is" (p. 136). Dropping the hedging "perhaps," Gwin asserts in her final paragraph: "Vyry's gesture of forgiveness does come too easily" (p. 148).

Schultz's essay represents a further advance in interracial sisterhood. Not only is it a century later, but the relations considered are, at least nominally, "friendships." Where Gwin's range runs from hatred to acceptance, Schultz's study contrasts superficial, ephemeral friendship with something deeper and more lasting. Schultz's survey of "interracial friendship" includes an explicitly lesbian relationship. Ann Allen Shockley's 1974 *Loving Her* presents an idyllic sexual love between black Renay and white Terry. Schultz does not separate this lesbian connection from other female bonds; in fact, she treats it in the same paragraph with another 1974 novel, about a casual friendship between a black and white woman with shared interests in clothes and boyfriends.

Schultz lumps these two novels together because neither "explores the racial dimension of the interracial friendship."[31]

Schultz considers "friendships" like those in these two 1974 novels inferior to the more difficult friendships worked out in *Tar Baby* and *Meridian*:

> Only *Tar Baby* and *Meridian* establish the open confrontation of racial stereotypes as the necessary basis for an interracial friendship. . . . [T]he women in *Tar Baby* and *Meridian* . . . make apparent that when the effects of racism . . . can be . . . acknowledged, then forgiveness is possible, then hope is possible, for then change is possible. For this hope we must applaud . . . Alice Walker and Toni Morrison. . . . [T]hey have created in their fiction models of interracial friendships that endure . . . in reality; not in fantasy, but in our common lives. (p. 82)

The ultimate interracial female bond is not lesbianism, but a friendship which does the hard work of confronting racism and difference.

Whether it is an ex-slave forgiving her cruel mistress or romantic love between a black and a white woman, the critical issue for Gwin and Schultz is the same. Is real life being oversimplified? Is difference being dissolved through wishful fantasy? Can the happy ending represent a usable model?

At the end of her essay, Schultz quotes Mary Helen Washington "insisting upon the priorities of shared experience" in an article entitled "How Racial Differences Helped Us Discover Our Sameness": "I do not want to see black women in opposition to white women as though that division is primary . . . or even relevant. . . . These are American lives."[32] Schultz remarks: "Yet Washington's assertions, like the friendship . . . in *Loving Her* . . . might seem merely sanguine."

Schultz contrasts Washington's position with Audre Lorde's. The chapter closes by quoting Lorde's "Open Letter to Mary Daly": "I invite you to a joint clarification of some of the differences which lie between us as a black and a white woman."[33] Having linked Washington's assertion with the unrealistic relationships in some novels, Schultz connects Lorde's gesture with the interracial friendships portrayed in *Tar Baby* and *Meridian*: "Lorde . . . reminds us . . . that black and white women must struggle, openly and painfully, as Ondine and Margaret, Meridian and Lynne have done, to appreciate the differences as well as the similarities in our common lives" (p. 83).

Conjuring's Introduction never so much as mentions interracial female connections. Pryse locates Gwin's reading of *Jubilee* and Schultz's essay as explorations of female bonding (race unspecified, contextually black). Might we then take Schultz's conclusion as valid not just for interracial bonds but for the female connections central to the volume? Perhaps it is not just women of different races, but even black women among themselves who, in order to truly and solidly bond, must "appreciate the differences as well as the similarities in [their] common lives."

The Introduction appreciates similarities. So much so that Hurston is assimilated to Walker, valued mainly for her similarities. So much so that no distinction is made between heterosexual female friends and lesbians. So much so that there is no mention of the fact that three of the chapters in the volume look at relations between women of different races.

These articles on interracial relations, in various ways, disrupt the volume. Amidst the chorus of praise for similarity, these reminders, of a difference between women that black women cannot deny, voice the hope or possibility of female connection that does not deny differences.

I have been reading *Conjuring* through and against the model proposed by its Introduction. That has, of course, been my technique for reading anthologies throughout the present book. But in this case, it is an inadequate if not downright false method. Marjorie Pryse, author of the Introduction, is only one of the book's editors; the other editor, Hortense J. Spillers, has also supplied the book with a frame, in an Afterword. Of all the anthologies that I looked at for the present study, this is the only one of those with more than one editor that allows the editors separate editorial statements. These two women do not merge their voices. On the level of greatest actuality, *Conjuring* stands out from the others of its genre, as a voice for female collaboration that does not deny differences.

I began this chapter with the fact that the Introduction begins and the last article ends with a quote by Alice Walker. I guess it would be fair to say that I began in deception. Barbara Christian's essay is, strictly speaking, the last article, but with that circular frame I closed Spillers's Afterword out of the volume. The book I have been reading up to this point is the anthology that would have existed had the volume opened with Pryse and closed with Christian, had there been just one editor, had the Afterword not been there.

I could say in my defense that this reproduces the linear experience of the volume, if one reads it in order. Having been given a structure by the Introduction, the reader tacks the various articles to that frame and the whole hangs together. Then, at the end, the reader encounters the Afterword which calls that whole into question, which causes the reader to rethink the volume.

Now, I realize that not every reader obediently reads the Introduction before and the Afterword after. What I am thus reproducing is my own reading experience. What is perhaps more interesting is that I had the same experience not only when I read the volume the first time, but upon rereading. Even when I knew the Afterword was coming, the same Prysian version congealed in my mind as I reread the collection, only to be disrupted, once again, after the fact, by Spillers.

The "Afterword" is subtitled "Cross-Currents, Discontinuities: Black Women's Fiction." While the Introduction places the fiction in a continuum, the Afterword explicitly looks at currents that run traverse to the mainstream, at discontinuities interrupting the tradition. A "cross-current" implies a main stream; a "discontinuity" only exists once a continuum is established: the Afterword could only take its effect *after*. Thus, it is not just that one editorial statement happens to be at the front of the book and the other at the back. Pryse's statement belongs before, as an organizing principle; Spillers's gesture only works after, as a reminder of what resists the organization.

The reading of *Conjuring* produced thus far is consistent with my procedures in the present book. Typically, I identify a central, hegemonic voice in the anthology, usually the editor(s)'s, which would organize all the voices into a unity and then I locate points of resistance within the volume to that unification. I place my weight behind those internal differences as a wedge against the centrist drive. Such a reading, which might be termed a deconstruction, consists precisely in seeking "cross-currents" and "discontinuities." *Conjuring*, we might say, comes with its own deconstruction.

As much as I am thus tempted to ally myself with Spillers against Pryse, I want to try and remember that the two are working together, that they have agreed to these respective roles as construction and deconstruction worker. That they jointly decided to produce a volume that lies between the two and thus belongs rightly to both and neither.

Pryse's "ancient power," the title's "Conjuring," Shinn's "Wise Witches," *The Salt Eater*'s woman healer, Petry's root doctor, all belong to a realm the Introduction specifies as a black, female, *folk* vision. We recognize this as alternative power and alternative knowledge, outside and opposite to elite cultural institutions.

Spillers's Afterword interrupts our admiration of this alternative knowledge. Her first paragraph states: "The American academy, despite itself, is one of the enabling postulates of black women's literary community simply because it is not only a source of income for certain individual writers, but also a point of dissemination and inquiry for their work."[34]

"Despite itself": Spillers recognizes that the vested interests of the academy, its belief in an elite of great men and their universal thoughts, might run counter to the interests of black women reclaiming the power of folk culture. But the fact is that the American academy not only makes it materially possible for some of these women to write, but also is where many readers first learn or learn more about these works, their tradition, even or especially the black, female, folk vision that this volume, for example, is delineating. Spillers wakes us from our folk vision to remind us of a few material facts: the critics in *Conjuring* are all academics, the collection is published by a university press, aimed toward an audience of professors and graduate students.

In an essay published two years after *Conjuring*, Barbara Christian asserts: "In no way is the literature Morrison, Marshall, or Walker create supported by the academic world. Nor given the political context of our society, do I expect that to change soon. For there is no reason, given who controls these institutions, for them to be anything other than threatened by these writers."[35] Spillers would agree that those who control these institutions have every reason to be "threatened by these writers"; that is the purport of her "despite itself." But the radical claim that "in no way is this literature supported by the academic world" must come up against a few facts. For example: Toni Morrison has taught at Columbia, Yale, and Princeton Universities; Paule Marshall has a permanent position at Virginia Commonwealth University; Alice Walker has taught at Wellesley and held a Radcliffe Institute Fellowship (with an appointment by the Harvard Corporation). And then we would have to talk of the courses which assign books by these writers, requiring their purchase as well as disseminating awareness of the writers and their work. And beyond the classroom, we would have to acknowledge a growing industry in academic articles and conference papers on these writers.

"The image of black women writing . . . is conduced toward radical revision. The room of one's own explodes its four walls to embrace the

classroom, the library, and the various mechanisms of institutional . . .
life, including conferences, the lecture platform . . . and collections of
critical essays" (Spillers, p. 250). Like Alice Walker, Spillers refers back
to Woolf's fundamental statement about women writers. *A Room of
One's Own*, delivered as a lecture at a woman's college by a nonacademic, is extremely mindful of the material and institutional infrastruc-
tures of knowledge and culture. Woolf offers the unforgettable image
of the woman writer's exclusion from the college library. In 1974 Walker
finds in her mother's garden a powerful alternative to institutionally
recognized culture. A decade later, Spillers points out that black women
writers are no longer locked out of the library.

"We are called upon to witness, then, the formation of relatively
new social and political arrangements that articulate fruitful contradictions" (Spillers, p. 249). Christian sees a contradiction between the
literary academy and black women's reclamation of their "ancient
power." Spillers also sees a contradiction here, but she imagines it can
be "fruitful."[36]

This idea of "fruitful contradictions" implies a dialectical vision of
history, where one moment's contradictions are precisely the sites
where the next moment's configurations are being distilled. Such a
vision of history underpins Spillers's reading of Paule Marshall's *Chosen
Place, Timeless People* in chapter 9 of *Conjuring*. "The novel . . . is the
situation of two *conflicting* principles that Marshall would confront.
Merle and Saul . . . are the wellspring of a dialectics in the making, one
that will discover in the agents' promised resolution of trouble, a new
way to flourish in Bournehills society, and in the USA" (p. 160). Two
conflicting principles are embodied in the characters Merle and Saul.
In their encounter, those "conflicting principles" produce a "dialectics"
which promises "resolution." That "promised resolution" will result in
something new and good: "a new way to flourish." Merle and Saul
exemplify Spillers's *fruitful* contradiction.

"Merle Kinbona, worldly black female, indigenous to Bournehills,
and Saul Amron, sophisticated Jewish anthropologist from academic
America, Stanford University specifically, are the principal agents. The
web of conflict between hostile cultures eradiates from their erotic
encounter. . . . [W]e are not allowed to forget that Merle and Saul stand
for their representative cultures, converging at a given moment" (p.
154). Spillers centers Marshall's novel on this symbolic encounter
between two "hostile cultures," represented by a Caribbean black
woman and a man "from academic America." The specific principles

embodied in Merle and Saul are very much to the point of *Conjuring*'s Afterword. The editor's chapter in the middle of the anthology could be taken as a figuration of the historical moment she describes in the Afterword: black female culture and American academic culture, "converging at a given moment."

As persuasive and worldly as I find her reading of Marshall's novel, let me here recall, if only in passing, the shadow of homophobia that briefly falls across Spillers's essay, consigned to but bursting at the seams of an overgrown footnote. The flip side of homophobia is heterosexism, a tendency to binarize the world into opposite genders which can then meet, resolve, and bear fruit. Of Merle and Saul the critic says, "They become the woman and the man of the New World" (p. 160). The two hostile cultures represented by "the woman and the man," the conflict can turn "fruitful." This in a novel where a destructive meeting of two cultures is symbolized by a lesbian relationship.

Pryse centers *Conjuring* on a continuum of black female bonding that ultimately can include lesbianism. Of all the articles in the volume, chapter 9, Spillers's reading of Marshall, least fits Pryse's frame. The problem is not primarily the question of literal lesbianism versus heterosexuality, but the fact that this essay prizes the encounter between a black woman and a white man, going so far as to suggest that Merle gets from Saul something that her countrywomen cannot offer her. Of all the characters in *Chosen Place*, the most likely candidate for Pryse's "ancient power" is Leesy Walkes, the old, black woman with whom Merle has a special relationship. Spillers specifically contrasts Leesy with Saul: "Merle . . . is led to acknowledgment by a foreigner and through the emotional hardware of a foreign culture. . . . Merle is 'read' by the man [Saul] in ways that Leesy Walkes, for instance, would never presume nor attempt. Merle's culture gives her sanctuary from offense and deliverance" (pp. 167–68). Leesy Walkes does not offend and cannot deliver. It seems that it is precisely the contact with "foreignness," with difference rather than similarity that can save Merle, can bring her out of her present contradictions.

Spillers's essay ends with a short paragraph: "Saul has a future, Bournehills has a future. Their mutual meeting and exchange demarcate the new dialectics of a New World culture that *Chosen Place, Timeless People* would contemplate." (p. 171). The final two pages of the article are devoted to Saul with no mention of Merle. As I read through the anthology, and reread, prepared by Pryse for a black, female folk vision, I recoil from this final sympathetic image of academic man.

It is Merle I want to hear about, preferably a Merle reclaiming the "ancient power" of Leesy Walkes. But why? What is so repellent to me about Saul Amron?

Merle is a black Caribbean woman; Saul is an American Jewish academic man. I am an American Jewish academic woman. Wanting Merle and refusing Saul, what game of desire and identity am I playing? Identifying with Merle against Saul, I reduce all identity to gender. If I would specify myself as other than some universalized woman, I might recognize Saul Amron as my brother.

In her long note Spillers comments that "'straight' or homoerotic" is not to the point of whether a relationship is productive or oppressive. If I were to credit her comment, as more than just defensive, then I could not use Saul's maleness to segregate his relation to Merle from mine to the black women I read. When Spillers compares Saul favorably to the old black woman, she specifically says "Merle is 'read' by him." When academic man moves into a New World through his contact with Marshall's fictional Caribbean culture, is he a figure for the white academic who is a likely reader of this anthology? Is Saul a figure for me reading *Conjuring*?

Reading backward from the Afterword gives the editor's essay on Marshall a central place in *Conjuring*. Not surprisingly, it embodies the editorial framework. But reading forward from the Introduction makes Spiller's article marginal and even inappropriate to the volume. The present chapter begins with the initial Prysian reading because I believe it also corresponds to and evokes in the reader, at least in the white female academic, a fantasy which orients our reading of black women. I want the conjure woman; I want some ancient power that stands beyond the reaches of white male culture. I want black women as the idealized and exoticized alternative to European high culture. I want some pure outside and am fool enough to think I might find it in a volume published by Indiana University Press, with full scholarly apparatus.

When I read *Conjuring* the first time, I was disappointed that the volume was so "academic." I disliked the references to Ovid, *The Golden Bough*, to deism. When I found an essay particularly "academic," tracing similarities to classical mythology or simply too dry in style, I would imagine that this critic must be white. Since I am a white academic, what sort of fantasy not only renders those attributes contemptible but, from an imagined identification with some righteous outside, allows me to cast them as aspersions on others?

Even when I reread the anthology, knowing how it ended, I half forgot the ending and gave myself over to the Introduction's imagining of a black, female *folk* vision. In this chapter I wanted to transmit this illusory take on the anthology because I consider this illusion central to our reading of black women. We must confront our wish to find this ancient power, this pure outside of academic culture, before we deconstruct or correct our illusion. Pryse's framing of *Conjuring* needs to take hold first before Spillers's reframing can take its effect.

The two editors' good cop/bad cop routine conjures up the image of that powerful outside and then catches me in full fantasy to recall that these critics are writing and I am reading them within the white man's academy. "Some of the fiction writers whose works are discussed here are (or were) also teachers in the academy, just as the critics are, so that the site of the institution becomes as crucial an aspect of the whole discussion as the audience toward which this volume of essays is aimed" (Afterword, p. 249).

Chosen Place, Timeless People produces its own small discontinuity in Barbara Christian's otherwise orderly historiography in *Conjuring*. Christian divides the history of Afro-American women's fiction into "phases." For the modern period, the first phase covers the fifties and sixties, "fiction in the early seventies represents a second phase" (p. 240), and "[b]y the mid-1970s, the fiction makes a visionary leap" (p. 241) into the third phase. In her discussion of mid-seventies fiction, after Morrison's 1974 *Sula* and Walker's 1976 *Meridian*, she turns to Marshall's *Chosen Place, Timeless People*, "[t]hough published in 1969." This is the only novel Christian's survey treats out of chronological order.

At the end of *Conjuring*, Christian places contemporary black women's fiction into a historical ordering. Immediately afterward, Spillers repositions the same fiction; her version of the history focuses on chronological discontinuities. Marshall's second novel, the subject of Spillers's chapter in the body of the collection, occasions a convergence between Christian's placement and Spillers's displacement.

In her 1987 article, Christian returns Marshall's 1969 novel to its proper historical moment. She recalls that when it was published, in the heyday of the nationalist Black Arts Movement, Nikki Giovanni "criticized the novel on the grounds that it was not black, for the language was too elegant, too white." At the same time, from the same cultural nationalist position, "[o]lder writers like Ralph Ellison and

James Baldwin were condemned because they saw that the intersection of Western and African influences resulted in a new Afro-American culture."[37] The nationalist position has the force of purity; black art is prized as totally outside Western culture. But, as Christian argues, this purist position could only condemn actual African-American culture, a new configuration of African *and* Western influences. From the nationalist position, one was either inside or outside the West, either wholly black or white.

In *Conjuring*, Christian remarks of Marshall's 1969 novel that it "depicts a black woman as both outside and inside the black world, as both outside and inside the West. As such, Merle becomes a spokesperson for her people . . . who do not always understand their own dilemmas" (p. 241). It is her partial discontinuity with her people, one of them and yet not one of them, that allows Merle to understand and speak for them. Merle is not Leesy Walkes, not just one of the folk, not wholly inside the black world. Her power is not the ancient power of black women but some new admixture of "black" and "Western."

The pure is attractive, not just for black nationalists but for white academics dreaming of an outside of Western culture. The pure is attractive, but we must try to affirm worldly impurity, inevitable mixity. Merle Kinbona, created during the nationalist sixties figures the sort of mixture we find in African-American culture: "both outside and inside the black world, both outside and inside the West."

Merle's past includes a life in London, as well as in the Caribbean, a primary relationship with a rich white Englishwoman as well as an African man. "Merle Kinbona, worldly black female, indigenous to Bournehills, [meets] Saul Amron, sophisticated Jewish anthropologist from academic America" (Spillers, p. 154). She is an "indigenous" black woman and he a first world male academic, but her worldliness matches his sophistication and produces not pure binary oppression but a fruitful dialectic.

The women writers *Conjuring* considers are more like Merle Kinbona than like Leesy Walkes. Alice Walker may have learned art in her mother's gardens, but unlike her mother she also has a B.A. from Sarah Lawrence where she learned to appreciate Anglo-American literature. *The Color Purple*'s heroine is wholly in and of the black folk; her author is not. "Without formal education Celie can't know what Walker does, that the earliest novels in English were also epistolary. Therefore Celie is not writing an 'epistolary novel.' She has simply found the form in which to . . . express . . . her deepest feeling" (Introduction, p. 19).

Attempting to celebrate Celie as an artist, the Introduction compares her to Walker's mother and to Zora Hurston, here going so far as to treat her as the author of the Pulitzer Prize-winning novel. Yet in the very promotion of Celie, meant to equalize her and her author, we are reminded of the difference: Walker's "formal education." Walker knows she is writing an "epistolary novel." And so does Pryse, offering us a bit of literary history in passing: "the earliest novels in English."

In the gesture that closes the anthology, Spillers speaks as an English professor: "In various literature courses that I have taught . . . one of the ways that I often distinguish between fiction written before 1925 and that written after that time in English-speaking traditions is to say that the latter tends to be a fiction of the classroom" (pp. 258–59). Speaking in the classroom, Spillers defines modern fiction as "of the classroom," meaning that, in order to be appreciated or understood, the fiction needs academic critical techniques, the sorts of reading one learns in college.

"Those of us trained in the graduate academy since the coronation of 'close reading' in the fifties were taught the same way, and nothing appears drastically out of place since my tenure at Brandeis University as a graduate student in English during the late sixties—early seventies" (p. 259). Merle Kinbona's convergence with a Jewish academic may also be a figure for the black woman who, at the time *Chosen Place, Timeless People* was published, studied English at Brandeis University.

This recollection of her professional training ends the paragraph which begins by recalling her professorial voice. In this long paragraph Spillers speaks as a literary academic about academic literary values which are mirrored by modern literature: "complexity," "ambiguity," "irony." Her tone is, as usual, complex, at times fairly drips with irony. The paragraph seems to belong to the genre of academic discourse taking an ironic or critical distance from academic discourse. When she speaks of "the 'tour guides' to writers whose *very goal* is obfuscation, the . . . playful new (and short!) critical pieces, and the rich proliferations of symbologies that threaten to enclose the literary/critical universe in a space of exclusionary and hieratic practices," it is not likely to make the literature or the academy sympathetic.

The next paragraph presents a refreshing alternative to this "academic" literature: "It appears that women's fictional work maintains, as a general rule, not only an allegiance to 'power to the people,' but also 'talking' to 'the people' in the now familiar accents of representation and mimesis. The work of black women writers is specifically notable in this regard." "Fiction of the classroom" is not only post-1925, it is male. Women's fiction, and notably black women's fiction, speaks to "the people," that is, can be understood without college literary instruction. The use of "people" echoes not only the political ferment occurring just outside the classroom during the period when Spillers was a student but also the "folk" of Pryse's vision of the black women's tradition. Here we have a political and non-elitist alternative to the classroom.

The dichotomy represented by these two paragraphs is familiar, as is the preference for women's "plain-speaking" over high-brow, obscurantist academics. The expression of such a preference by a self-avowed academic comes as no surprise. Left-leaning academics have long spoken ironically of the academy, romantically of the politicized and populist. But there remains one more paragraph to Spillers's Afterword, one last paragraph to the anthology. And the third paragraph places these two into dialectical convergence. Thesis: fiction of the classroom—antithesis: (black) women's fiction "talking to the people." Synthesis:

> The day will come, I would dare to predict, when the black American women's writing community will reflect the currents both of the new new critical procedures and the various literatures concurrent with them. . . . More than that, this literature of the future . . . might not renounce, either, its inexorable ties to the drama of the "tremendous strivings" of a people. If that happens, then the academy meets life, and life the academy, in a situation of emphases neither of whose resonance and value we can afford to deny in our own small strivings. (pp. 259–260)

Academy and life would meet. Black women's fiction will not only enter the classroom (as it has) but will also be "of the classroom," modernist/postmodernist, complex, hard to read, supporting and needing critical explication. Yet at the same time it would be tied to the life drama, the political "strivings of a people." "We in our own small strivings," that is, we literary critics can afford to deny neither the demands of life (politics and populism) nor the demands of the academy (criticism and complexity).

Parenthetically in this last paragraph, Spillers says: *"The Salt Eaters*, I believe, already anticipates some of the future moves." Hull's reading of Bambara's novel bears out the sense that this is a novel of the classroom. The critic begins her essay with the recognition that "many people have difficulty with it. They . . . give up after muddling through the first sixty-five pages twice with little comprehension. . . . Lost and bewildered, students decide that it is 'over their heads' and wonder what made the teacher assign it in the first place" (p. 216). Hull takes up her responsibility as "teacher" and tries to explain as well as possible "what" Bambara "is doing." Frequent reference to readers' problems suggests she writes in response to those problems. "Teaching it well can be a political act. However, Toni Cade Bambara has not made our job easy. *Salt* is long, intricately written, trickily structured, full of learning, heavy with wisdom" (p. 217).

Hull's reading of *The Salt Eaters* is the last chapter in the anthology before Christian's and Spillers's overviews. Thus the volume actually reflects the editor's sense of the direction of black women's fiction, of a progress toward the future. Where Pryse begins with Walker's 1982 novel and reads the tradition backward from there, Spillers ends with Bambara's 1980 novel and points the tradition forward.

Spillers closes the anthology by returning to the idea of tradition and giving it a final twist: "'Tradition,' as I would mean it, then, is an active verb, rather than a retired nominative, and we now are its subjects and objects. Quite correctly, 'tradition' under the head of a polyvalent grammar—the language of learning woven into the tongue of the mother—is the rare union of bliss toward which African-American experience has compelled us all along" (p. 260).

The assertion that "tradition" is a verb rather than a noun certainly runs up against traditional grammar. Her "quite correctly," her "subjects and objects," and her use of the word "grammar" make her flaunting blatant. Spillers is wittingly and willfully constructing something that does not already exist. Tradition here is, radically, not what we assume it to be; it is here, literally, invented. We recall the insistence at the beginning of the Afterword that "Traditions are not born. They are made. . . . [T]hey are not, like objects of nature, here to stay, but survive as *created social events* only to the extent that an audience cares to intersect them" (p. 250). The end of the Afterword goes beyond the insistence on constructedness to suggest that traditions only exist while still under construction, they only survive as long as we keep working on them. A literary tradition cannot rest on its laurels; it belongs not to the past, but to the near future. Spillers's sense affirms and makes explicit the volume's willful constructions of the tradition. It is this construction work, not the passive description of what preexists, that is for Spillers the job of the literary critic.

This editorial posits African-American experience in retrospect as heading toward "the rare union of bliss." The tradition is structured to lead to this happy ending. The Afterword and the volume close on this ultimate image for the pleasures of dialectical synthesis.

Just before bliss, a more arresting image of the synthesis intercedes, literally breaking the flow of the sentence: "the language of learning woven into the tongue of the mother." "The language of learning" is academic culture; "the tongue of the mother" is the "ancient power" of black women, black female folk culture. The image joins grammar to Granny's voice, while the work of synthesis is figured as "weaving," traditional women's art/work.

The image not only interrupts the sentence, it also questions the happy ending. Moving from the Latinate "language" to its Anglo-Saxon synonym, the literal body appears. And then, literally, weaving into the mother's tongue evokes the most unspeakable pain. This embellished tongue might be not more articulate but—bleeding, swollen, and scarred—barely if at all able to speak: a trained and disciplined tongue.

The final sentence of the Afterword, with its troubling tongue, recalls the final sentence of the Introduction: "We propose our volume's title, *Conjuring* . . . as a reminder . . . of the oath we all must take to continue the work of speaking with each others' tongues in our mouths" (p. 22). The sentence alludes to a folksay from Hurston's *Their Eyes Were Watching God*: "mah tongue is in mah friend's mouf."[38] Hurston's phrase describes stories being passed on from woman to woman and thus figures an oral literary tradition. But before the final sentence of the Introduction recalls the phrase, Pryse lesbianizes it through *The Color Purple*, calling forth a bodily tongue: "Quite literally these are 'kissin'-friends' whose tongues are in each others' mouths" (p. 18). When the phrase returns to close the Introduction, the literal, *Purple* tongue conjures up a disturbing possibility: engaged in such a soul kiss, how could one speak?

As each editor reaches her climax and gestures out toward the critical future, the tongues trouble her say. Both end up with a tongue which might not be able to speak. Both final images involve the intrusion of the tongue of the other: for Pryse, another woman; for Spillers, the literary academy's "tongue," Latinized and disembodied into "language." Pryse and Spillers are, ultimately, tongue-tied, linked through their attempts to open their speech to the other.

Pryse asserts a powerful sisterhood of black women, a tradition of folk knowledge outside of and opposed to white malestream institutions. Yet although that move empowers black women writers and readers, it also threatens to silence any difference within. The soul kiss between sisters can pass on a powerful and pleasurable oral tradition, but it might also operate as a gag on the woman who wants to speak out.

Spillers asserts a mixed heritage; the power of the black mothers converges with the American academy. The encounter with difference gives the black woman access to a powerful language. But this encounter with the white man's institution also could be, like so many before, a brutal imposition on the body of the black mother.

Two opposing strategies frame this book. Both have great potential and entail real danger, and both are the necessary antidotes to each other. *Conjuring* joins them, not in some sanguine synthesis, but in their mutual fears. Each strategy needs the other to protect against an internal threat to speech. In its uncanny tongue work, *Conjuring* must battle both the suffocation of similarity and the violence of difference.

11
The Attraction of
Matrimonial Metaphor

In 1985, Showalter's anthology *The New Feminist Criticism* was published; that same year another anthology appeared, subtitled *Feminist Literary Criticism*, likewise promising to represent the breadth of feminist criticism.[1] Whereas all the essays collected by Showalter had been published before (mostly in 1980–1981), all except one of the chapters of Gayle Greene and Coppélia Kahn's *Making a Difference* appear there for the first time, more truly situating this anthology in the mid-eighties. The single exception is Bonnie Zimmerman's "What Has Never Been" which, first published in *Feminist Studies* in 1981, can also be found in *The New Feminist Criticism*. The version Showalter includes is essentially what was published in *Feminist Studies*. For the Greene and Kahn anthology, "What Has Never Been" has been brought up to date, including two references for 1984, and many for 1982 and 1983. And it is not only the bibliography which has been updated. Comparing Zimmerman's piece in these two 1985 anthologies highlights differences not only between two editorial perspectives but, more significantly, between two moments of academic feminist literary scholarship, the first around 1981, the second around 1985.

In Zimmerman's 1981 essay, we read:

> to me it seems imperative that lesbian criticism develop diversity in theory and approach. Much as lesbians, even more than heterosexual feminists, may mistrust systems of thought developed by and associated with men and male values, we may, in fact, enrich our work through the insights of Marxist, structuralist, semiotic, or even psychoanalytic criticism. Perhaps "male" systems of thought are incompatible with a lesbian literary vision, but we will not know until we attempt to integrate these ideas into our work.

The passage is identical in *The New Feminist Criticism*.[2] These sentences conclude a paragraph that begins by discussing the theoretical influence of lesbian separatism on literary criticism. Although Zimmerman feels that separatism has been an invigorating and empowering influence, she believes that (in 1981) lesbian criticism needs "diversity." Such diversity would entail the use of "'male' systems of thought," a move from separatism to "integration." She imagines resistance to her suggestion, in that lesbians are more likely than heterosexual women to mistrust anything associated with men. Lesbians and male thought may be "incompatible," but Zimmerman advocates a trial association in order to "enrich" lesbian thought. According to lesbian theorists such as Adrienne Rich, throughout history, women who prefer women have been forced to associate with men for economic reasons.[3] Zimmerman nominates Marxism, structuralism, semiotics, and psychoanalysis as likely candidates for such integration, although she implies that the last is probably the least acceptable of the bunch (alluding to its long connection with psychotherapeutic attempts to cure lesbians of their abnormality).

Zimmerman's 1981 passage is followed by a footnote (number fifty-nine): "For example, a panel at the 1980 MLA convention in Houston, 'Literary History and the New Histories of Sexuality,' presented gay and lesbian perspectives on contemporary French philosophies." What Zimmerman advocates has begun, could be seen in December, 1980, shortly before Zimmerman wrote this article. What in the text is named as "male systems of thought" gets exemplified in the footnote by "contemporary French philosophies." At the moment Zimmerman writes, the American literary academy was increasingly feeling the influence of something that could be named "contemporary French philosophies," that could also be named "Marxism, structuralism, semiotics, and even psychoanalysis." Zimmerman is proposing lesbian criticism enrich itself through an alliance with the variously named "theory" that has come to power in literary studies.

Let us now read this Zimmerman passage as it appears in the Greene and Kahn anthology: "increasingly, lesbian criticism has developed diversity in theory and approach, encorporating the insights of Marxist, structuralist, semiotic and even psychoanalytic criticism. Although lesbians, perhaps more than heterosexual feminists, may mistrust systems of thought developed by and associated with men and male values, our work is in fact richer and subtler for this incorporation" (p. 198).

The development of diversity that Zimmerman was promoting in 1981 has become a *fait accompli.* Lesbian thought no longer needs enrichment; it "is in fact richer and subtler." Before integration, male systems of thought were desirable for the riches they would bring; in light of the accomplished association, it appears they bring not only riches but "subtlety," a concept new to the passage, a value learned since "the development." In 1981 we read: "lesbians, *even* more than heterosexual feminists, may mistrust systems of thought developed by and associated with men and male values"; by 1985 one word has been changed: "lesbians, *perhaps* more than heterosexual feminists, may mistrust systems of thought developed by and associated with men and male values." It is possible that lesbians still mistrust male thought more than heterosexual feminists, but it is no longer so certain. The question of "incompatibility" ("perhaps 'male' systems of thought are incompatible with a lesbian vision") has been dropped entirely. The revised passage ends with the word "incorporation," but in the preceding sentence we read the non-word, almost-a-word "encorporate," that uncivilized signifier perhaps the last bit of (someone's) unconscious resistance to the union of lesbian criticism and "systems of thought developed by and associated with men and male values."

In 1981, Showalter's "Feminist Criticism in the Wilderness," in its survey of the current state of feminist criticism, celebrated gynocentrism and advocated a continuing mistrust of male systems of thought.[4] Four of the nine chapters in the Greene and Kahn anthology explicitly take that article to task for limiting the horizons of feminist criticism. In their introductory chapter, the editors allow that gynocriticism "may be a necessary stage" but decidedly "an intermediary stage" (pp. 24–25). *Making a Difference* occupies a moment that is very self-consciously beyond Showalter, and which considers itself richer and subtler for that.

Greene and Kahn's anthology is part of Methuen's New Accents Series.[5] The penultimate paragraph of the general editor's Preface discusses the series' title: "Finally, as its title suggests, one aspect of *New Accents* will be firmly located in contemporary approaches to language" (p. viii). A legitimate member of the series, *Making a Difference* presents us with feminist literary criticism "firmly located in contemporary approaches to language." One of Greene and Kahn's major complaints against Showalter is her ignorance of such approaches to language: "Implicit in Showalter's argument is the assumption that the text, and language itself, are transparent media which reflect a pre-existent objective reality, rather than signifying systems" (p. 25).

If *Making a Difference* would take us beyond Showalter, or beyond 1981, its first step is into "contemporary approaches to language." After Greene and Kahn's introduction, the first chapter is Sydney Janet Kaplan's survey of gynocriticism which culminates in a discussion of

Showalter's work. Kaplan's chapter is immediately followed by Nelly Furman's essay focused specifically on language.

Furman discusses Showalter along with Sandra Gilbert and Susan Gubar, two other major gynocritics included in Showalter's and Abel's anthologies: "For Gilbert and Gubar, as for Showalter, there is no doubt that literature reflects life. . . . When literature is viewed as a representational art whose function is to 'picture' life, what is ignored or pushed aside is the part played by language" (p. 63). I am not certain why or how there can be "*no* doubt," but this is an oft-repeated contention about these gynocritics made by critics in tune with "contemporary approaches to language." Furman then presents an alternative to this view of literature: "Literature may be thought of as a representation of life, but literature can also be viewed as a non-referential linguistic system" (p. 64).

Furman's essay may in fact present an exemplary case of non-referential language: I often could not tell what she meant. But a few things were clear. For her, how we view literature is not just a simple choice, as the last quotation might imply. There is a politics to that choice, and the choice made by Showalter, Gilbert, and Gubar is incorrect, in unwitting collusion with patriarchal ideology. One other thing is clear, if puzzling in its implications: the "working metaphor" of this chapter is marriage.

The choice of marriage as central metaphor is explicitly connected to the view of language: "a study of marriage as a linguistic operation could help us understand language as a non-referential system. Both the marital vow and the ceremony which enacts it will serve as the working metaphors of this chapter" (p. 64). Although Furman's reader could use "help" in understanding, her "study of marriage" does not explain why feminists should choose to see literature as nonrepresentational or language as a non-referential system. Nonetheless the fact of her choice of marriage as topic for study stands out.

Whereas Furman claims that it is specifically the marital vow and ceremony that will be her "working metaphor," the editors' abstract which heads off her chapter mentions neither vow nor ceremony but rather talks simply about "marriage." Six of the ten sentences in the one-paragraph abstract are about marriage, giving it proportionally much more space than it has in the chapter itself. The abstract begins: "In our culture, marriage is a privileged place for the interaction of the sexes" (p. 59). This sentence in fact corresponds to something Furman does not say until the last page of her essay, but its position opening the abstract suggests that the article is going to be about marriage as the interaction of the sexes.

The abstract continues with two more sentences from the last page of Furman's article: "Marriage can be viewed as the blissful coming together of equal voices speaking in unison, or as an ongoing dialogue between individuals affirming their differences. In the first instance, marriage is seen as a social structure where equality and unity can be achieved; in the second, it is the place which allows the play of difference" (p. 59). Although these two views of marriage differ, both are attractive, endowing marriage with differing but equally glowing qualities, depending on one's taste for bliss or dialogue. Yet these sentences in the abstract leave out an essential element from their appearance in the chapter. Furman writes: "whether one views marriage as the blissful coming together of equal voices speaking in unison, or as the site of an ongoing dialogue between individuals continuously affirming their differences, we cannot escape the structure it imposes, the patriarchal society it sustains" (p. 76). The two alternative "views" of the abstract are, in the text, equally opposed to something else that is not called a "view," that is less visible, but more important: not our view of marriage but marriage as a structure and its relation to patriarchy. The two lovely alternatives, blissful coming together or dialogic affirmation of differences, are both set by Furman in the ironic context of their inability to "escape" the structural position of the institution of marriage in patriarchal society. Leaving out that structural framework, the abstract endorses a romantic vision of marriage, and of "the interaction of the sexes."

While the abstract proposes two alternative views of marriage, Furman's essay suggests three: two within romantic discourse plus a structural perspective. If the abstract reduces three to two, that may, in part, be accountable to a certain counting difficulty within the chapter. The final quotation of Furman's chapter has Jacques Derrida tell of "an implacable destiny which immures everything for life in the figure 2" and of the dream of escaping that closure (pp. 75–76). Perhaps dreaming that escape, Furman's essay resists the figure two but also assists in editorial reduction to that number, producing a difficulty in counting, a stubborn confusion between two and three, particularly during the dense last page where Furman seems ready to state her position about marriage and—perhaps more to the point (at least my point here in this book)—about feminist criticism.

Immediately after the sentence with two romantic views of marriage both likewise unmindful of its place in patriarchy, we read the following paragraph, the penultimate of Furman's essay:

> Whether viewed as the place which can allow for equality, or conceived as an agonistic setting for the expression of difference, marriage may also serve as an allegory of our feminist critical practices. While the egalitarian argument in feminist criticism calls for equal representation in literature of women's and men's experience of life, post-structuralist feminism challenges representation itself as already a patriarchal paradigm, thus positing the existence of a different discursive practice. (p. 76)

This apparently simple paragraph is made up of just two sentences, each opposing two positions. But the pairs in the two sentences do not line up. The first sentence contrasts the egalitarian and the differential view of marriage, the pair represented in the editorial abstract. The paragraph's second sentence opposes egalitarian and poststructuralist feminist criticism. If poststructuralist feminism sees representation itself as "already a patriarchal paradigm," then it is not in the position of the agonistic affirmation of differences (dialogue), but in the third position (that forgotten by the abstract) which recognizes both the egalitarian and the dialogic view as enclosed within patriarchal structures.

Furman is undoubtedly trying to link the sort of criticism practiced by Showalter with a naive egalitarianism. She is also clearly tying poststructuralist feminism with an analysis that does not forget the patriarchal construction of the "interaction between the sexes." The problem is that whereas there are three views of marriage, there are only two feminist critical positions.

Since the abstract offers only two versions of marriage, blissful merger or affirmation of difference, when it later quotes Furman's sentence opposing egalitarian and poststructuralist criticism, one can only understand poststructuralist feminism as analogous to the dialogic view of marriage. This conforms to the anthology's explicit affirmation both of poststructuralism and of "difference," leading us precisely to believe that poststructuralism will "Make a *Difference*."

Furman carries some of this connection between poststructuralism and difference in the last clause of her paragraph when she affirms that poststructuralist feminism posits "the existence of a *different* discursive practice." Despite this connection, in Furman's argument, poststructuralism is never unambiguously linked to the dialogic model. The structure of her two-sentence paragraph nonetheless leads one to superimpose the contrast between egalitarian and poststructuralist criticism upon the opposition between egalitarian and dialogic marriage. But before suggesting that analogy, Furman quietly effects a change in her description of the marriage of difference. What in the last sentence of the preceding paragraph is called "the site of an ongoing dialogue between individuals continuously affirming their differences" becomes, in the first sentence of this paragraph, "an agonistic setting for the expression of difference." Although these two expressions undoubtedly refer to the same concept, dialogue has become agonistic, difference has become combative opposition. This suggests a less rosy conception of marriage, part of the ironic rather than romantic tradition.

The abstract closes with two sentences, neither of them from anything Furman exactly wrote: "Marriage, like criticism, is a locus of interaction for the two sexes. Marriage thus can serve to illustrate how differing modes of feminist criticism relate to our patriarchal culture and its language" (p. 59). The abstract closes as it began, speaking of interaction for the sexes, which Furman mentions only once, while two of the abstract's ten sentences are devoted to it. In its repetition, this promotion of interaction for the sexes refers not only, or primarily, to marriage, but more relevantly to criticism.

The abstract's last sentence however reminds us that marriage is not, as romantics would have it, about either blissful heterosexual merger or dialogic sexual difference but, particularly in feminist analysis, about a patriarchal institution. Criticism, as the abstract itself tells us, is the locus of interaction between feminism and patriarchal culture. If feminist literary criticism finds its allegory in marriage, is it because masculine and feminine literature there interact? Or is it because feminist criticism finds its voice and status defined by its place within the patriarchal institution of literature? Although the abstract certainly ends on the latter choice, the promotion of dialogic marriage would lead to simple affirmation of a dialogic relation between male and female literature, masculine and feminine criticism, within an unanalyzed and unrecognized patriarchal institution. As this anthology variously promotes difference *within* a now poststructuralist, academic literary institution, the tendency to celebrate a marriage of difference while forgetting the structural analysis of the institution leads me to wonder in fact what difference it makes.

It is not only in Furman's chapter that marriage functions as an allegory for feminist criticism. Greene and Kahn, in their opening chapter, choose as their "working metaphor" Isak Dinesen's short story "The Blank Page," a story focused on women's relation to the institution of marriage: "the contrast between the story told by the spotted bridal sheets and that which speaks in the silence of 'the blank page' may be seen as a metaphor for the two major foci of feminist scholarship" (p. 6). "The blank page" refers to an unspotted bridal sheet displayed in a convent gallery of mounted and framed bridal sheets. Greene and Kahn suggest that these two contrasting bridal stories be taken as a metaphor for the two kinds of feminist scholarship. Like marriage in Furman's essay, this is a "working metaphor": in which "women's work"—the convent's weaving of fabric for sheets, the women's art symbolized by the blood-paintings—is a metaphor for feminist work, our scholarly work, but also in which marriage is a metaphor for our economic condition, the institutions in which we work.[6]

Dinesen's story is well-known in feminist critical circles, thanks to its analysis by Susan Gubar in an article which, like Showalter's "Feminist Criticism in the Wilderness," is anthologized both in *Writing and Sexual Difference* and in *The New Feminist Criticism*.[7] The only essays to appear in both these anthologies, they might be taken as exemplary of the moment I like to call 1981. *Making a Difference* repeatedly dwells upon Showalter's article, but we might also see in this choice of Dinesen's story as framework for the volume's introduction another attempt by this anthology to rewrite that moment.

A reference to Gubar's 1981 article finally shows up on the penultimate page of Greene and Kahn's introductory chapter and in fact constitutes the last of the chapter's many references to feminist scholarship outside the anthology. Greene and Kahn cite Gubar's calling the blank page "subversive" and give Gubar's explanation of why and how it is subversive. Their next paragraph begins: "It is also subversive in that it is unnamed, without an author, for, as Barthes suggests, 'To give the text an Author is to impose a limit on that text'" (p. 27). Greene and Kahn go beyond Gubar, beyond 1981, beyond gynocritics with its interest in women authors. And that move beyond is here underwritten by the authority of Roland Barthes.

After the editors' Introduction, the first essay in *Making a Difference* is Sydney Kaplan's thoughtful account of feminist criticism as the study of women writers. Author of one of the earliest of the feminist books on women's writing,[8] Kaplan serves as a representative of gynocriticism. Kaplan's essay is followed by: (1) Furman's account of "contemporary approaches to language," (2) a chapter on French feminine theories by

Ann Rosalind Jones, (3) Judith Kegan Gardiner's survey of psychoanalytic feminist criticism, and (4) an analysis of socialist feminist criticism by Cora Kaplan. After those four we reach Zimmerman's "overview of lesbian feminist criticism." If we take Sydney Kaplan's chapter to represent a sort of separatist criticism, then between it and Zimmerman's updated article falls precisely the "incorporation" of the "systems of thought" of which Zimmerman's 1985 version tells: "encorporating the insights of Marxist, structuralist, semiotic and even psychoanalytic criticism" (p. 198).

After Zimmerman comes Susan Willis' study of black women writers. The book does not end on this gesture toward not-yet-incorporated otherness, but has one last chapter. While a study of black women writers might not give the anthology happy, rounded closure, the final essay, by Adrienne Munich, seems designed to do just that. It takes up one last time the attack on Showalter and gynocriticism sounded in the Introduction and in Furman's chapter. Its tone toward gynocritics is more antagonistic than Furman's or Greene and Kahn's. Whereas Furman attacked Showalter, Gilbert, Gubar et al. on the grounds of "contemporary approaches to language," Munich attacks gynocriticism for not reading men, for forbidding feminist critics from reading men. Munich indicts Showalter for "polarizing literary criticism into gynocentric and androcentric criticism" (p. 243) and goes on to a joint, not contrasting, reading of the wisdom to be found in Miguel de Cervantes' *Don Quixote de la Mancha* and Toni Morrison's *Sula*. Munich can follow Willis because both offer us readings of *Sula*. The opening onto black women prepares the final match between white and black, male and female, father of the novel and successful young daughter, canonical monument and outsider/newcomer to the literary institution. In place of politicized difference, in place of separatism and polarization, we can celebrate the resolution of those differences.

In an anthology, editorial position asserts itself particularly in the order of the essays. No exception, *Making a Difference* may have a clearer narrative line than most, taking us from Sydney Kaplan's gynocentrism to Adrienne Munich's return to the male canon, not to the old androcentrism of the sacred canon, but to a reading that will allow men and women to touch. This narrative trajectory is disturbingly familiar.

Not only "separatist," Kaplan's position is an extremely affirmative version of lesbian criticism. Not in the way Zimmerman usually means, criticism of lesbian literature, but criticism that is itself lesbian, that expresses a woman's passion for women. Kaplan begins her essay: "For some of us, feminist criticism originated in a recognition of our love for women writers" (p. 37). This textual preference, prohibited by the academy, still somehow stubbornly survived: "If we entered academia . . . such secret loves had to be abandoned. . . . I soon discovered that even the rigorous conditioning [graduate education] had imposed had not destroyed my hidden preference for . . . women writers" (pp. 38–39). Twentieth-century heterosexism has all too frequently meant the application of "rigorous conditioning" to cure lesbians of their unfortunate "preference." More humanistic variants of such conditioning have tended to believe in the effect of continual enforced exposure to male beauty.

The narrative of *Making a Difference* represents an even more tolerant version of heterosexism, this one likewise not unfamiliar. Freud held the liberal view that homosexuality was neither sinful nor in fact abnormal. On the one hand offering it a place within normal human sexuality, Freud would contain it by relegating it to a minoritized place. For Freud, homosexuality was an adolescent stage, a stage of development prior to adult reproductive heterosexuality.[9] In 1985, Zimmerman finds that "lesbian criticism has *developed* diversity in theory and approach" (p. 198), moving beyond separatism. Greene and Kahn relegate the gynocentric criticism of Showalter, Gubar, and Sydney Kaplan to "an intermediary stage on the way towards a more comprehensive literary criticism which considers both male and female traditions in their interactions" (p. 25). As we saw in the editors' abstract to Furman's chapter, "marriage is a privileged place" for such "interactions."

Let me make it clear that I am not accusing *Making a Difference* of literal heterosexism. At stake here is not sexual but textual preference. Many gynocritics are practicing heterosexuals, just as many lesbians prefer to write about male texts. Let me echo a note to Zimmerman's article: "The sexual preference of the authors is, for the most part, irrelevant; this is an analysis of lesbian feminist ideas, not authors."[10]

Making a Difference derives its developmental narrative from the three-"stage" model for women's history, found in Gerda Lerner's book *The Majority Finds Its Past*. Although the book is devoted to the theory and practice of women's history, of studying women, Lerner imagines a final stage which would unite women's history with men's. The last paragraph of *The Majority Finds Its Past* begins: "What is needed is a new universal history, a holistic history which will be a synthesis of traditional history and women's history." The paragraph ends: "Only a history based on the recognition that women have always been essential to the making of history and that *men and women* are the measure of significance, will be truly a universal history."[11] Lerner ends her book on the grand, encompassing "universal history" and ends with an emphasis on "men and women," the two conjoined.

I do not so much want to question the desirability of "universal history" as to remark that such grand resolutions of difference tend to crop up at the end of feminist books, in the very position of marriage as the happy narrative resolution of another genre which women have written and read with like verve and pleasure.

Judith Mayne suggests that we "submit theory to the test of narrative." Finding a "fit between theory and narrative," Mayne attributes it to a like desire behind the two. "This is not to say that there is something 'wrong' with that desire," but "[h]owever much the projects of theory and narrative might overlap, it is the task of theory to interrogate the patterns of opposition and resolution, not to replicate them."[12] I would like here to consider two more examples of happy endings from widely-read books of feminist theory: Carol Gilligan's *In a Different Voice* and Virginia Woolf's *A Room of One's Own*.[13]

Gilligan's influential book stresses the importance of attending to the contrasts between women and men, their differing developmental histories, and their differing ethical thinking. The very last page of that book brings the two back into contact, supplying a particular and familiar mode of closure. The penultimate paragraph begins: "To understand how the tension between responsibilities and rights sustains the dialectic of human development is to see the integrity of two disparate modes of experience that are in the end connected." In Gilligan's book they are literally "connected in the end," through a telling image. Here is the last sentence of *In a Different Voice*: "Through this expansion in perspective, we can envision how a *marriage* between adult development as it is currently portrayed and women's development as it begins to be seen could lead to a changed understanding of human development and a more *generative* view of human life."[14] Lerner ends by imagining women's and traditional history interacting; envisioning an analogous synthesis of traditional and women's developmental theories, Gilligan calls their connection "a marriage," which although not literal will, hopefully, have a nonetheless *generative* outcome.

The different voice ends up saying something uncannily familiar. Is there any relation between this closing image and the popularity of the book? Is the image being generated by the narrative drive for an upbeat ending? How does the insistence upon difference look when finally inscribed into a model of heterosexual complementarity? Is this the difference feminists want to make?

The heterosexual ending of *A Room of One's Own* begins not on the last page, but with the last chapter. On the second page of that last chapter, a "girl" comes from one side of the street, a "young man" from the other; the two meet and get into a taxi-cab. Woolf then comments: "Perhaps to think, as I had been thinking these two days [the fictional time of the rest of the book, the other five chapters], of one sex as distinct from the other is an effort. It interferes with the unity of the mind. Now that effort had ceased and that unity had been restored by seeing two people come together and get into a taxi-cab."[15] Although the image of the couple and the taxi may seem transitory, it is intimately related to the main theme of the book's concluding chapter: androgyny.

Woolf goes on to theorize about her pleasure in seeing the "two people come together"; her theory is disturbingly familiar:

> When I saw the couple get into the taxi-cab the mind felt as if, after being divided, it had come together again in a natural fusion. The obvious reason would be that it is natural for the sexes to co-operate. One has a profound, if irrational, instinct in favour of the theory that the union of man and woman makes for the greatest satisfaction, the most complete happiness. But the sight of the two people getting into the taxi and the satisfaction it gave me made me also ask whether there are two sexes in the mind corresponding to the two sexes in the body, and whether they also require to be united in order to get complete satisfaction and happiness. (pp. 101–102)

The union of the two sexes in the mind is what she has famously called androgyny. Less has been said about its status as internalized heterosexuality. What she calls a "theory" here is a rather purely distilled form of heterosexist ideology. Not only is heterosexuality "natural" (the word twice repeated), "a profound, if irrational, instinct," but it is superior in that it provides "the greatest satisfaction, the most complete happiness." The passage begins in a more traditional heterosexism grounded in biologism and the morality of reproductive sex, but "the obvious reason" is succeeded by a discourse of pleasure. The repeated words "satisfaction" and "happiness" praise heterosexuality not for its reproductive capacities, but for its orgasmic potential.

In the 1920s pleasure was called upon to reinforce marriage, transforming it from a bond with reproductive goals to a pleasure bond.[16] Writing during that moment, Woolf actually reenacts the transformation in this passage, moving from the discourse of "nature" to the discourse of "satisfaction." We today are more familiar with a similar (hetero)sexual revolution that took place in the 1960s. In a lucid, witty analysis of the ideology of that more recent period, Meryl Altman links the sixties to the twenties and tellingly exemplifies the period's strategies with quotations from Dr. David Reuben: "basically all homosexuals are alike . . . looking for sexual satisfaction where there can be no lasting satisfaction."[17] In retrospect, Woolf's emphasis on "complete satisfaction" echoes Reuben.

Let us recall that in the fifth chapter, last but one, of *A Room of One's Own*, Woolf discovers in the writing of her fictional contemporary, Mary Carmichael, the words "Chloe liked Olivia." Innocent enough out of context, or even with the explicit context Woolf supplies (lab partners, one married with two children). But Woolf's tone certainly suggests something shocking: "Are there no men present? Do you promise me that behind that red curtain over there the figure of Sir Chartres Biron is not concealed? We are all women, you assure me? Then I may tell you that the very next words I read were these—'Chloe liked Olivia . . .' Do not start. Do not blush. Let us admit in the privacy of our own society that these things sometimes happen. Sometimes women do like women" (pp. 85–86). From this camped-up sense of scandal and secret, it would be hard not to infer lesbianism.[18]

After the chapter on Mary Carmichael's novel, the story of Chloe and Olivia, comes chapter 6 and the relieved retreat into heterosexuality. Perhaps because in Woolf's book this final move occupies so much more than just a page, we in fact find more than just formulaic heterosexism. Woolf moves from biologistic to hedonistic heterosexism. Yet there is more in her discussion of heterosexual satisfaction than the echo of Dr. David Reuben might lead us to believe.[19]

Occurring three times in two sentences, the word "satisfaction" marks the passage with a particular insistence: "The union of man and woman makes for the greatest satisfaction, the most complete happiness. But the sight of the two people getting into the taxi and the satisfaction it gave me made me also ask whether there are two sexes in the mind . . . and whether they also require to be united in order to get complete satisfaction and happiness." It is worth noting exactly whose satisfaction Woolf is talking about. "The union of man and woman makes for the greatest satisfaction": for whom? The two sexes in the mind "require to be united in order to get complete satisfaction":

for whom? Only the second of the three "satisfactions" is actually attributed. The only actual satisfaction in this passage belongs neither to the man nor to the woman who "come together," but to the woman who watches. The only attested pleasure arises not from heterosexuality, but from voyeurism. The insistence of the number two, the fact that the word "two" occurs three times in the last sentence ("two people," "two sexes in the mind corresponding to the two sexes in the body"), serves to hide the fact that there are three parties to this encounter.

Perhaps the draw of heterosexuality, the pleasure it supplies as happy ending for women's stories, is not the pleasure ideology would have us believe. Perhaps women like to watch the heterosexual couple, to read it, to imagine it. The spectacle of heterosexual coupling, the thought of it, may give women enormous pleasure. Not necessarily because they identify with the woman they watch.

This voyeuristic scenario is not so marginal to the argument of *A Room of One's Own*. The *ménage à trois* returns in the final paragraph of the main text, in the description of androgyny as a marriage in the mind: "Some collaboration has to take place in the mind between the woman and the man before the act of creation can be accomplished. Some marriage of opposites has to be consummated. . . . The curtains must be close drawn. The writer . . . once his experience is over, must lie back and let his mind celebrate its nuptials in darkness. He must not look or question what is being done" (p. 108). The man and woman in the mind will consummate a marriage. One generally thinks of this androgynous mind as split into two opposite-sexed halves which then conjugally reunite. But in fact, there are three parties here, the two spouses *and* "the writer." There is some part of the writer left out of the nuptials who would be in a position to watch, except "he must not look." Looking is explicitly forbidden here, and with insistence: "the curtains close drawn," the "darkness." With such precautions, one suspects there must be a voyeuristic drive about.

Remark that the writer here is male. We recall that the writer who, in Woolf's mind, managed to celebrate these nuptials with most complete satisfaction was William Shakespeare. *A Room of One's Own* is not only the source book of feminist literary criticism, not only a tale of British women writers, fictional and real, over four centuries. It is also the founding text of feminist criticism of Shakespeare. And like most feminist criticism of Shakespeare, and unlike most feminist criticism of other male writers, it is laudatory rather than critical of the bard.

It is perhaps only fitting that Shakespeare should be centrally there at the beginnings of feminist literary criticism. In a 1981 article, Gayle Greene feels that she can use feminist reading of Shakespeare as a synechdoche for feminist criticism as a whole: "While feminist criticism of Shakespeare is in some sense unlike other sorts of feminist criticism, in that it is more a matter of reassessing than of rediscovering a literary canon, still we found that we could, on the basis of our work with Shakespeare, describe elements of a feminist approach to literature that applied to the enterprise as a whole."[20]

The "we" in Greene's sentence refers to Greene, Carolyn Ruth Swift, and Carol Thomas Neely, the co-editors of the 1980 anthology, *The Women's Part: Feminist Criticism of Shakespeare*. Also in 1980, Coppélia Kahn co-edited *Representing Shakespeare: New Psychoanalytic Essays*. If *Making a Difference* in some way represents the marriage of those two earlier anthologies, its central chapter is Judith Kegan Gardiner's survey of the intersection of psychoanalysis and feminism. Gardiner's essay is the only chapter of the book to mention Shakespeare, despite nearly two decades of diverse and influential feminist readings of Shakespeare. Discussing psychoanalytic approaches to female literary characters, Gardiner writes: "Prolific as a goddess, Shakespeare attracts psychoanalytic feminist character critics" (p. 118). Speaking in terms of textual attraction, Gardiner would seem to construe feminist criticism of Shakespeare as a lesbian relationship, if not entirely between mortals.

Aside from Gardiner's idealizing feminization, there is a general forgetting of Shakespeare studies, particularly odd in a volume edited by two Shakespeare critics. The history of criticism constructed by the volume implies that feminists have largely devoted themselves to women writers and that now we must also turn our attention to male writers of the canon. Yet one canon father has had his share of attention since the beginning of feminist criticism and all through its history. Unless we don't count him because he is actually a mother.

Making a Difference ends with Adrienne Munich's call for feminists to read "male-authored works of the literary canon" (pp. 238, 240). The last sentence of her essay, the last sentence of the book, militantly proclaims: "The canon has been owned by a monopoly, but acts of repossession have begun" (p. 257). So, in 1985, feminists are just beginning this repossession of canonical literature. And Munich makes it clear that, like any radically new, vanguard action, this gesture is especially dangerous: "Rereading the canon involves great costs and requires great courage, since one risks being cast out, like Sula, by man and woman alike" (p. 255).

Perhaps in the fields in which Munich works (Browning, Virgil, Tennyson, Joyce, Gilbert and Sullivan, according to notes on contributors) feminist criticism is still new, risky, and marginalized. But feminist readings of Shakespeare have been influential, recognized both by Shakespeareans and by feminist critics ("by man and woman alike"?). Munich never so much as mentions feminist Shakespeare criticism. Perhaps she is unaware of it, but Greene and Kahn certainly are not. By closing their book with Munich's impassioned plea, they construct a feminist literary criticism that, in 1985, urgently needs the very thing they have been doing for years.

In 1981, Greene states that feminist Shakespeare criticism, despite the fact of its concentration on a canonical (male) author, can represent the entire field of feminist literary criticism. This is not 1981 as Showalter would define it. Greene and Kahn would seem to accept Showalter's definition in order to propose this other feminist criticism not as contemporary with Showalter's but beyond it, the next stage, not an alternative, but a further step into maturity.

A transformation of alternatives into sequential stages can also be seen in the editorial treatment of Sydney Kaplan's essay.[21] Not only is it positioned first, placing all the other sorts of feminist criticisms after it, but the abstract preceding it reconstructs Kaplan's argument so as to place gynocriticism in a sequential progression.

The abstract opens: "Feminist criticism begins, according to Sydney Janet Kaplan, in the personal response of women readers to women writers. . . . *It then branches* into several paths: revisionary criticism of the canon, the study of neglected or lost women writers, and the articulation of a distinctive female literary tradition" (p. 37, emphasis added). Feminist reading of male canonical texts finds its place in the second moment of the abstract, after a singular origin has "branched."

Kaplan's chapter actually begins: "For some of us, feminist criticism originated in a recognition of our love for women writers. In this we diverge from many of our sister critics whose awakening was hastened by their urge to reveal the diverse ways women have been oppressed, misinterpreted and trivialized by the dominant patriarchal tradition, and to show how these are reflected in the images of women in the works of male authors" (p. 37). Kaplan posits a double beginning for feminist criticism: for some it begins in loving readings of women writers; for other "sisters" it begins in angry readings of male authors.

This angry reading of "images of women" is not what Munich is calling for, nor does it describe most feminist criticism of Shakespeare. But let us at least note that for Kaplan reading women and reading men are contemporary activities practiced not by different generations but by sisters with differing textual preferences.

Sydney Kaplan associates loving reading women with childhood, with the period before she entered the academic institution of reading. For Kaplan this is, however, only half the origin of feminist criticism; this early love is coeval with angry readings of men authors. By isolating the bond between women readers and writers, the editorial abstract constructs an originary moment of feminist critics loving women authors, feminist criticism as a sort of pre-Oedipal relation between women readers and women writers with no men about.

According to Munich, Showalter "prohibits women's writing about literary tradition. This particular limitation reinforces . . . a primitive patriarchal taboo forbidding women to approach sacred objects" (p. 243). Munich's point about leaving patriarchal culture untouched and sacred is well-taken. But is another "primitive" story about taboo also getting told here? Munich is angry that Showalter would prohibit her access to sacred patriarchal objects. In a heterosexual Oedipal configuration the daughter resents her mother for barring access to the father.

One of the editors of *Making a Difference*, Coppélia Kahn, in her article in *The (M)other Tongue*, takes up recent feminist psychoanalytic theories. According to Kahn, following Chodorow, "mothers represent regression and the lack of autonomy".[22] Kahn then subscribes to a pre-Oedipal revision of the infamous concept of "penis envy": the girl "desires a penis as a crucial sign of difference, to serve as a defense against the undertow of merger with the mother. . . . She wants a penis, then, insofar as she wants to detach herself from her mother and become an autonomous person" (p. 76). Is this then the difference we are trying to make?

In the same article, Kahn terms penis envy "that bugaboo which has justifiably angered many feminists and regrettably alienated them from psychoanalysis" (p. 75). Feminists were right to be offended, but Kahn regrets their estrangement from psychoanalysis. Perhaps this interpretation can help undo the alienation.

While Kahn has worked to remedy the split between feminists and psychoanalysis, her partner has argued for an "alliance" between feminist and Marxist criticism. In a 1981 article in *Women's Studies* Greene presents a reading of Shakespeare's Cressida in order to "illustrate the way a Marxist and a feminist reading of a work *complement and complete one another.*"[23] Incomplete in themselves, when joined, Marxist and feminist readings will be whole. Admittedly, "[i]t does seem that at this point, Marxist criticism has the most to gain" (p. 41); but Greene is addressing this argument to feminists, publishing it in *Women's Studies*, trying to persuade feminists to enter into this alliance.

In making her argument for a Marxist feminist criticism, Greene quotes from a "now classic essay": "Feminist criticism is, as Lillian Robinson describes it, 'criticism with a cause, engaged criticism . . . revolutionary.'"[24] The same quotation serves as an epigraph to the chapter on socialist feminist criticism in *Making a Difference*. Cora Kaplan gives the complete quotation, showing us what Greene elides: "Feminist criticism, as its name implies, is criticism with a Cause, engaged criticism. But the critical model presented to us so far is merely engaged to be married. It is about to contract what can only be a *mésalliance* with bourgeois modes of thought and the critical categories they inform. To be effective, feminist criticism cannot become simply bourgeois criticism in drag. It must be ideological and moral criticism; it must be revolutionary." Robinson's "engaged" feminist criticism is actually far from "revolutionary."

Robinson worries that feminist criticism will be turned away from its revolutionary promise, rendered academic, coopted by bourgeois modes of thought. Kaplan feels that "Robinson's astute pessimistic prediction is worth remembering" (p. 147), but her real use of the quotation involves mining the resources of Robinson's metaphor. She follows the Robinson quotation with a second epigraph: "The 'Marriage' of marxism and feminism has been like the marriage of husband and wife depicted in English common law: marxism and feminism are one and that is marxism. . . . [W]e need a healthier marriage or we need a divorce."[25]

The juxtaposition of these two epigraphs undercuts the differences and emphasizes the similarities for feminists between ties to bourgeois institutions and ties to Marxism. Kaplan's chapter then begins in fun: "In spite of the attraction of *m*atrimonial *m*etaphor, reports of feminist nuptials with either *m*ild-*m*annered bourgeois criticism or *m*acho *m*ustachioed *M*arxism have been greatly exaggerated" (p. 147, emphasis added). The excessive alliteration signals the high-spirited camp. "Mild-mannered" alludes to Clark Kent, "mild-mannered reporter for the Daily Planet," and implies that the contrast between "bourgeois criticism" and "Marxism" is deceptive. However much *L*ois *L*ane might desire

Superman and spurn Clark Kent, the informed reader knows they are in fact the same. The repeated initial m's not only contribute to this joke ("mild-mannered," "macho mustachioed") but help it spill over onto "Marxism" itself, robbing that term of its usual seriousness.

The phrase "reports of feminist nuptials . . . have been greatly exaggerated" alludes to Mark Twain's "reports of my death have been greatly exaggerated." Putting "nuptials" in the place of death recalls "the conventional narrative resolutions of marriage or death"[26] and suggests that for feminism such a marriage would be equivalent to death. As for the other pair of m's, what in fact is "the attraction of matrimonial metaphor"? Although Kaplan playfully dismisses that question in the first phrase of her essay, it remains pressing here. We have found this attraction operative in Furman's essay, in *Making a Difference* as a whole, and, beyond that, in diverse books of feminist theory. Agreeing that we feminists are attracted to matrimonial metaphor, I would add that there is not only a desire for but also a pleasure taken in such metaphor, as witness the delightful opening of Cora Kaplan's essay. *A Room of One's Own* suggests that the appeal of such metaphor should not be confused with a satisfaction in or even a wish for matrimony itself. What then is the character of this attraction to, this pleasure in matrimonial metaphor?

Whatever the pleasures of this metaphor, for Kaplan in 1985 it no longer signals danger as it did to Robinson in 1971 or Hartmann in 1979: "the present danger is not that feminist criticism will enter an unequal dependent alliance with any of the varieties of male-centred criticism" (p. 147). Abandoning matrimonial metaphor as she ends her first paragraph, Kaplan turns to the current dilemma of liberal feminist criticism, the dominant voice in academic literary feminism. "Without the class and race perspectives which socialist feminist critics bring . . . liberal feminist criticism . . . will unintentionally reproduce the ideological values of mass-market romance" (pp. 147–48). Still in danger of becoming bourgeois, feminism no longer needs Marxism to save it. As Kaplan puts it, "this reactionary effect must be interrogated and resisted from within feminism" (p. 147).

Seriousness aside, the double m's of "mass-market" recall Kaplan's opening play. Certainly no genre of writing better attests to women's attraction to and pleasure in marriage as "conventional narrative resolution." "Mass-market romance" burgeoned in the same period that saw the rise of academic feminist criticism. Both are genres where women write to the pleasure of women readers, not however in some separatist utopia, but through the mediation of male-controlled institutions.[27] No wonder these sister genres bear a family resemblance.

Kaplan goes on to describe the characteristics of mass-market romance:

> In that fictional landscape the other structuring relations of society fade and disappear, leaving us with the naked drama of sexual difference as the only scenario that matters. . . . Even where class difference divides lovers, it is there as narrative backdrop or minor stumbling-block to the inevitable heterosexual resolution. Without overstraining the comparison, a feminist literary criticism which privileges gender in isolation from other forms of social determination offers us a similarly partial reading of the role played by sexual difference. (p. 148)

The critique is extremely well-taken. Feminist discourse has tended to emphasize gender and disregard all other differences. The similarity to romance is instructive, not only, I would hope, because it is humiliating to have our "high" cultural production compared to so-called "trash." If the isolation of gender "leaves us with the naked drama of sexual difference," it might be because we enjoy contemplating this "naked drama." Our pleasure may be linked to "the inevitable heterosexual resolution." When class difference operates as "narrative backdrop or minor stumbling-block," might not the "heterosexual resolution" also be serving to resolve this other social division? And might not the promised ending be agreeable precisely because it can resolve this other difference? Do we prefer sexual difference because this particular difference conventionally promises narrative resolution?

Perhaps our desire is not fundamentally for sexual difference but rather simply for "inevitable resolution." And gender is the only difference we know that includes that promise. No wonder we are attracted to matrimonial metaphor. If we can drape our various oppositions, contradictions, the terms of our troubled wishes, in the trappings of sexual difference, then we have a conventional scenario to imagine a happy ending. And who does not want a happy ending?

Cora Kaplan does, but she is trying to write a different scenario, resolution with a twist that is neither heterosexual nor inevitable. The dilemma that spurs her writing is "the polarization of social and psychic explanation" (p. 154) within feminist criticism. She tells of two "admirable recent essays" on Charlotte Brontë's *Villette*.[28] Mary Jacobus' psychoanalytic reading explores "psyche, desire, and fantasy" while "the social meanings fade and all but disappear" (p. 153). Judith Lowder Newton "privileges the social meanings of the novel" but "stigmatizes the psychic level" (pp. 153, 154). Casting the two as complementary, Kaplan leads us to hope for a feminist reading that could "integrate" them. The body of her essay explores and analyzes the history of this polarization. Concluding her chapter by reading another Brontë novel, *Jane Eyre*, along with *A Room of One's Own*, she writes: "I want to end this chapter with an example of the kind of interpretative *integration* that I have been demanding of feminist critics" (p. 169, emphasis added).

Just as Greene concludes by interpreting Cressida in order to "illustrate the way a Marxist and a feminist reading of a work *complement and complete one another*," Cora Kaplan helps us dream the marriage of Mary Jacobus and Judith Newton. Before introducing the two brides, she announces: "[p]sychoanalytic perspectives have yet to be *integrated* with social, economic and political analysis" (p. 152, emphasis added). Coppélia Kahn wanted feminist criticism to take up psychoanalysis; Gayle Greene hoped we would learn from Marxism. Kaplan might just be speaking the dream behind this anthology.

Although beginning in matrimonial metaphor, she never expressly ties it to what she calls "integration." They certainly occupy the same narrative position. "For liberal humanism," writes Kaplan, "feminist versions included, the possibility of a unified self and an integrated consciousness . . . is represented as the fulfilment of desire, the happy closure at the end of the story" (p. 152). Although this may seem simply part of an attack on liberal feminism, Kaplan believes this desire for unity and integration to be shared by Newton and Jacobus, both of whom she explicitly associates with socialist feminism: "Neither Newton nor Jacobus argues for the utopian possibility of a unified subjectivity. But the *longing* to close the splits that characterize femininity is evident in the way each critic denies the opposing element" (p. 154, emphasis Kaplan's). She does not expose their covert wish for wholeness in order to accuse them of bourgeois liberalism. She shares this wish, speaks it with her own "demand" for "integration."

Trying to satisfy that demand, she closes with a reading of *Jane Eyre* and *A Room of One's Own*, a performance that thrills as we watch her combine social and psychic explanation. She reads two books central to feminist literary history: Woolf's founding text and the Brontë novel that served Sandra Gilbert and Susan Gubar the working metaphor for a history of women writing in the nineteenth century.[29] Both books also exemplify "inevitable heterosexual resolution." We've already looked at how marriage functions at the end of *A Room*. The plot of *Jane Eyre* looks like a formula immensely popular with romance readers in the mid-1980s: the heroine in love with and fleeing "the magnetic advances of an impetuous employer."

The last quotation is from an advertisement for a new series of romances launched in 1984.[30] As academic feminists dream of integrating the social and the psychic, the major producer of mass-market romances offers its readers books that focus on and resolve the contradiction between the work plot and the love plot. As Leslie Rabine puts it: "The very facts that the hero is both boss and lover, that the world of work and business is romanticized and eroticized, and that in it love flourishes suggest that the Harlequin heroines seek an end to the division between the domestic world of love and sentiment and the public world of work and business" (p. 250). Harlequin heroines, romance readers, Cora Kaplan, Greene and Kahn, feminist critics, how many of us in the mid-1980s long to wed the psychic and the social?[31]

Although Kaplan may have meant the analogy to romance as an embarrassment for liberal feminists, Rabine, another socialist feminist critic writing in 1985, has a healthy respect for Harlequin's sophistication in representing our wishes: "The genius of the Harlequin Romances is to combine the struggle for the recognition of feminine selfhood and the struggle to make the work world a home for that self" (p. 260). With more success than feminist critics, Harlequins combine the psychic and the social struggle. But, as Kaplan suggests, they combine them by eroticizing the social struggle so that both can be resolved through the old heterosexual happy ending. Whatever contradictions can be fit into the heterosexual formula can find happy fictional solution.

Cora Kaplan begins by rejecting matrimonial metaphor and the marriage of Marxism and feminism, and advocating instead an alliance between socialist and liberal feminism. She satisfies our longing for resolution by wedding two female protagonists who have been polarized into opposition: first Jacobus and Newton, finally Brontë and Woolf.

A similar move can be admired in Lydia Sargent's anthology, *The Unhappy Marriage of Marxism and Feminism*. Beginning with the title metaphor, the book proceeds to ring a dozen variations on it, typical of a more general response to Hartmann's seminal essay. As Lise Vogel puts it at the beginning of her contribution in the middle of the volume: "Others have informally embellished the sexual metaphor of a marriage between marxism and feminism. In place of an unhappy marriage they offer a string of humorous, if faintly bitter, alternatives: Illicit tryst? Teenage infatuation? May–December romance? Puppy love? Blind passion? Platonic relationship? Barren alliance? Marriage of convenience? Shotgun wedding? and so on."[32] Carrying on the tradition, Vogel suggests we view the relationship as a "trial separation." But the last essay in the book "refocuses the discussion," as the editor puts it. Zillah Eisenstein talks of a different couple, one not channeled into metaphors of sexual difference. Like Cora Kaplan, Eisenstein proposes we pursue an alliance between liberal and socialist feminism.

This metaphoric lesbian marriage certainly supplies a new twist to heterosexual teleology, but like the old formula it still demands terms in pairs, mapping difference onto the figure two. As with Furman's chapter, there is some difficulty counting in "Pandora's Box." Kaplan's chapter begins with two kinds of feminist criticism: liberal and socialist. A few pages later two kinds of feminist criticism are represented by Jacobus and Newton. Since both Jacobus's and Newton's essays are "informed by socialist feminist concerns" (p. 152), this must not be the same opposition. Newton's position would seem to typify socialist feminism, as Kaplan describes it. She terms Jacobus's position, variously, psychoanalytic, semiotic, Lacanian, post-structuralist. This is, in fact, a third type of feminist criticism. But the charm of polarized couples makes it hard to keep the three-term typology in mind.

Where does poststructuralist feminism fit into the original opposition between liberal and socialist? On the one hand, Jacobus's position is nominally considered socialist (although the exact phrase "informed by socialist feminist concerns" is somewhat vague). On the other hand, poststructuralism is linked to the liberal position: "The appropriation of modern critical theory—semiotic with an emphasis on the psychoanalytic—can be of great use. . . . But those theories about the production of meaning in culture must engage fully with the effects of other systems of difference than the sexual, or they too will produce no more than an anti-humanist avant-garde version of romance" (p. 148). When Kaplan says of Jacobus's reading that "the social meanings fade and all but disappear" (p. 153), we must recall her description of romance (and liberal feminist discourse): "In that fictional landscape the other structuring relations of society fade and disappear" (p. 148). Kaplan positions Jacobus as both liberal and socialist and as neither.

She does actually articulate the three different sorts of feminist criticism: "psychoanalytic and semiotically oriented feminism" represents a definite advance over "humanist feminism," but still has "been correctly criticized from a socialist feminist position for the neglect of class and race" (p. 149). In another mapping of the three terms, we find that although "the Marxist critic . . . assumes that author and text speak from a position within ideology . . . [s]emiotic and psychoanalytic theories of representation go even further in rejecting the possibility of authentic mimetic art" (p. 161). In some ways, socialist feminism is more advanced; in other ways, poststructuralist feminism goes further. This all seems an accurate and reasonable assessment, yet this complex relation between three terms, three sorts of feminist criticism, remains hard to read, partially covered by charming tales of fighting and mating.

This is not the only counting difficulty in "Pandora's Box." Following the discussion of romance ideology, Kaplan writes:

> Masculinity and femininity do not appear in cultural discourse, any more than they do in mental life, as pure binary forms at play. They are always, already, ordered and broken up through . . . other categories of difference. . . . Class and race ideologies are, conversely, steeped in and spoken through the language of sexual differentiation. . . . To understand how gender and class—to take two categories only—are articulated together transforms our analysis of each of them. (p. 148)

First, the passage moves beyond the heterosexual binary; then we encounter the general, open plural, "other categories of difference." The plural then becomes specified as a threesome: class, race, and sexual difference. And finally we end with a new pair: "class and gender."

"To take two categories only": Kaplan is explicit about both the reduction and its arbitrariness. But this heuristic reduction always takes the same form: we continually move from the generalized plural, the specified threesome to the same pair, a choice perhaps determined by the pair's aptitude for analogy with the other couples in "Pandora's Box." Kaplan believes the task for socialist feminist critics is "to put class and gender, social and psychic together in a non-reductive way" (p. 163). We want to make a match that in no way diminishes either of the parties. When it comes to "putting together," we tend to imagine terms in pairs. "Class and gender" can line up with "social and psychic," either in apposition (class : social :: gender : psychic), or at least as a double date.

The urge to couple, the drive to resolution, repeatedly drops race from the equation.[33] It may, however, return in Kaplan's term for resolution. Certainly the word has its various abstract, psychological, and mathematical meanings, but the one specific social sense of "integration" connotes the longing to heal the split between races.

Whereas "Marxism and feminism," "class and gender," "psychic and social," fit smoothly into narrative scenarios, it is much harder to tell the story with three terms. Grappling with this narrative problem, Gloria Joseph begins her essay in *The Unhappy Marriage*:

> Hartmann's essay speaks of an "unhappy marriage between marxism and feminism" but makes no mention in the title, and does not acknowledge in the essay, the incestuous child of patriarchy and capitalism. That child, now a full grown adult, is named racism. Thus, a more appropriate title of an article that attempts to create a theory that transcends marxism and feminism would be "The Incompatible Ménage à Trois: Marxism, Feminism, and Racism." . . . while Hartmann's essay represents an attempt to transcend the limitations and shortcomings of both marxist analysis and feminist analysis, I lament the absence of analysis of the Black woman and her role as member of the wedding. (p. 92)

In this opening paragraph, Joseph constructs scenarios for imagining a three-way relation. Racism is "the incestuous child of patriarchy and capitalism." This provocative formulation suggests that patriarchy and capitalism are related (siblings? parent and child? more distant relations?). Racism is not a third extrinsic ill but the direct result of the interaction of patriarchy and capitalism.

Joseph then goes on to suggest "a more appropriate title," in fact proffering the title of her own article. The relation is now named a "ménage à trois," the classic term for a three-way "marriage." This new construction does not necessarily contradict the original idea of two parents and a child. The child, "now a full grown adult," has become a sexual partner to her parents, redoubling the original incest. Yet it is not only the "ménage à trois" that is incompatible. There is a continuity problem between the two triads: the first comprised of capitalism, patriarchy, and racism; the second of Marxism, feminism, and racism. The first two terms of the second triangle name the struggles against the first two terms of the first triangle; the third term in both are identical. This can of course suggest that, as far as racism goes, Marxism and feminism are no more advanced than capitalism and patriarchy. A powerful indictment, but it nonetheless does not jibe with the notion of capitalism and patriarchy as racism's parents. Certainly Joseph does not intend to put Marxism and feminism in that position as well. Racism may in fact be incompatible with Marxism and feminism precisely because they are not kindred.

This opening paragraph ends with an image of "the Black woman as member of the wedding." The third term here is no longer "racism" but "the Black woman," victim and resister of racism, as well as capitalism and patriarchy. In Carson McCullers's *The Member of the Wedding*, white thirteen year old Frankie Addams would like to accompany her brother and his wife on their honeymoon. We see their wedding through her eyes, but we also see it through the eyes of the black cook. Joseph's use condenses this desire for an incestuous ménage à trois with a black woman's perspective on the white heterosexual union.

Packed with meaning, images jostle against each other in Joseph's opening paragraph. She is trying to juggle three terms without dropping the matrimonial metaphor. Each of her triadic variations on the metaphor works, but the disconcerting shifts from one to the other mark a story that is hard to tell, a story that does not fit smoothly into narrative convention.

Joanna Russ, committed to telling new stories, has helped us understand a writer's difficulties in trying to move outside conventional plots:

> Something that has been worked on by others in the same culture . . . provides a writer with material that has been distilled . . . and . . . clarified. A developed myth has . . . its own cues-to-nudge-the-reader. When so much of the basic work has already been done, the artist may either give the myth its final realization or stand it on its head, but in any case what he does will be neither tentative nor crude and it will not take forever; it can simply be done well.[34]

Russ uses the term "myth," from Aristotle's *mythos*, for what I have been calling plot or conventional narrative to imply that, like myths, these story structures carry the cultural belief system we call ideology. We may want to question the implication that uses of conventional narrative are never "tentative nor crude" and that they are simple to do well. But this essay in feminist poetics by a fiction writer, rather than a critic, suggests that when we discover writing difficulties, we might consider them as marks of someone trying to write outside the myth.

While Joseph's tale begins with the noisy incompatibility of her three terms, it ends with the vision of a reduction to a more manageable two terms: "The possibility of an alliance between black and white women can only be realized if white women understand the nature of their oppression within the context of the oppression of Blacks. At that point we will be able to speak of 'The Happy Divorce of Patriarchy, Capitalism, and Racism,' and the impending marriage of Black revolutionary socialism and socialist feminism" (p. 102). The "alliance" between black and white women is not in itself a resolution but rather an intermediary stage on the road to a happy ending. Once the shameful incestuous bond is dissolved in "happy divorce," we can get ready for proud and joyous nuptials. The incompatibility which throughout this essay speaks eloquently for the lack of any theory that can "put together" race, gender, and class "in a non-reductive way" is, in the last phrase, resolved by the transformation of three terms into two: "Black revolutionary socialism and socialist feminism." Whereas three occasioned sin, shame, and bumpy writing, the figure two betokens fictional happiness and resolution.

As Joseph writes, "an alliance between Black and white women" has not yet been realized; it is only a "possibility," but just as she begins to envision it, she rushes beyond to a more conventional, more heterosexual narrative resolution. The penultimate chapter of the anthology *Making a Difference* also marks some sort of alliance between white and black women. It is literally the place reserved for white academic feminists to attend to black women's writing. Susan Willis, a white critic, guides us through the distinctive contours of black women's narrative fictions. *Making a Difference* does not stop there, but moves beyond to an ending in which this very recent inclusion of black women can serve to help us imagine Munich's two-sexed world, where Toni Morrison can join Miguel de Cervantes.

Rather than push on to the conventional resolution, I would like to linger with this penultimate moment to see what difference it makes. Like Munich, Willis gives us a role model in Morrison's protagonist Sula: "Sula's challenge is, finally, directed to the reader—to imagine Sula and Nel's adolescent twosome evolved into adulthood. The real challenge, of course, would be for them to bond as adult heterosexual women" (p. 234). Impressed by the bond between Nel and Sula, Barbara Smith, in her classic essay "Toward a Black Feminist Criticism," termed the relationship and the novel lesbian.[35] Similarly impressed by this bond, Willis comes up with an interpretation that also makes a place for the manifest heterosexuality of the two friends. As I tried to show earlier in this chapter, heterosexism can take on the tolerant guise of relegating bonds between women to adolescence, making a place for lesbianism as the penultimate stage before full heterosexual maturity. This model can then be applied not only to actual adolescents but to adult lesbians and/or separatists who are considered "arrested" in their development, stuck in "an intermediary stage." How then to imagine a primary bond between women that could forcefully challenge this insistent developmental narrative? "The real challenge, of course, would be for them to bond as adult heterosexual women."

Sula's "challenge" concludes the penultimate section of Willis's chapter. Immediately following that section, a short ending entitled "Utopian Visions" begins:

> While Sula is the halcyon figure of challenge, there is, at the heart of the novel, an alternative vision which Sula does not perpetuate, but which nevertheless nurtured her and made it possible for her to articulate a radical perspective on heterosexuality. I am referring to the three-woman household, comprised of Sula's grandmother . . . her mother . . . and Sula herself. The three-woman household is a living arrangement that crops up throughout Morrison's writing to suggest an alternative and utopian possibility for redefining the space and the relationships associated with social reproduction. (p. 234)

Although the household in *Sula* is made up of three generations of mothers and daughters, Willis cites examples from *The Bluest Eye* and *Song of Solomon* which involve three women of the same generation. "The three-woman household" is a version of the "ménage à trois." The French word "ménage" has two basic meanings: the household and the couple. "Ménage à trois" tries to keep the two meanings together: "an arrangement in which three persons share sexual relations especially while they are living together" (Webster's). But by insisting on the "trois," could we not begin to pry the household apart from the couple?

Marriage is a household and a couple; it represents both an economic and an emotional relation. Promising to fulfill both our emotional and economic needs, marriage seduces women trying to integrate the social and the psychic. But, more often than not, matrimony closes these splits simply by denying them until the contradiction rends not only the bond but the partners. If we could pry apart the couple and the household, if we could separate the complementary figure of difference from the economic institution, perhaps we could begin to articulate the relation between psychic and social needs rather than leaping across the gap to a fictional happy ending.

12

History is Like Mother

Within the literary academy, the term "criticism" refers to what, by the 1960s, was certainly the most commonly practiced form of scholarship: textual interpretation. Outside of literary studies, "literary criticism" is more likely to mean some form of evaluation (the book review) and "criticism" unmodified has the primarily negative sense of fault-finding. When, within the academy, the term "criticism" takes on objective, neutral connotations, the word "critique" takes over the negative functions served by "criticism" outside academic discourse. Feminists writing about literature described our practice as "criticism" in order, I believe, to take advantage of the double sense of the word. It could imply, when necessary, that we were engaged in a negative evaluation, a "critique," of a cultural institution; it could also signify, when appropriate, that we were simply doing what students of literature did. This double sense worked well for a group located on the margins of an institution, expressing our position as at once critical of and obedient to the discipline.

The last anthology we will consider, published in 1987, is entitled *Feminist Issues in Literary Scholarship*. The word "scholarship" in this title replaces the ambiguous "criticism" of the earlier collections. Inside the volume, "scholarship" is most frequently used in an essay by Lillian Robinson, itself entitled "Feminist Criticism." Robinson's thoughts in that piece come out of her "experience as one of five collaborators on a . . . study of feminist scholarship in its first decade." Five feminists working in different academic disciplines produce a book called *Feminist Scholarship: Kindling in the Groves of Academe.*[1] However volatile "feminist scholarship" might be, it is clearly to be found *within* "the groves of academe." "Scholarship" is a general term to describe the practice of academics in diverse disciplines. The phrase "literary scholarship," used by Robinson in her essay and picked up in the anthology's title, locates criticism as one among other academic disciplines.

For the first time, an anthology of feminist literary criticism names itself as academic. These are "Feminist Issues," but they are "Feminist

206

Issues *in* Literary Scholarship." This 1987 anthology is located in the aftermath of the institutionalization of feminist literary study.

In *Feminist Issues* Jane Marcus cites an earlier essay by the collection's editor: "Shari Benstock suggests . . . that academic feminist critics are not marginal in the least."[2] The Benstock essay cited refers to "those of *us* inside the circle (academics who practice feminist literary criticism)."[3] This 1983 essay, Benstock's first statement as editor of *Tulsa Studies in Women's Literature*, notes that Marcus's "work has informed this editorial in a way that will become more apparent, I think, with the publication of Volume 3 of *Tulsa Studies*, a special issue . . ., a volume to which Jane Marcus is contributing an essay" (p. 149 n. 7). This 1983 editorial is also the call for papers for "Volume 3," the 1984 special double issue called "Feminist Issues in Literary Scholarship" which is republished in 1987 as an anthology by the same name. Not just a contributor among others, Marcus "informs" that volume's very conception.

Marcus's contribution to *Feminist Issues* points to another connotation for the title's "scholarship" besides the academic identity we have been pursuing. Earlier in the history of literary studies, criticism and scholarship had been polemically opposed alternatives. By the time feminist "criticism" enters the scene, the terms can be used synonymously to refer to the literary academic's production.[4] Although scholarship and criticism are no longer at odds, by the 1980s a new opposition polarizes literary studies. Marcus opposes "scholarship" to "theory."

Marcus takes theorists to task for slighting scholars: "At present the scholars generously acknowledge the theorists, but theorists, like their brothers, follow the fashionable practice of minimalism in footnoting, often slighting years of scholarship, textual editing, and interpretation without which their own work could not begin" (p. 90). Feminist theorists, no better than their brothers, are modish, impolite, and ungrateful. As bad as all that might be, it is in fact worse. What in the text appears a breach of etiquette, in the footnotes gets politically colored as exploitation:

This minimalism in annotation has the political effect of isolating the critic or theorist from scholars and from the history of scholarship. If present practice in footnoting is a legacy of nineteenth-century capitalist recognition of the ownership of ideas, the minimalism of theorists, as opposed to scholars, represents a new economy of critical exchange in which the work of scholars is fair game (like exploitation of third world countries) and the Big White Men only acknowledge each other. (p. 96 n. 23)

Theorists slight not only scholarship but also "interpretation," i.e., criticism, yet "the critic or theorist" can be isolated from scholars and scholarship. In the polarization of literary studies, the "critic" can go either way. Marcus wants her sister critics, socialist feminist critics she usually calls us, to align ourselves with the scholars. She is acutely aware of the historical antagonism between criticism and scholarship: "It is an ironic turn of events when one declares that a socialist feminist criticism should defend its old enemies, the very bibliographers, editors, textual scholars, biographers, and literary historians who wrote women writers out of history to begin with. But without the survival of these skills and the appropriation of them, women will again lose the history of their own culture. Theory is necessary and useful but is not superior to other literary practice or immune to historical forces" (p. 87). At this point in the history of literary studies, Marcus fears that the old antagonism may lead criticism to a fatal misalliance.

Marcus is not so much attacking theory (she notably concedes here that it is "necessary and useful") as she is arguing against a critical siding with theory against scholarship. The anthology's titular substitution of "scholarship" for "criticism," cementing an alliance between the two terms, is most certainly "informed by Marcus's work." This collection has been taken as an attack on theory,[5] but I see it more precisely, here in Marcus's specification, as a resistance to an alliance with theory that would isolate criticism from scholarship. And what is rather insistently at stake, according to Marcus's formulation, is "history."

"Theory is not immune to historical forces." If Marcus needs to assert something so obvious, it is because she fears that theory is, precisely, passing as transhistorical. "Why this defensive bristling at the historical nature of our enterprise?" she asks (p. 90).

Debunking theory's transcendent immunity, Marcus constructs an intriguing family romance:

I would also like to see a more sisterly relationship develop between feminist theorists and feminist scholars. At present the scholars generously acknowledge the theorists, but theorists, like their brothers, follow the fashionable practice of minimalism in footnoting, often slighting years of scholarship, textual editing, and interpretation without which their own work could not begin. This is a denial of the place of one's own work in literary history, asserting as virgin births interpretations which have ancestry. As Virginia Woolf claimed of art, "masterpieces are not single and solitary births," so one may claim that criticism itself has a familial and cultural history. Perhaps theorists, like the characters in Oscar Wilde's plays, want to be orphaned. It increases the cachet of avant-gardism. (p. 90)

This passage begins by treating theorists and scholars as "sisters," albeit as estranged sisters. The next sentence, quoted earlier, adds brothers to the family. The theorists, not close enough to their sisters, are all too close to their brothers. At this point although the relations are familial, all parties are of the same generation; the significant difference is gender. With the third sentence, theorists are now denying not sisters but "ancestry." Other generations enter the portrait along with "history." "Criticism has a history," and that history is not only cultural but "familial." Returning to the ingrate modishness of "theorists," Marcus claims they want to be not only "virgin births" but "orphans." The scholars who began as unacknowledged sisters have become scorned, denied, or wished-dead parents. The denial of history is here synonymous with the refusal of filial obligation; cultural history parallels familial.

Marcus's essay cites one of the other essays in the anthology. The editor's own essay also cites only one of the other contributions, the same one as Marcus does, Judith Newton's "Making—and Remaking—History." Newton's article is a fine example of research into cultural and familial history. She too is troubled by an ahistorical tendency in feminist criticism. Newton urges us, whom she might with Marcus call "socialist feminist critics," to resist this trend: "We have implicitly committed ourselves to resist English Department formalism—the view that literature and literary critics are divorced from history—a view still perpetuated, despite their air of currency and French fashionableness, by the forms of criticism now dominant in Britain and the United States."[6]

As in Marcus's discussion, denial of history is accompanied by "fashionableness." Newton, however, expects something better from "fashion": "*despite* their fashionableness." Fashionableness after all is precisely the embrace of the historical moment, the rejection of the "unchanging." The problem here is not modishness but that the "currency" is simply an "air," a surface affectation below which remains the conservative belief in the unchanging. Whereas for Marcus, trendiness is negative in its rejection of the past, for Newton it might be, if it were not a sham, a commitment to change and the historical moment. Yet Newton too drapes her cultural history in the trappings of family romance. Where Marcus is offended by a lack of respect for older generations, Newton would set us against "divorce."

Catharine Stimpson's Introduction to this anthology mentions Newton's article first of the volume's essays, before she even gets to the presentation of the collection's contents: "We must . . . act, politically and culturally, in order to change history. Theory and practice must meet, engage each other, wed. Judith Newton's strong essay . . . details such an imperative" (p. 2). In a move explored at length in the preceding chapter, Stimpson would resolve the theory/practice dilemma through matrimonial metaphor. Although she likely means that Newton's essay "details [the] imperative" to change history, the intervening sentence also suggests that Newton's text carries a matrimonial imperative. Such an imperative might indeed view "divorce" in a negative light.

Newton is not the only writer in *Feminist Issues* explicitly to resist divorce from history. Elizabeth Fox-Genovese concludes: "The account of the black woman's self cannot be divorced from the history of that self or the history of the people among whom it took shape."[7] I am not questioning the necessity, which Newton and Fox-Genovese are here affirming, of thinking texts in relation to history. I am, however, interested in the way that, in a feminist context, a separation which is considered objectionable is repeatedly imaged as "divorce."

Fox-Genovese's essay is the first of three at the end of the 1987 volume which were not in the original *Tulsa Studies* special issue, the only one of the three not previously published elsewhere. It is in fact a slightly different version of a chapter in another anthology edited by Benstock a year later.[8] In the context of the 1987 collection whose title locates us within the literary academy and in the context of the present study, we might note that Fox-Genovese, alone of all the writers anthologized in the volumes we have been studying, is from another academic discipline: she is a historian.

Along with Gerda Lerner, Joan Kelly-Gadol, and Nancy Cott, Fox-Genovese is cited as a "theorist of feminist historiography," in Elaine Showalter's contribution to *Feminist Issues*.[9] Appearing immediately after the editor's own contribution, Showalter's essay is an attempt, as its subtitle puts it, at "Writing the History of Feminist Criticism." In this anthology, feminist criticism must attend not only generally to history but first and foremost to its own historicity. Marcus asserts, "criticism itself has a familial and cultural history" (p. 90); and Showalter can be seen precisely as mapping that double history for us.

Showalter begins by claiming for feminist criticism an anomalous family history: "There is no Mother of Feminist Criticism" (p. 31). The absence of a mother is not in itself, in this context, anomalous; the other modern criticisms to which she compares us have no mother either, but they all have, according to her, a father. "We do not derive our charter from a single authority or a body of sacred theoretical texts. There is no . . . fundamental work against which one can measure other feminisms."[10] Feminist criticism is, in the familial terms with which this book likes to express our cultural history, an orphan. Showalter clearly considers this a real advantage; we are freer because we have no model to obey.

Not every feminist critic prefers us unmothered. In 1981 Jane Marcus asserts: "As a literary critic, Virginia Woolf is the mother of us all."[11] Toril Moi, in her 1985 book, shares Marcus's sense of the homage due Woolf: "she has yet to be adequately welcomed and acclaimed by her feminist daughters in England and America. . . . A feminist criticism that would do both justice and homage to its great mother and sister: this, surely, should be our goal."[12]

In Benstock's volume, Marcus's discussion of the desire to be orphaned focuses specifically on two theorists who "reject explicitly Woolf's role as foremother of feminist criticism in *A Room of One's Own*. There she outlines 'thinking back through our mothers' as writing practice for feminist critics . . . and shows us how to do feminist criticism. . . . What they seem unable to accept is their own daughterhood as critics to Woolf's role as the mother of socialist feminist criticism" (p. 89). For Marcus, there is a mother as well as a "fundamental work against which one can measure other feminisms." That "foremother" prescribes, precisely, that we "think back through our mothers."

The 1978 anthology *Feminist Criticism* opens with Margret Andersen's statement: "the literary critic who first used feminism as a criterion was, to my knowledge, Christine de Pisan."[13] Pisan, Andersen goes on to tell us, was born in 1364. We are then lead on a quick tour of six centuries of feminist criticism which concludes: "It is evident from this brief survey that a tradition of feminist critique exists" (p. 4). A decade later, Stimpson—introducing *Feminist Issues in Literary Scholarship*—

repeats Andersen's gesture, upping the *ante*. The 1987 anthology opens: "Feminist literary criticism in the West . . . begins with Sappho in the mid-seventh century B.C." (p. 1). After some verses from Sappho, Stimpson's second paragraph begins: "Despite the length of its lineage, feminist criticism did not become a force with a name until the mid-twentieth century A.D. One of its two major texts was *A Room of One's Own* . . . the second was *The Second Sex.* . . . Signifying the lack of a history that might have bonded women to each other was the brevity of *The Second Sex*'s one-sentence response to the prior text."

For the presentation of feminist criticism, Andersen and Stimpson go back and claim a long "lineage" precisely to repair the absence of a "history." The difference between the two terms is not so much that "lineage" is familial, since feminist critics repeatedly cast our history in familial terms, but rather a matter of record, of recognition and "naming." When Marcus's theorists deny their ancestry, they refuse to record their lineage in "history."

Stimpson's Beauvoir bears a certain resemblance to Marcus's theorists. Not only does she slight the work that went before her, but "notably, even notoriously, Beauvoir's language . . . balloon[s] towards 'brotherhood' while jettisoning 'sisterhood.' . . . *The Second Sex* erases women from history" (p. 2). Stimpson sees contemporary feminist critics "negotiating between" Beauvoir and Woolf, "although writers within colleges and universities are more apt to resemble Beauvoir." Herself well within the academy—at the time of publication, a dean; as I write, the president of the MLA— Stimpson clearly prefers Woolf, and not just for reasons of style. "Woolf's grasp of history, if narrower than de Beauvoir's, is often hardier" (p. 1).

Having taken us from Sappho to Beauvoir and Woolf, having shown us where Woolf goes beyond Beauvoir, Stimpson, in a move typical of anthology introductions, segues from the lineage to a discussion of the essays which follow: "Such ideas form the matrix for much of the thinking in *Feminist Issues in Literary Scholarship*. In 'Still Practice . . .' an act of homage to Virginia Woolf, Jane Marcus calls for critics to accept the '. . . authority of the female text.' Marcus must be read against Judith Kegan Gardiner's study of the ambivalence of one female creator, Doris Lessing, towards the mother, an authority in the female text and time" (p. 3, second ellipsis Stimpson's).

"Such ideas" is ambiguous: it might refer to Woolf's ideas in *A Room*, discussed in the paragraph which immediately precedes this statement; it might refer to all the ideas of the lineage discussed up to this point in the Introduction. In either case, the "matrix" is a sort of "thinking back through our mothers"; we might recall the etymological sense of "matrix." Stimpson then, immediately, mentions Marcus's essay. The phrase Stimpson quotes from Marcus directs us to this sentence: "these critics deny the authority of the female text, they deny the motherhood of the author of the text" (p. 89). "Marcus must be read against Gardiner's study": Stimpson wants us to attend to this contrast in attitudes toward female authority. If some critics prefer us mothered, some writers are ambivalent on that head.

Stimpson's appositive to the mother in Gardiner's study—"an authority in the female text and time"—is quite puzzling. The phrase "authority in the female text" recalls the previous sentence's "authority of the female text," bringing the two close together so we might better read them "against" each other. The "time," however, both evocative and ambiguous in the extreme, does not refer to anything else in the paragraph. Does "and time" mean "in the female text and the female time" or does it mean "and an authority in time"?

The first reading does not strike me as particularly likely, but it does connect to the phrase "women's time," which Showalter features prominently in her essay:

> We need to begin by seeing feminist criticism from within . . . women's time instead of as a subset of standard critical time. The history of feminist criticism is more than a history of ideas or institutions; it takes in events on many levels of women's daily lives. But to limit ourselves to women's time would be equally misleading, since feminist criticism is also constituted by the histories of the academy, the discipline, and modern criticism itself. . . . [F]eminist criticism . . . has both a Mother and a Father time. (Showalter, p. 33)

"Women's time" would seem to refer to the "many levels of women's daily lives" as opposed to "a history of ideas or institutions." At the end of this passage it is personified as Mother Time. "Mother" here might be said to be, in a certain uncertain interpretation of Stimpson, "an authority in the female time."

Showalter is playing with the classic personification of time as Father Time, reminding us that history has been "his story," not hers. A similar gesture is made in the 1978 anthology which begins with Christine de Pisan where the dedication reads: "To MOTHERTIME whose pendulum is beginning to swing." Yet Showalter also makes women's time a mother in order rhetorically to strengthen her assertion that we need two models: one male and one female. "Women's time" could remain separate from what she calls not "men's time" but "standard critical time"; these two phrases belong to radically different associations. But when she wants to persuade us not to "limit ourselves" but to embrace both models, her metaphor appeals to our ideological "common sense": you can't have (or you wouldn't want?) a mother without a father. Mother Time ought not be divorced from Father Time?

Let us return to the second possible interpretation of Stimpson's phrase: "the mother, an authority in time." This reading, which seems the more likely to me, is unclear in its reference. Half a page later, Stimpson again uses the word "time," equally ungarnished, when she lists differences among women not yet sufficiently addressed by feminist critics: "religion matters; colonization matters . . . time matters" (p. 3). In this case, "time" would seem to mean something like "historical moment," and she would thus be calling for an attention to historical change and specificity like Newton does. In any case, I assume that "time," in the maternal authority context, must be connected to "history." Such a vague yet powerful connection echoes an entire register of Gardiner's article which functions as a sort of matrix for the present chapter. Although Gardiner often, and variously, links mother and "history," only once does she use the word "time" in connection to the mother, and then in the most offhand of manners.

"Time" shows up in Gardiner's discussion of Lessing's potboiler *Particularly Cats*: "Talking of cats, it seems, Lessing allows herself to slip into careless conventions that she otherwise examines more scrupulously. This carelessness helps the critic, because it means that here Lessing leaves unprocessed chunks of ideology lying exposed in her prose. . . . Time and time again, Lessing judges her cats by how well they mother their kittens."[14]

What Lessing is careful not to say directly about human females, she feels free to say about cats. One of the "chunks of ideology" exposed is Lessing's subscription to the belief that, to be good, a woman must be a good mother. Gardiner throws in the phrase "time and time again" to emphasize repetition. The phrase itself is, to be sure, utterly marginal to the discussion of motherhood and ideology Gardiner is pursuing, but the very notion of repetition, the idea that "time again" will be just like "time," is in fact central to the difficult nexus she is here trying to think through.

These "unprocessed" chunks of ideology are lying around, it is implied, because Lessing has not yet worked them through. The ideology is residual, belonging to an earlier idea of women than otherwise characterizes Lessing's thinking. Lessing repeats these ideas, unprocessed, unwittingly. She repeats them precisely because she does not process them. In order not to repeat we must process: "History is like mother: if we don't understand her, we are doomed to repeat her" (p. 121).

Gardiner's consideration of Lessing's cats is also a reconsideration of "mothering theory." We could take as the fundamental text of mothering theory Chodorow's 1978 *The Reproduction of Mothering* which, as the title implies, is about repetition. The ideologically supported mode of parenting produces daughters with fluid boundaries between themselves and their mothers. This prepares those daughters to grow up to be good mothers, capable of the sort of empathy which the institution of motherhood demands. Thus, time and time again, motherhood reproduces itself.

Gardiner finds mothering theory useful but also critiques it: "I think the chief defect of mother-daughter theory is that it separates empathy from history, according to conventional stereotypes: women become their mothers; whereas men go off to conquer the world. . . . According to this theory, empathy belongs to women, history to men" (p. 117). Mothering theory supports a gendered dichotomy: one can either become mother or join history. Four pages later, in her closing paragraph, Gardiner provocatively asserts "history is like mother," insisting upon a connection between the separate spheres.

If, in her discussion of Gardiner's essay, Stimpson uses the word "time" with such vague reference it is perhaps because there is an aspect of Gardiner she wants to represent even if she doesn't precisely know how. "Gender, Value, and Lessing's Cats" is centrally about both mother and history. Gardiner closes her essay with a plea to connect the two. The final paragraph begins with the stunning "History is like mother," then briefly summarizes the relation between history and empathy in the works by Lessing she has considered. Then, without even a paragraph break, she goes on: "And this returns us to the importance of the paradigms through which we understand our world. If we do not incorporate gender into our model of history, we may relapse into . . . sexism. . . . But if, on the other hand, we feminists do not incorporate history into our model of gender, we are doomed to simple repetition" (p. 122). Not only must we, living our lives, try to connect the separate domains of empathy and history, but our theorizing must likewise attempt to combine mothering theory with the study of history.

Gardiner's essay ends here, with this call to double our paradigms, and is immediately followed by Judith Newton's essay. Newton's first two pages decry feminist criticism's tendency toward unchanging, essentialist constructions, and then she begins a new paragraph on a positive note: "there have been important counters to this." The "important counters" to ahistorical formalism are represented as dual by Newton's next two sentences:

> Theories of gender construction advanced by feminist theorists like Nancy Chodorow, Dorothy Dinnerstein, and Jane Flax have re-emphasized the idea that gender identity and ideologies of gender . . . are socially constructed. . . . Feminist history by historians like Mary Ryan and Judith Walkowitz, meanwhile, has countered the ahistorical quality of much feminist psychoanalytic theory by illuminating the ways in which constructions of gender . . . have changed with changing historical situations. (pp. 125–26)

After these two separate if not quite equal sentences, Newton's paragraph concludes: "Together these developments in feminist theory and feminist history . . . provide a more adequate and helpful model . . . than our current implicit focus on the unchanging, the universal, and the monolithic." All three of the "feminist theorists" listed in the first sentence in fact specifically do "mothering theory." Like Gardiner, Newton proposes a combination of mothering theory and history as the basis for feminist criticism.

That Judith Gardiner and Judith Newton should take up this same position is particularly interesting when read against the roles they play in the roughly contemporaneous Greene and Kahn anthology. *Making a Difference* came out in 1985; *Feminist Issues in Literary Scholarship* was published in 1987, but both Gardiner's and Newton's essays were included in the 1984 *Tulsa Studies* special issue. In the Greene and Kahn volume, where each essay represents a different trend within feminist criticism, Gardiner's contribution represents psychoanalytic feminism, in particular mothering theory and its impact on literary criticism. Not a contributor to the 1985 anthology, Newton nonetheless plays a major role in the article immediately following Gardiner's, Cora Kaplan's consideration of socialist feminist criticism. Discussing the split between the social and the psychic in feminist criticism, Kaplan contrasts Newton's reading of *Villette* with Mary Jacobus's: Jacobus's is psychoanalytic, Newton's historical.

In 1985 Kaplan is longing for a feminist criticism that could combine psychoanalysis with history. Gardiner, who could speak for psychoanalysis with not a worry about history, and Newton, who is seen as disregarding the psychic for the sociohistorical, meet to express the same wish as Kaplan, in another book, but at the same moment in the history of feminist criticism. When we join Newton not to Jacobus but to Gardiner, we bring history together not only with the psyche but with mother.

Gardiner closes her essay in *Making a Difference* by bringing us back to her title, "Mind mother," commenting, "as daughters and sons, we automatically resent such a demand."[15] Contrasting Marcus and Gardiner in *Feminist Issues*, Stimpson repeats the word "authority": "Marcus calls for critics to accept the 'authority of the female text.' Marcus must be read against Judith Kegan Gardiner's study of the ambivalence of one female creator, Doris Lessing, towards the mother, an authority in the female text and time" (p. 3). Accepting authority, especially maternalized authority, can mean obeying, minding mother. The mother's "authority in time" might mean that since she is older, has more experience, she must be accepted as knowing better, and followed. That obedience can be conservative, dooming the daughter to repeat the mother. History might function as the same sort of authority. The phrase "history tells us" has been used to rule out possibilities, keeping us within the confines of what has already been.

Both mother and history, for Gardiner, function as models. There are two ways to embrace a model: imitate it or study it. In "thinking back through our mothers," as Marcus recommends in Woolf's words, do we think in identification with our mothers? Or do we think them through, analyze them, so we, in Gardiner's words, "can understand [our] mothers and change to become better mothers than [our] own mothers were" (p. 122)? A decade earlier Gardiner wrote: " 'We think back through our mothers.' . . . We have yet to think forward through them."[16]

Feminist Issues in Literary Scholarship resounds with the call to history. Sometimes history is opposed to theory, in this volume; sometimes there is the demand or the wish that the two be conjoined. In either case, the call and its intrication with the question of theory typifies this moment of academic feminist criticism, a moment we might locate around 1985.

In the pages of this anthology, Stimpson, Showalter, Nina Baym, Marcus, Gardiner, Newton, Robinson, and Fox-Genovese all call feminist literary criticism to an accounting with history. Beside this clarion call can also be found traces of a quiet rebellion against history. Whereas Newton and Fox-Genovese insist that literature ought not be divorced from it, a few critics in the collection seem to find some sort of liberation in an escape from history.

Between Marcus's and Gardiner's essays lies Josephine Donovan's cultural feminist program, "Toward a Women's Poetics." In this attempt to characterize a women's writing practice, appearing first in the 1984 *Tulsa Studies* special issue, Donovan refers to another article she published that same year on Sarah Orne Jewett: "Using [the] notion that the traditional woman's sense of time is repetitive or cyclic rather than linear (the time of the quest), I suggest that Jewett's plots be understood as reflective of the traditional woman's consciousness. Ultimately, I argue, Jewett's greatest works concern an escape from the androcentric time of history into transcending gynocentric space."[17]

The gendered contrast between repetitive and quest time is the same one we find in Gardiner between reproducing mother and "going off to conquer the world." But whereas Gardiner urges us to escape repetition and become part of history, Donovan seems to value the escape from history. The notion of women's time here resembles the one used by Showalter. Showalter recommends constructing a history according to women's time, but Donovan sees this time leading us ultimately, and in the best cases, beyond history, perhaps even beyond time itself. The framing of the escape—"from the androcentric time of history into gynocentric space"—does not logically imply but nonetheless rhetorically suggests that time itself, in contradistinction to space, is androcentric.

Although cultural feminism might wish to escape time, and thus history as change through time, as well as history as dramatic world-conquering event, it does not seek to escape the past. On the contrary. Donovan's women's poetics is based in "traditional women's experience and practice in the past" (p. 100). Cultural feminist theory tends to imply that what women have been and done is what women ought to do or be. Respect for our history in the sense of what has been here threatens our participation in history in the sense of movement in time.

Jewett's escape from time into space is echoed elsewhere in the volume. Showalter divides feminist literary criticism into two types, gynocritics and gynesis: "Gynocritics is, roughly speaking, historical in orientation. . . . Gynesis rejects . . . the temporal dimension of women's experience . . . and seeks instead to understand the space granted to the feminine in the symbolic contract" (p. 37). "Gynocritics," her own coining, is used to name what Showalter herself and others like her do. She borrows Alice Jardine's word "gynesis" to represent feminist critics working under the sign of French poststructuralist theory.[18] Showalter's "gynesis" closely resembles what Marcus calls theory. Marcus's two examples of theorists who deny their own history—Gayatri Spivak and Peggy Kamuf—are avowed poststructuralists both. Although Showalter makes an attempt to be fair to this other side, and is certainly less dismissive of poststructuralist feminism than she was in 1979 or 1981,[19] her preference remains unmistakable.

Donovan's challenge to history could perhaps be overlooked as merely a token inclusion of the cultural feminist perspective which, if a major force in 1980s feminist thought, is wrong-headed and ahistorical ("comedic essentialism," Newton calls it, p. 125). Gynesis's rejection of the temporal dimension is likewise included as part of an attempt to give some time (if not quite equal) to the other side. Neither of these seriously challenge the hegemony of historicism in *Feminist Issues in Literary Scholarship*. But there are two other escapes from history in the volume, which cannot be dismissed quite so easily: one from the periphery and the other echoing it from the very center. I will turn to the margins first.

Laurie Finke's 1986 response to the 1984 "Feminist Issues in Literary Scholarship" locates in that *Tulsa Studies* special issue a "center" and "margins": "The 'center' of the issue is taken up with nine articles, all by prominent white female critics. . . . In the margins of the text are the book reviews to which are relegated women of color (there is one review on works by black feminist critics), lesbians (there is one review of a book on Radclyffe Hall), men (three of the reviewers are men and four books by men are reviewed), and women writers before 1800 (three reviews)" (Finke, p. 254). When the issue comes out as a book in 1987, none of the reviews are included, but one of the reviewers now has an article in the collection. The only one to survive marginal status is Hortense Spillers, author of the "one review on works by black feminist critics."[20]

Finke's tableau is slightly more complicated than its binary distinction might suggest. When Finke turns to the margins, it at first appears that subject matter is what counts. For the first two marginal categories she mentions only subject, however when she reaches the third category, she counts both author and subject. In the final category, she need not specify. Finke, in fact, is the author of a book review, on writers before 1800, in this issue of *Tulsa Studies*.

Finke does not mention the subject matter of the "central" articles; here she focuses instead on the authors' identity. Aside from the issue of author versus subject, only two of her marginal categories reply directly to her portrait of the center. She does not comment on the sexual orientation of the central critics and she could hardly complain that they all write after 1800. Finke characterizes the center as "articles by prominent white females." Benstock publishes Finke's critique in *Tulsa Studies* in 1986. Looking at the 1987 version, following Finke, I would say that Benstock seems interested in remedying the "white" but not the "female."[21]

The nine articles of the *Tulsa Studies* special issue are, in the 1987 anthology, followed by three additional articles, which thus literally occupy the place of the 1984 book reviews. All three of these new articles deal with black women and/or race. But the middle one is also written by a "woman of color," by the only nonwhite female writing in the 1984 *Tulsa Studies*, Hortense Spillers.

Spillers's essay, originally published in *Feminist Studies* in 1983, is a study of three novels: Zora Neale Hurston's *Their Eyes Were Watching God* (1937), Margaret Walker's *Jubilee* (1966), and Toni Morrison's *Sula* (1973). Before turning to the novels, Spillers warns her readers: "The scheme of these observations . . . is not strictly chronological."[22] In fact, Spillers's "scheme" is in rebellion against chronological order. One of her central points is that Janie, the heroine of the 1937 novel, is located midway between Walker's Vyry Ware and Morrison's Sula. And in terms that have to do with development and progress: *Jubilee*'s female protagonist is traditional; Sula is something new; Hurston's heroine falls right in-between. Spillers's explicitly anti-chronological method runs directly counter to Judith Newton's exhortations to understand a work in its time.[23]

Ending the paragraph which begins with her warning that she will not be "strictly chronological," Spillers makes it clear that this is not a casual gesture but implies a certain politics: "Ironically, it is exactly the right *not* to accede to the simplifications and mystifications of a strictly historiographical time line that now promises the greatest freedom of discourse to black people, to black women, as critics, teachers, writers, and thinkers" (p. 183). Her repetition of the adverb "strictly" contrasts effectively with "freedom" to suggest history might also be a discipline in the sense of that which keeps us in line.[24]

Spillers is not the only critic in the volume to suggest violating chronological order. The first essay in the collection, "Beyond the Reaches of Feminist Criticism," proposes we read Hurston's contemporary, Gertrude Stein, out of order: "If we take Stein out of her modernist setting . . . Stein seems to be one of our contemporaries" (pp. 25–26). This critic is working to free Stein from other feminist critics: "Her work has been recovered by . . . feminist critics who, however refreshing their sensitivity to Stein as a woman within a patriarchal framework, have continued to discuss her work within the confines of the modernist project. That is, her work has been viewed as the product of her historical situation; she has remained 'contemporary' with her contemporaries" (p. 25). The word "confines" here could suggest, like Spillers's "strictly," that respect for historical context can operate as a form of constraint.

I have used Finke's mapping to show how Spillers exemplifies the margins of Benstock's anthology. We might be prepared to see this black challenge to historicism join cultural feminism and poststructuralism as token inclusions, of restricted effect upon the volume's hegemonic center. But the reader of Stein who joins Spillers in her lack of respect for chronology is none other than Shari Benstock, the volume's editor, herself.

In counting nine articles as the center, Finke does not include Benstock's which, presented as "From the Editor's Perspective" in the 1984 *Tulsa Studies*, looks like some sort of introduction. Although Finke never mentions Benstock's essay, we might still use her mapping to locate it. If the book reviews, after the articles proper, are a marginal edge of the special issue, so too is this text, preceding the real articles, which is about Gertrude Stein and treats her writing as specifically lesbian. We might thus keep Finke's notion that lesbians are relegated to the margin. But we would be forced to contemplate the possibility of an editor marginalizing herself.

In 1987, when the issue is republished as a book, Benstock's text is essentially unchanged. But the tag "From the Editor's Perspective" has been removed and the piece is now preceded by Stimpson's Introduction. Like Spillers, Benstock moves from margin to full-fledged article. Yet it strains our notions of tokenism to see the editor's inclusion as merely token. In order to understand this editor and her "marginal" place in her own anthology we may have to rethink marginality and editorial authority. In 1983, Benstock's first text under the tag "From the Editor's Perspective" ends with her call for the special issue that would become "Feminist Issues in Literary Scholarship." In the last sentence of that first editorial, she writes: "Most especially, I hope that *Tulsa Studies* will resist the re-establishment of the old centrality under a new guise."[25]

In the present study, "around 1981" locates a moment when feminist criticism attains some sort of centrality. And, in the present study, that moment is centrally connected to the figure of Elaine Showalter. Showalter is, in every sense of the word, framed by the present book which describes a structure radiating from that moment. In that moment, the first section of this book, are two anthologies: Showalter's *New Feminist Criticism* and Abel's *Writing and Sexual Difference*. Showalter's strategy as an editor is unabashedly to claim centrality for herself. Her anthology contains not only her introduction but two other pieces by her, each heading a section, each interpreting and directing the path of feminist criticism. One of those Showalter texts, the one dating from 1981 ("Feminist Criticism in the Wilderness"), also appears in Abel's anthology, immediately following Abel's introduction. At the back of Benstock's 1987 collection, in the notes on contributors, we read that Elaine Showalter "is editor of *Writing and Sexual Difference* and an anthology, *The New Feminist Criticism*" (p. 234).

Showalter's essay in *Feminist Issues in Literary Scholarship*, like her essay in *Writing and Sexual Difference*, appears directly after the editor's text and is, like "Feminist Criticism in the Wilderness," an overview of feminist literary criticism. Benstock repeats Abel's placement of Showalter; the lapsus in the contributors' notes might then imagine the most dramatic marginalizing of an editor from her own anthology.

Of all the anthologies we have considered, *Feminist Issues in Literary Scholarship* is the only one to have an introduction by someone other than the editor. Benstock has given up the privilege (or the responsibility) of taking stock of and speaking for the collection as a whole. Her own contribution is entitled "Beyond the Reaches of Feminist Criticism: A Letter from Paris," thus doubly suggesting something from outside American feminist criticism. And if "gynesis" names something marginalized in this volume, it is worth noting that Benstock opens with an epigraph from Jardine's "Gynesis."[26]

Referring to the male theoretical masters (French, poststructuralist) behind "gynesis," Benstock has occasion to discuss marginality: "If some of these men align themselves and their theoretical practice with *les marginaux* in western culture, we suspect it is only to secure for themselves a firmer grip on the center of theoretical discourse" (p. 9). She thus suggests one possible motive for self-marginalization: in order better to occupy the center. Yet Benstock does not simply align herself with the margins.

Benstock explicitly asks: "Do we claim the center for ourselves (taking up the modernist project) or do we redefine the limits of authority by which the center constitutes itself (taking up the post-modernist project)? Or do we, like Gertrude Stein, try to do both?" (p. 12). Refusing to claim the center for herself, Benstock would be a thoroughly postmodern editor. Yet it is pretty clear that, to the extent that Benstock marks one of the alternatives as superior, the right answer is "try to do both, like Gertrude Stein."

Virginia Woolf is Marcus's model for feminist criticism; Benstock's model is Gertrude Stein. Benstock's essay cites Catharine Stimpson as someone "currently at work on a book-length study of Stein." If Benstock asks Stimpson to replace her in the Introduction, it undoubtedly has something to do with the Stein connection. In the Introduction Stimpson names Stein as a model for the feminist criticism she would like to see and links that model to a certain Woolf: "Calling its own premises and proto-canons into question, such a revisionary feminist criticism would *honor* both the more ironic, ludic Virginia Woolf and the radically innovative Gertrude Stein. It would *follow Stein's injunction*: . . . 'Act so that there is no use in a center'" (p. 5, emphasis added). Despite the anticentric content of her "injunction," Stein, like Marcus's Woolf, appears here as an authority we ought to follow.

How does one *follow*, especially how does one *honor* "radical innovation"? Where Stimpson asks us to "follow" Stein, giving her priority, Benstock's rebellion against history might make it possible to think of Stein as following us. When she imagines Stein as a postmodernist, as one of our contemporaries, she recreates Stein in our image; we become the model for Stein.

Benstock would seem to belong to the perhaps marginal camp in this collection who rebel against authority in time. Marcus, on the other hand, is squarely among those who call us to account for being disrespectful of history and our elders. Yet we cannot in any way simply polarize Benstock and Marcus. Not only does the editor credit Marcus with "informing the conception" of the anthology, but there is also a solidarity between Marcus's model feminist critic and Benstock's postmodern Stein.

Marcus proposes an approach she calls "still practice": "*A Room of One's Own* is 'still practice.' . . . This concept of 'still practice' . . . is a model for feminist criticism. It demands the suppression of the critic's ego in a genuine attempt at explicating the signs of the subject, her body, her text. It is a frustrating and selfless activity" (p. 80). It is precisely this selflessness which rejoins Benstock's Stein: "Oddly enough, this new reading of Stein writes an ironic afterword to that early Stein criticism that accused her of having an ego as big as the Ritz. In order to make the kind of . . . discoveries I am claiming she did make, Gertrude Stein had to renounce ego" (p. 26).

Whereas Marcus's feminist critic renounces ego in order to listen to "oppressed women," Stein "submitted her will to language" (pp. 80, 16–17). I do not want to deny the crucial differences between these two renunciations: the one moral, the other postmodernist. Yet I find the connections striking and I credit them particularly because of the way Benstock and Marcus cite each other in such comradely fashion. Whether or not Marcus's "selfless activity" can describe Stein, it might more properly characterize Benstock, the heterosexual critic speaking in defense of a lesbian's power. According to Marcus, the feminist critic ought to speak on behalf of her more marginalized sisters, "women of color and lesbians" (p. 79).

Marcus's title—"Still Practice, A/Wrested Alphabet"—comes from Shakespeare's *Titus Andronicus*. Raped, without tongue or arms, Lavinia makes bodily gestures to Titus, her father, who asserts: "I, of these, will wrest an alphabet,/And by still practice learn to know thy meaning."[27] Marcus comments: "The story is not a pretty one, but it does give us a vivid image for the feminist critic and her relation to oppressed women" (p. 80). I am struck by Marcus's placing "the feminist critic" outside the category of "oppressed women." "Oppressed women" are those not only raped but silenced; because the feminist critic still has her tongue and arms she is not oppressed. It is our responsibility to speak for, care for, and defend "oppressed women," like Titus, the father.

Perhaps Titus can be the father of feminist criticism because his "still practice" in attending to his daughter is so motherly. Unlike fathers or children, mothers have traditionally been valued for their selfless activity in caring for others. It is this resemblance to the ideological construction of the good woman as good mother even more than Titus's gender that disturbs me in Marcus's construction of the good feminist as selfless caretaker of those who cannot speak for themselves.

Stimpson's Introduction asks us to read Marcus against Judith Gardiner. The latter seems particularly aware of the ideological functioning of motherliness. Her study of Lessing's work begins with the 1960 story "Our Friend Judith." Her reading of that story concludes with a paragraph that contains one or two of the enigmatic but suggestive phrases that I consider Gardiner's critical signature:

> The story does not devalue Judith for being unmarried; rather, it shows her as an admirable new woman. However, its attitudes to motherhood are ambivalent. . . . [T]he incident of the cat who killed her kitten exposes Judith's thwarted maternity as the essence of her character. Only in attending the birthing cat . . . does she evoke our sympathy. . . . We, the motherly, understand people as do the narrator and her friend Betty. Judith does not. . . . [S]ince she cannot understand others, she is doomed to remain a fictional character, not a motherly creator. (p.119)

Suddenly, in the middle of the interpretation, a first person plural pronoun appears, representing a community of readers. Its first occurrence is ordinary enough: "evoke our sympathy." But with its next appearance this collective subject particularizes itself in a rather startling way: "we, the motherly." Not just those who may have read the story but those who are, as opposed to those who aren't, "motherly."

I find the phrase—"we, the motherly"—powerful and puzzling. It probably is to be taken ironically since Gardiner criticizes a certain ideological complicity here. It clearly includes Gardiner and is perhaps part of some sort of self-criticism. I recall that, in the biographical sketches of the 1978 anthology *Feminist Criticism*, the entry for Judith Kegan Gardiner concludes: "Her mother and two daughters are among her heroines, she states" (p. 354).

Gardiner concludes her reading of Judith on the diacritical distinction "a fictional character, not a motherly creator." Here the irony is even less certain. The categories are theoretically fascinating if not referentially clear. My association is to Gardiner's pithy and evocative formulation "The hero is her author's daughter," the refined distillation of her attempt to apply psychoanalytic to literary theory.[28] Since "creator" seems the more attractive category, "motherly" would be a positive trait. Or else, and I cannot disallow this possibility, the irony has extremely wide repercussions.

"A fictional character, not a motherly creator" joins "the hero is her author's daughter" and "history is like mother" as phrases by Gardiner which unleash in me a flood of thought. Gardiner tends to set these jewels in her prose with little explanation. For me they sparkle with the promise of a wealth of understanding, like minimalist poems, tight and compact, set in but discontinuous from a discursive context. Of all these, "we, the motherly" is probably the most minimalist of all. I can barely begin to imagine what Gardiner wishes to suggest by it. But, if puzzling, it is nonetheless pertinent, for it is not the only "motherly we" in the volume.

Criticizing the place allotted to the mother in psychoanalytic feminist theory, Nina Baym writes: "Of course we all know, in our rational moments, that the mother's influence lasts far beyond the age of five. But even if we were to grant its waning at that age, we surely know that the mother's role in the child's earliest life is not so simple as this pre-Oedipal model makes it out to be. (At least we who have been mothers know.)"[29] The passage begins by evoking a community of reasonable people, or at least of people who have rational moments. The first "we" is broadly inclusive, rhetorically calling her readers to join her in finding this psychoanalytic model ridiculous. The "we" insists, occurring four times in the space of three sentences. The insistence builds ("we all know," "we surely know"), implicitly mocking not only the pre-Oedipal model, but anyone who might abstain from the "we." And then the parenthesis renders the "we" exclusive.

Baym's "motherly we" reads mothering theory: "recent feminist literary work on mothers and daughters . . . provides testimony, often unwitting and in contradiction to its stated intentions, of the deep-seated hostility of daughters to mothers. (Mothers do not speak of daughters in this discourse.) Adrienne Rich's *Of Woman Born* . . . is strikingly cold when not silent on the writer's own mother. Nor does Rich's poetry speak to her mother" (p. 57). The parenthesis in this passage perhaps refers to the one a page earlier, quoted above. In contradistinction to Baym's text, mothering theory is not spoken by a motherly subject. "We who have been mothers" read this discourse and remark the hostility to mothers: "What purpose does the theory . . . serve? It minimizes the mother" (p. 56). The motherly reading ultimately unveils the pre-Oedipal mother as itself Oedipal, constructed according to the daughter's classic Oedipal wish: "The matricidal impulse could not be plainer" (p. 58).

The citation of Rich is surprising. Rich, after all, writes *Of Woman*

Born explicitly as a mother, albeit as a mother of sons. Baym, however, reads not Rich the mother but Rich the daughter. The latter is not appreciative enough. The comments about Rich bespeak another aspect of motherly discourse; the flip side of self-suppression is bitterness and resentment. Here is a tone likely to produce guilt in "today's feminist daughter-critic" (p. 58).

Baym is worried about the future: "There is no future for a commonality of women if we cannot traverse the generations" (p. 58). Marcus specifically closes her essay on a model of generational traversal: "One after the other [feminist critics] have climbed in the pantry window of literary criticism taking note of the muddy footprints of their predecessors. It is in this way that literary criticism moves from one generation to the next, affirming its mothers' works and moving them along" (p. 94).

Although Baym's explicit complaint, and Marcus's too, would seem to be with theory, that protest is accompanied by a psychologically more effective complaint: feminist critics are not good daughters to their mothers. Whereas Baym largely restricts herself to negative examples, Marcus cites appropriate daughterly behavior. If Woolf is the mother of feminist criticism, Marcus nominates Sylvia Townsend Warner as number one daughter: "[Townsend Warner's] 'Women as Writers' is not a seductive sapphistry like *A Room of One's Own*, but in its own dry, wryly ironic way it continues the work of its predecessor as feminist criticism. It modestly apprentices itself (we might say 'daughters itself') to its mother text and brings up to date the history of women writers" (p. 92).

The feminist critic must renounce ego not only in the service of (more) oppressed women but also in apprenticeship to the predecessor. Daughterliness is next to motherliness. If the good daughter modestly apprentices herself to the good mother, then she will be a good feminist. We, the daughterly, resemble the motherly, but as pale imitations, dry rather than seductive, lacking the mother's power, except through identification.

Feminist Issues in Literary Scholarship gives another example of good daughterly writing. According to Spillers, "*Jubilee* is, in effect, the tale translated of the author's female ancestors. This is a story of the foremothers, a celebration of their stunning faith and intractable powers of endurance. . . . The source material for the novel is based on the life story of the author's great-grandmother, told to her by her grandmother in the best tradition of oral his/herstory" (pp. 191, 205). Walker's heroine, Vyry Ware, is heroically maternal: "Vyry and Randall Ware . . . have two children . . . and Ware makes plans for their liberation. His idea is that he or Vyry will return for the children later, but Vyry refuses to desert them. Her negotiation of a painful passage across the countryside . . . groans with material burden. . . . Vyry travels with the two children— Jim toddling and the younger child Minna in her arms" (p. 190). Not only a literal good mother, Vyry is figuratively and symbolically motherly: "Vyry Ware belongs to, embodies, a corporate ideal. The black woman in her characterization exists for the race, in its behalf, and in maternal relationship to its profoundest needs and wishes" (p. 182).

Neither the daughterly Walker nor the motherly Ware are Spillers's heroes. Sensitive and appreciative with all three of the novels she considers, Spillers makes her preference clear, from the first paragraph: "*Sula* . . . is, to my mind, the single most important irruption of black women's writing in our era. . . . the novel inscribes a dimension of being, moving at last in contradistinction to the tide of virtue and pathos that tends to overwhelm black female characterization in a monolith of terms and possibilities. I regard Sula the character as a literal and figurative *breakthrough* toward the assertion of what we may call, in relation to her literary 'relatives,' new female being" (p. 181).

Spillers celebrates Sula as a "breakthrough" precisely in contradistinction to the "ideal" exemplified by Walker's Vyry Ware. "If Vyry is woman-for-the-other, then Sula is woman-for-self" (p. 182). This contrast is articulated specifically in relation to motherliness: "Vyry Ware . . . embodies a corporate ideal. The black woman in her characterization exists for the race . . . and in maternal relationship to its profoundest needs . . . . Sula, on the other hand, lives for Sula and has no wish to 'mother' anyone, let alone the black race in some symbolic concession to a collective need" (p. 182).

Sula is a bad woman. Her "badness" (p. 183) involves her "nubile *singleness* and refusal of the acts and rites of maternity" (p. 200). A white academic critic articulates her own badness in similar terms: "I enjoyed thinking of myself as a bad woman; never until recently, did I admit that it was never 'bad' to refuse to be 'good' in the self-mutilating way young women were raised to be in the 1950s. I never wanted to be a caretaker; I never saw myself as a wife or a mother, and I never was one."[30]

Like the article on Sula, this statement by Nina Auerbach was not in the 1984 version of "Feminist Issues in Literary Scholarship." The acknowledgments to the 1987 volume state that, of the original *Tulsa Studies* articles, Auerbach's and Baym's are "in slightly altered forms." Although the alterations to Baym's piece are indeed "slight," not noticeable in a casual reading, Auerbach's 1987 piece is a substantially different text. In fact only about a quarter of her 1984 text is even included in the much longer 1987 text.

Between 1984 and 1987, Auerbach, like Spillers and Benstock, moves from the periphery toward the center of the volume. If the center of the *Tulsa Studies* special issue was made up of nine articles, Auerbach's was the last of these, right before the book reviews. Just as we might see Spillers as central to the margins, Auerbach, in 1984, was at the edge of the center. Spillers's was the only book review to have endnotes; Auerbach's was the only of the central texts with no notes. Auerbach's 1984 text was not actually a full-fledged article: it was a mere four pages long, shorter, in fact, then Spillers's six and one-half page Review Essay. In 1987, Auerbach's text is not only more than doubled in length, with fourteen endnotes; it is followed by three additional articles so it is no longer on the edge.

According to Finke's typology, relegated to the margins of the 1984 issue are not only women of color, lesbians, and writers before 1800, but also men. Both versions of Auerbach's contribution make the point that, unlike the mainstream of feminist criticism, unlike gynocriticism, she writes about men's books.

Auerbach's 1987 text associates gynocriticism with Sandra Gilbert and Elaine Showalter. Auerbach contrasts not only her work but her life with these two other feminists of her generation. Showalter, for example, was an "obedient good woman" and "a caretaking faculty wife" (p. 151). Auerbach is referring to the 1983 English Institute talk published in *Feminist Issues in Literary Scholarship*, where Showalter opens her life history: "In 1968 I was a faculty wife with a small child" (p. 34). Auerbach's adjective "caretaking" specifically refers to Showalter's motherhood. Gynocritics here lines up with "we who have been mothers."

Between 1984 and 1987 Auerbach gives her contribution a new title: "Engorging the Patriarchy." One of the few passages remaining essentially unchanged from her 1984 essay glosses this title: "Probably, I share the primitive superstition that by writing about the patriarchy, as by eating it, I engorge its power."[31] This sentence would suggest that reading men could be an act of dominance rather than submission. As a sister hearty appetite, I am, first of all, taken with the oral character of her act. Where the caretaking woman feeds others, this woman eats. The good woman nurtures men; the bad woman feeds off them.

This hearty oral scenario is shadowed by another I find more troubling. When, in 1987, Auerbach elevates the verb "engorge" to her title, presenting it thus first of all out of context, it becomes even more likely that a phallic double entendre might occur to us. One of the meanings of "engorge" is "to congest or fill to excess, as with blood." But even if we bracket the phallic possibility, the oral scene itself can become ambiguous. "Engorge" as a transitive verb can mean "to devour greedily," but it can also mean "to feed (as an animal) to repletion."[32] Auerbach does not comment on these shadow meanings. How can we know for sure if her "engorging" consumes the patriarchy or feeds it full?

Whatever the status of this ambiguity in and for Auerbach specifically, it resonates more generally in the position of the bad woman in patriarchy. Does the bad girl break out of the strictures demanding woman's obedience or does she just titillate the patriarchs? Engorging their power?

The valence of the bad girl left ambiguous, the good girl turns out to be no less trouble. Although this anthology seems at any moment ready to range us in good girls against bad (we, the motherly, against the bad daughters; scholars against theorists), the oppositions neither hold nor actually break down. There is angry, moral discourse and ironic, superior discourse, both of which have the effect of dividing the world into opposing camps. But, taking the volume as a whole, it is hard to tell not only who is good and who bad, but what set of values might consistently apply.

As I have constructed the volume, Baym and Auerbach would represent opposite poles on the scale of good womanhood as motherliness. Yet to leave the two Ninas in opposition would be to ignore a major commonality: both term themselves "pluralists" and are angered by an orthodox position which would define what a feminist critic should or should not do.[33] In 1984, Auerbach defines feminist pluralism as "insisting on the differences that allowed us to say no in the first place to what we were told women were" (p. 153). This pluralism could be seen as a bad girl's stance.

As I have constructed the volume, Baym is in league with Marcus in shaming us into appropriate daughterly behavior. Others have grouped

Baym and Marcus together in an anti-theory camp; yet this togetherness can only be achieved by ignoring what Baym explicitly says about Marcus.[34] Baym begins her final paragraph: "I am, evidently, a pluralist. Essays in feminist journals are permeated with musts and shoulds" (p. 59). At this point, we are directed to her final note: "See Jane Marcus in her attack on pluralism, 'Storming the Toolshed' . . . : 'she must . . . she must . . . she must.' If that *she* is *me*, somebody (once again) is telling me what I '*must*' do to be a true woman. . . . I've been here before" (p. 61, Baym's ellipses in internal quotation). Baym rebels against Marcus's prescription of appropriate behavior.

When Auerbach presents herself as a pluralist in 1984, she explicitly derives the term from Annette Kolodny's 1980 article "Dancing through the Minefield." Baym never explicitly mentions Kolodny's article but, in introducing the concept of pluralism, writes: "Pluralists 'dance'; theorists 'storm'" (p. 45). The first verb would seem to allude to Kolodny's article; the second to Marcus's "Storming the Toolshed" which appears in Baym's final note. Marcus's "Storming" in fact discusses Kolodny's "Dancing" and her pluralism: "In 'Dancing through the Minefield,' Kolodny's liberal relaxation of the tensions among us and the tensions between feminists and the academy reflects a similar relaxation on the part of historians and political activists. What this does is to isolate Marxist feminists and lesbians on the barricades while 'good girl' feminists fold their tents and slip quietly into the establishment."[35] Whereas with Baym and Auerbach pluralists were the bad girls rebelling against authority, when we turn to Marcus pluralists are the "good girls."

Perhaps there are two kinds of good girls: good daughters of the mother and good daughters of the father. The "'good girl' feminists" who "slip quietly into the establishment" are, presumably, good in the sense of respectful of paternal authority. On the other hand, Marcus and Baym would have us respect *maternal* authority. Marcus makes that quite explicit. Yet when she complains that theorists "assert as virgin births interpretations which have ancestry" or that theorists "want to be orphaned" (p. 90), the issue begins to seem not maternal as opposed to paternal authority but recognition of parental authority.

The good/bad split, in feminist discourse, is shot through with irony. First of all, it is, by and large, bad to be a "good girl." Probably no feminist wants to be a "good girl," although no one really wants to be bad. Probably most every feminist fears that she is good and/or that she is bad. Out of that double bind we get feminists accusing other feminists of being "good girls" which implies that they are bad feminists, i.e., bad girls.

Center and margins interact with the good/bad dichotomy. If we take the center/margin structure straight, the center defines itself as good and relegates its others, presumed bad, to the margins. But in feminist (or postmodernist) discourse the center tends to be suspect, i.e., bad, and the margins have the moral authority, that is, it is good to be marginal. Thus marginalized by her badness, the bad girl is good.

The center/margins dichotomy also interacts with pluralism. Marcus quotes Gayatri Spivak: "Pluralism is the method employed by the *central* authorities to neutralize opposition by seeming to accept it. The gesture of pluralism on the part of the *marginal* can only mean capitulation to the center."[36] Pluralism's valence depends upon whether one is located in the center or the margins. Like the poststructuralist identification with *les marginaux*, pluralism enhances the center's power. On the other hand, it diminishes the margin's resistant force. If pluralism has become a focus for debate in the academic feminist critical community, if it seems to carry with it the highly moralized if nonetheless ambiguous opposition of good and bad girls, it is probably because feminist literary criticism is no longer simply marginal while still not comfortably central.

The final essay in the 1987 anthology is a telling case in point. Three essays were added to the 1987 collection, replacing the book reviews: the first two consider African-American women's writing; the last article is on the Euro-American modernist poet H.D. Given much attention by more than a decade of feminist criticism, H.D. has practically entered the bisexual modernist canon. The supplementary articles in the 1987 volume seem like an attempt to include the margins. What, we might ask, is H.D. doing in those margins?

The most immediate answer to this question is that Susan Stanford Friedman is examining H.D.'s relation to African-Americans. Friedman, who has written two books on H.D. and edited a volume of her letters, gives an exhaustive account of the places in the poet's life and writings where black people appear. In many ways, this gesture of returning to a canonical white writer after considering black women's texts seems right. First of all, it ensures that black women are not completely on the periphery of the volume. But beyond that superficial gesture, if we white women are going to turn to racial questions, it is essential that we counteract "the implication that only women of color possess a racial identity that has to be understood by the critic" (Robinson, p. 147). As Robinson goes on to say, "[i]n fact, in a society divided not only by racial differences but by racism, all writers have a significant racial identity." It would seem that the anthology absorbs Robinson's lesson and goes on from the consideration of those women who have had expressly to bear the burden of race to see what light such considerations might shed on a member of the default race.[37]

But as much as turning the question of race on ourselves and our white sisters seems an appropriate response to the awareness that black feminists have forced upon us, I find myself embarrassed by Friedman's essay. Friedman supplies us with detailed evidence from life and work, calling the two sections of her essay "The Biographical Record" and "The Literary Record." But this evidence is "for the record" not so much in the sense of an objective study but in the sense of a legal brief, not scholarship but advocacy. Friedman explicitly sets out to defend H.D. from charges of "political escapism." She theoretically locates the case within the feminist questioning of a gendered understanding of political activism which excludes a lot of women's more personal style of political practice. Although the theoretical point is certainly well-taken, this defense appears at the end of the 1987 anthology not because of the general issue of political engagement but because of the almost exclusive concentration on the single political issue of white/black race relations. Friedman musters all her documentation to prove that, in her relations to black people and in her views on race, H.D. was good, perhaps not perfect by our 1980s standards, but definitely better than the others in her milieu.

A few examples will demonstrate the tone of unabashed advocacy: (1) "Although Bryher's wealth and the interracial erotics in H.D.'s circle constituted the conditions of white paternalism, the Harlem Renaissance did not function for H.D. as a fashionable excursion into the dangerously exotic and erotic world of Otherness." (2) "A narrative that focuses on a young white girl who loves the family's black servant dangerously evokes the conventional stereotyped script. . . . What is interesting about the issue of race in *HER* is the degree to which H.D. avoids the familiar pattern." (3) "This focus on politics as it permeates the inner life is partially responsible for the degree to which H.D. avoided exploitative objectification of blacks that characterized the fascination of so many wealthy white liberals involved in the Harlem Renaissance."[38]

In a remarkably bland sentence, Stimpson's Introduction links

Friedman's essay to another in the collection: "Susan Stanford Friedman and Paula A. Treichler show specifically how being a woman can mark poems and stories" (p. 3). Nothing else is said in the Introduction about either of these essays. The sentence closes a paragraph; the next paragraph discusses the danger in universalizing the category of woman and not attending to things like sexual orientation and race.

Treichler's essay is a reading of Charlotte Perkins Gilman's "The Yellow Wallpaper," a text canonized by feminist criticism. In 1989, Susan S. Lanser discusses Treichler's article along with other feminist readings of the story published between 1973 and 1986 (the very period covered by the present study) as a way of tracing the mainstream of feminist literary criticism through its discussion of this privileged text. Pointing out that none of these diverse and inspired interpretations ever wondered why the wallpaper was yellow, Lanser connects the color to racial questions and carefully documents Gilman's racism. Lanser does not demonize Gilman or her later day feminist critics but rather calls upon us to recognize her and our contradictory places as subjects *in* ideology and history. Lanser's reading of Gilman responds to the same historical forces as Friedman's reading of H. D. but seems willing to look upon our foremothers' shame in order not to repeat, unwittingly, their errors.[39]

Friedman had published an earlier attempt to show that H.D. was "good," although in quite a different sense. A 1975 article argues for her inclusion in the (male) modernist canon, emphasizing her commonalities with those already included:

> H.D. is part of the same literary tradition that produced the mature work of the "established" artists—T. S. Eliot, Ezra Pound . . ., D. H. Lawrence. She in fact knew these artists well. . . . Like these artists, H.D. began writing in the aestheticism . . . characteristic of the imagists; and like them, she turned to epic form and to myth. . . . I . . . insist . . . that H.D. was a serious prolific poet exploring the same questions as her famous counterparts and thus inviting comparison with them.[40]

In the essay included in the Benstock anthology, first published in 1986, Friedman worries about these same connections: "No one has yet associated H.D.'s politics with the views of many of the male modernists she knew well—Ezra Pound's anti-Semitic fascism, T. S. Eliot's reverant [sic] Toryism . . . , D. H. Lawrence's flirtations with racism and fascism. . . . It is possible, however, that people will come to regard H.D.'s politics as a gentler version of the generally reactionary direction of these men" (p. 209). Friedman's essay is a concerted attempt to forestall this very possibility.

Although I am contrasting Friedman's two defenses of H.D., I do not believe they contradict each other. It is not Friedman's understanding of H.D. that has changed; it is the critical context in which a white academic feminist critic writes about a white woman poet. In the mid-seventies, the critic wanted to prove her poet was "good" by male modernist aesthetic standards; by the mid-eighties she wants to prove her poet "good" by color-conscious feminist political standards. Or, to put the same story another way: in the mid-seventies white women modernists were marginal and critics struggled to make them central; by the mid-eighties white women modernists are practically central and critics want to align them with the margins.

Friedman's 1986 essay concludes: "Working through issues of race played a significant role in the development of [H.D.'s] political syncretism, a modernism of the margins rather than the reactionary center. H.D.'s particular modernism developed out of her identification with all the others who have been 'dispersed and scattered' by the forces of history: blacks, Jews, Indians, homosexuals and lesbians, women, even artists" (p. 227). "The reactionary center" is the modernism of Eliot, Pound, and Lawrence. What is H.D. doing in the margins, I asked? Hers is a "modernism of the margins," replies Friedman; she identifies with "all the others" that Benstock, in her Letter from Paris, calls "les marginaux."

The first article in Feminist Issues in Literary Scholarship defines the modernist project as "claiming the center" and, defying chronological order, saves Stein as a postmodernist. The last article in the anthology finds, in addition to "a modernism of the center," a "modernism of the margins" and locates H.D. there. In the first article, the volume's editor defines the modernist project as centrist explicitly in relation to the question of where we, today's feminist critics, should position ourselves: "Do we claim the center for ourselves (taking up the modernist project)"? (p. 12). At the end of the volume, as Friedman pleas for H.D.'s marginal identity, she does so, I would wager, for the sake of our position as prominent white female critics.

"With all this jostling in the margins," asks Marcus, "who is in the center?" She then supplies a sort of answer: "Shari Benstock . . . suggests that academic feminist critics are not marginal in the least, compared to black outsiders or writers excluded from the academy" (p.

87). Marcus is referring to Benstock's 1983 editorial, the seed text for *Feminist Issues in Literary Scholarship*, the text where Benstock gives Marcus credit for informing her conception of the collection. Somewhere around the birth of this 1984/1987 anthology, somewhere between Shari Benstock and Jane Marcus, is a recognition that academic feminist critics are no longer marginal. We might read the anthology as a very complex response to this ambiguous fact.

Citing but not quoting Benstock, Marcus lists two sorts of writers more marginal than academic feminists: "black outsiders or writers excluded from the academy." The first group is, at least in a token way, included between 1984 and 1987. And looking beyond this specific anthology, I would say that a major gesture of academic feminist literary criticism in the mid-1980s has been the inclusion of "black outsiders." White feminist critics by the dozens have turned to writing about black women writers. Finally, we started listening to what black feminists had been saying for at least a decade (if not a century), although too often listening just long enough to rush out and quickly try to do the right thing. It is possible that, not long after I write these words in 1990, we might envision an inclusion of black women writers in the literary academy paralleling the inclusion of white women writers in the 1980s. But Marcus's second category, "writers excluded from the academy," could pose a more troubling problem for us academic feminists, if we understand it not as those contingently excluded (the writers we fight to get into the canon) but as the structural, institutional exclusion of the nonacademic, of those who might challenge our values, those who are excluded by the processes which constitute our inclusion.

It is specifically in relation to our centrality and its complicity with this exclusion that Marcus suggests we identify with Titus Andronicus: "It is a frustrating and selfless activity that must include, as in the case of Titus, a recognition of one's own complicity in the silencing of the subject" (p. 80). If I am embarrassed by Friedman's attempt to prove that H.D. is (and by implication we prominent white female critics are) good and marginal, I find myself equally uncomfortable with Marcus's moral imperative that, in recognition of our guilty centrality, we suppress our selves in the service of our silenced, marginalized sisters.

According to Friedman, H.D. learns her own marginalization and finds her feminism by identifying with racially oppressed others. Auerbach's 1987 text tells a similar story: "Putting aside my private, lifelong and often enjoyable rebellion, I accepted my oppression as a woman after living with a racist and class oppression that included men as well. I recognized myself as a victim when I saw others victimized. In the best female, caretaking tradition, I learned to fight for myself by fighting for others" (pp. 154–55). This is definitely *the* "female tradition": in the nineteenth century, white women got the idea of fighting for their "emancipation" by working for the abolition of slavery; in the 1960s, white women got the idea of fighting for our "rights" from working in the black "civil rights" movement.

A page earlier, Auerbach states: "I never wanted to be a caretaker; I never saw myself as a wife or a mother, and I never was one." Never wanting to be a caretaker, she finds herself "in the best female, caretaking tradition." We are more familiar with the feminist story of "good women" learning to claim something for themselves. Auerbach is telling a different story: about how a "bad woman" gave up her private rebellion, in order to fight as a woman for women. But in going from rebellious to caretaking, Auerbach is not simply crossing the line from bad girl to good. Auerbach redefines the "female, caretaking tradition" so it is not synonymous with self-suppression, so it includes fighting "for myself."

"It was never 'bad,'" Auerbach realizes, "to refuse to be 'good' in the self-mutilating way" (p. 152). The opposition between good girls and bad has historically set women against each other. Although the standards that determine good girls have varied over the last century or so, and in relation to specific subcultures, the moralized, adversarial opposition has remained powerful in its ability to paralyze individual women and to obstruct alliances between women of differing groups.

Within our ideology of normative femininity, middle-class and white, as it has played itself out since the 1830s, the black female has not only been excluded from pink femininity, she has been suspended as the "bad woman" from the burning cross of sex and race. Dialectically attempting to free her sisters from that violent marginalization, the African-American woman writer has, since she started writing, constructed the black heroine as good woman. Yet if the bad woman is marginalized, the good woman approaches the center only at the expense of her self. For Spillers, Sula takes the risk of being bad so that the black woman not be confined to the self-sacrifice of good womanhood.

Not only race, but class difference, sexual orientation, ethnicity, among other less theorized differences, all have been interpreted through the bad girl/good girl dichotomy. The split serves patriarchy not only by marginalizing disloyal women, not only by setting women nearer the center of power against those less domesticated, but by ensuring that the women closest to power renounce their selves in order to keep that proximity. One of the constants behind the good girl/ bad girl dichotomy is that it is bad to have power. The moralized split, if left unanalyzed, unfortunately reappears within feminism, interpreting differences between women, for example, marginalizing some women as not feminist (enough): bad or "good girl." And I fear, as some few women approach a sort of peripheral centrality, specifically for our present concern, as some feminist critics find a secure place within the literary academy, we will be forced to choose between selfish individualism and selflessness for the sake of our more oppressed sisters.

I have, throughout my career as an academic feminist, enjoyed the role of bad girl. Yet if to affirm one's identity as bad girl can be a first step in breaking out of obedient femininity, it seems necessary to get beyond that posture in order to challenge the good/bad divide that makes the assertion of female self too often private and destructive, too often at the expense of other women.

History is like mother. As I read the 1984 special issue "Feminist Issues in Literary Scholarship," "history" seemed very much "like mother." Both words, differently but in insistent if not fully articulated connection, seemed to carry moral imperatives, produced guilt/resistance/resentment in me, the bad daughter-critic, not daughterly or motherly enough, insufficiently historical. When I read the 1987 volume, I noted in Spillers a rebellion against both history and the motherly. I wanted to use Spillers/Sula to break the power of the volume's center, to rebel against maternal authority. I wanted this newly included black critic to speak my rebellion, rendering it not bad but good, giving it another sort of authority. Marcus, on the other hand, correctly urges us: "The white woman critic must be careful not to impose her own alphabet on the art of women of color" (p. 80).

History is like mother. Gardiner and Newton, polarized in *Making a Difference*, surprisingly coincide in the wish for a feminist criticism both psychologically and historically informed. If indeed I could bring those two terms together, then I could also bring together two different versions of my own project. One version dates from around 1984 and is centered in psychological categories, interpreting feminist critical relations in familial and psychoanalytic terms, in particular the mother-daughter relation. The other version dates from around 1987 and sees feminist critical positions in terms of institutional history.

History is also not like mother. Despite my attraction to Gardiner's oracular pronouncement, I am beginning to realize that feminists need to stop reading everything through the family romance. If we are going to understand our relation to the academic institution within which we think and teach and speak, we need to recognize its specific dynamics which are obscured in the recourse to familial metaphor.

We must again risk being "bad" and recognize that we are operating outside the family, outside the realm of romance, outside woman's traditional place, that we are "pros," workers and authorities, in the literary academy and that what we can most effectively say and do as feminists is mediated through that institution, its ideologies, values, structures, and its location in the world.

Afterword

The present book stops around 1987. And, in fact, most of the 1987 anthology was already published by 1985. Thus the present book does not take us up to "the present," certainly not to your present of reading (whenever that might occur), but not even to my present of writing (around 1991).

To be sure, I had to stop sometime in order to finish. I had to say "no more anthologies" in order to produce this book. But, in retrospect, where I stopped may also be the end of a certain story, the very one I would here tell, the story of feminist literary criticism.

From around 1975 to around 1983, the mainstream of academic feminist criticism focused on women's writing in the Euro-American high cultural tradition. This book tells the story of that period, from the preparations for it up to its dismantling. In the early seventies we see the dilemmas and choices leading to that focus; in the mid-eighties we see the confusions and challenges as that implicit definition gets called into question. By looking, all along, at resisting edges, I tried to make it clear that feminist criticism never simply was the study of literature by women. But if reductive of actual plurality, this profile was operative. People took feminist criticism for the study of literature written by women. And that received definition had definite institutional effects: the focus on Euro-American high cultural "literature" made feminist criticism fit in the literary academy.

During the late 1980s this implicit definition was challenged from three different directions. All three have been both unsettling and immensely productive. I want to take a last moment to indicate these three trends.

The most powerful has been the exposure and condemnation of an implicit prejudice in "women's literature" that in fact only considers writing by Euro-American women. The last half-decade has witnessed a massive turn to literature by other women, first and foremost African-Americans but then also, more recently, moving to other ethnic groups and other nationalities.

This trend has already begun in the final period studied above, the

240

final section of this book, around 1985. That year saw the first academic literary critical anthology devoted to black women's writing. In the past two years alone, at least three such anthologies have appeared.[1] It is the more recent insistence of this move which brought about my decision to do a chapter on *Conjuring*. When published, that anthology did not represent the mainstream of academic feminist criticism (and was not in fact widely read). But, in retrospect, it represents the first gathering of what would, by the time of the present book, join the main stream. Thus although *Conjuring* literally belongs to the period around 1985, it is most significant and thus appears here as a harbinger of what goes beyond this book, of feminist criticism around 1990.

Thus, the last section of this book not only looks at the end of a certain moment in feminist criticism, but also and at the same time catches the beginning of another moment, the centralization of race and black women's writing to academic literary feminism. This moment, which continues as I write this in early 1991, already has to its credit two major accomplishments: the inclusion of questions of race in critical considerations of gender and the inclusion of writings by African-American women in academic practice—critical and pedagogical, feminist and mainstream—in particular, the works of Hurston, Walker, and Morrison.

These inclusions substantially alter both feminism and criticism. But, subject to these revitalizing corrections, what remains is still the study of literature by women. Having answered over and over again, and in chorus, the question "Ain't I A Woman?" with a resounding affirmative, academic feminist criticism has improved the concept of "women," expanded it beyond its racialist provincialism. And although it does wondrous good to view black women as the producers of the highly valued cultural product "literature," questions about the boundaries of the literary realm, about the possible elitism of the category itself are deferred by the inclusion of these exemplary representatives of the doubly oppressed.

If the mainstream of academic literary feminism has proceeded from Euro-American "gynocritics" (with or without poststructuralist theory) to African-American "gynocritics" (with or without), it is probably not irrelevant that, at the moment the study of women's literature was being challenged, this move to something clearly more progressive and radical preserves both "women" and "literature." The two other trends of the late 1980s call one and the other, respectively, into question.

In recent years, there has been a push from "women" to "gender." A 1986 anthology is entitled *Gender and Reading*; a 1989 collection *Gender and Theory*, to cite just two volumes at random from my bookcase.[2] This move too is already at play in the last moment of the present book, around 1985, particularly in *Making a Difference*, with its narrative progression from women to women-and-men. That 1985 anthology would go beyond the definition of feminist criticism as the study of writing by women, beyond gynocritics, beyond Elaine Showalter. But the latter, with her own excellent sense of timing, in 1989 edits an anthology entitled *Speaking of Gender*.[3]

My reading of *Making a Difference* voices a suspicion of heterosexist anxiety, but this feminist consideration of gender has also been a valuable opening. In particular, there has been a real contribution to the understanding of masculinities and a new insight into men as gendered rather than falsely generic. A recent anthology is entitled *Engendering Men* and although the title is richly ambiguous, one of its meanings is this reinscription of men as gendered.[4] A new generation of male literary academics, students of feminist critics, have responded to the power of feminist thought not simply in the cooptive, dismissive mode of their elder brothers but in a way really marked by feminist knowledge. Rather than studying women as a means of mastery, they investigate men, masculinity, and even their own will to mastery. Part of this move intersects with the rise of gay (male) studies in the late 1980s. There is a border where gay studies and gender studies overlap and there is anxiety about the relation between gay studies and feminist criticism, but that is another story.

This turn within literary studies is part of a larger academic shift from women's studies to gender studies. The word "gender," infrequent in literary criticism before the mid-eighties, has been a central concept in feminist social science. Although it is theoretically invaluable for feminist scholars to intervene in the understanding of men, within literary studies, this tends to mean work on canonical authors which however nuanced a notion of gender we may get, also contributes to the ongoing status of these authors. When we study their ambiguous and multiform gender, we often lose sight of their cultural authority, all the while contributing to it. Criticism can ambiguate and complexify gender in literary texts to the point that literature, once again, appears to be beyond the cruel binarized oppressions of the world. Within literary studies, I fear, "gender," unlike "women," tends to reinforce the superiority of the literary.

During the period with which the present book is concerned, the question of why study literature rarely was posed. By the late eighties, "literature" as object of feminist criticism no longer goes without saying. Feminist criticism has participated in a more general move from literary to cultural studies. In the late eighties feminists have turned to study popular writing and, linking up with feminist film criticism, also to look at media. Within cultural studies, literature is looked at as one among various signifying practices rather than as a privileged site of "culture."

This third challenge is theoretically the most radical in that it calls into question the very grounds and ideology of the discipline. But it also must be said that feminist cultural criticism in the late 1980s is taking place in the context of a literary discipline that is interrogating itself and transmuting into cultural studies.

From the standpoint of this challenge to the elitism of high culture, the claims that Euro-American women or even African-American women can produce high culture seem merely reformist. But it also must be remembered that, in an academy which takes itself and is taken by the larger society as a purveyor of a culture that is better, it is of significant effect to associate that highness, however we might also and at the same time want to call it into question, with representatives of inferiorized groups, for example women and people of color.

We may want to use our limited but real cultural authority, as purveyors of "better culture," teachers for example, both to link women to culture, wisdom, and knowledge in order to chip away at hierarchies which associate us with nature, body, the menial and yet also to use that same authority to call the ideology of high culture into question.

Between 1975 and 1983 the mainstream of academic feminist criticism implicitly defined its enterprise in a way that fit the literary academy. Cooptation or strategy? We may not be able simply to decide what motivated this fit. But we live in the legacy of that period; we benefit from it. It allows us not only radically to call its terms—"women" and "literature"—into question but to be heard through an institution's channels of transmission when we do so.

From the point of view of these contemporary trends, feminist literary criticism of the classic period looks irretrievably tame. But we must also see, looking retrospectively at that period, that, once in-stalled, feminist criticism was precisely free to move in these three more radical directions and it immediately did so. Although they often are merciless about the blind spots of the 1975–83 period, these chal-lenges are in fact possible because of the solid institutional foothold gained through the tame definition of feminist criticism.

Now that we are comfortable enough to ask these questions and be heard, let us use this position not to accuse each other of being too academic or elitist or reformist but to articulate these questions with the institution in which we work and through which we interact with society. As a step in that direction I have tried, in this book, to look at where we are and how we got here, we feminists in what is still, until further notice, the literary academy.

Notes

Introduction

1. Toril Moi, *Sexual/Textual Politics: Feminist Literary Theory* (London: Methuen, 1985), and Janet Todd, *Feminist Literary History* (New York: Routledge, 1988).

2. Meaghan Morris, *"in any event . . ."* in Alice Jardine and Paul Smith, eds. *Men in Feminism* (New York: Methuen, 1987), p. 179.

3. K. K. Ruthven, *Feminist Literary Studies: An Introduction* (Cambridge: Cambridge University Press, 1984), pp. vii, 6–7.

4. Rereading this phrase, I realize its unusual wording recalls the following statement by Janet Todd: "there is on the whole little upfronting of the historical enterprise of criticism. . . . in Showalter's *The New Feminist Criticism* and in many other anthologies, composition dates of the essays are hidden away in footnotes or even in closely printed acknowledgments in the front"—*Feminist Literary History*, p. 91.

5. Cf. Gayatri Chakravorty Spivak, "French Feminism in an International Frame," *Yale French Studies* 62 (1981), p. 177, reprinted in Spivak, *In Other Worlds: Essays in Cultural Politics* (New York: Routledge, 1988), p. 149.

6. Cf. Spivak's sympathetic symptomatic reading of the work of the Subaltern Studies group: "I remind the reader that, in my view, such 'cognitive failures' are irreducible. . . . [I]t is not therefore my intent to suggest a formula for correct cognitive moves"—*In Other Worlds*, p. 202.

7. Patrocinio Schweickart, "What Are We Doing, Really?—Feminist Criticism and the Problem of Theory," *Canadian Journal of Political and Social Theory* 9 (1985), pp. 160, 164 n. 35.

8. Todd, *Feminist Literary History*, p. 1.

9. Gloria T. Hull, "Researching Alice Dunbar-Nelson: A Personal and Literary Perspective" in Hull, Scott, and Smith, eds., *All the Women are White, All*

the Blacks are Men, But Some of Us Are Brave: Black Women's Studies (Old Westbury, NY: Feminist Press, 1982), p. 194.

10. Moi, *Sexual/Texual Politics*, p. 80.

11. Myra Jehlen, "Archimedes and the Paradox of Feminist Criticism" in Keohane, Rosaldo, and Gelpi, eds., *Feminist Theory: A Critique of Ideology* (Chicago: University of Chicago Press, 1982), pp. 200–201, originally published in *Signs* in 1981.

1. The Difference Within

1. Elizabeth Abel, "Introduction," *Critical Inquiry*, Vol. 8, No. 2 (Winter 1981), p. 178. The entire issue was reprinted as the anthology *Writing and Sexual Difference*, ed. Elizabeth Abel (University of Chicago Press, 1982) along with two additional articles and four "Critical Responses" to the original issue, including an earlier version of the present chapter. The quoted sentence (which appears on page 6 of the 1982 book) no longer concludes the introduction for it is followed by a paragraph which describes the Critical Responses. All subsequent cited page numbers are from the anthology.

2. See Jacques Lacan, "The Signification of the Phallus," *Ecrits: A Selection*, trans. Alan A. Sheridan (New York: Norton, 1977), pp. 286–87.

3. Jean Laplanche, *Life and Death in Psychoanalysis*, trans. Jeffrey Mehlman (Baltimore: Johns Hopkins University Press, 1976), p. 24.

4. Barbara Johnson, *The Critical Difference: Essays in the Contemporary Rhetoric of Reading* (Baltimore: Johns Hopkins University Press, 1980), p. 13.

5. See Jane Gallop, "Phallus/Penis: Same Difference" in *Thinking Through the Body* (New York: Columbia University Press, 1988), pp. 124–31.

2. The Problem of Definition

1. Elaine Showalter, ed., *The New Feminist Criticism: Essays on Women, Literature, and Theory* (New York: Pantheon, 1985). Page references will appear parenthetically in the text.

2. Annette Kolodny, "A Map for Rereading: Gender and the Interpretation of Literary Texts," p. 61 n. 26.

3. Elaine Showalter, "Women's Time, Women's Space: Writing the History

of Feminist Criticism," *Tulsa Studies in Women's Literature*, Vol. 3, Nos.
1–2 (1984), p. 35, emphasis added. This special issue of the journal has
been reprinted as *Feminist Issues in Literary Scholarship*, Shari Benstock,
ed. (Bloomington: Indiana University Press, 1987) where the quotation
can be found on page 36. Further references will be to the 1987 volume.

4. *Feminist Literary History*, p. 49.

5. Josephine Donovan, ed., *Feminist Literary Criticism: Explorations in Theory* (Lexington: University Press of Kentucky, 1975).

6. See p. 267 n. 1. The subtitle is omitted in the original publication of the
essay: Elaine Showalter, "Feminist Criticism in the Wilderness," *Critical
Inquiry*, Vol. 8, No. 2 (Winter 1981), p. 179 n. 1.

7. See p. 142, n. 7. This date is incorrect in the original publication of the
essay: Elaine Showalter, "Toward a Feminist Poetics" in Mary Jacobus,
ed., *Women Writing and Writing about Women* (New York: Barnes and
Noble, 1979), p. 40, n. 7.

8. 1975 here is the date of Showalter's review of feminist criticism in *Signs*:
Elaine Showalter, "Literary Criticism," *Signs* 1 (1975); pp. 435–60.

9. In her 1984 article, Showalter writes: "The point at which the difference
or specificity of women's writing was conceptualized as the focus of
feminist criticism was, in my opinion, the single most important breakthrough in its history" ("Women's Time, Women's Space," p. 39). The
paragraph which includes this sentence is followed by an unusual note
which reads: "In this paragraph I have adapted Juliet Mitchell's statement
about the discovery of the unconscious in psychoanalysis, p. 322" (p. 244
n. 29). This gesture, unique in Showalter's accounts of feminist criticism,
marks the importance of this historic moment by implicitly comparing
it to Freud's discovery of the unconscious. On page 322 of Mitchell's
Psychoanalysis and Feminism: Freud, Reich, Laing, and Women (New
York: Pantheon, 1974) we can read "Freud made history, he was not made
by it."

10. Adrienne Rich, "Compulsory Heterosexuality and Lesbian Existence,"
Signs 5 (1980); pp. 648–49, quoted by Zimmerman, p. 205.

11. Sigmund Freud, *New Introductory Lectures on Psychoanalysis*, *The Standard Edition of the Complete Psychological Works*, Vol. 22 (London:
Hogarth, 1964), p. 113.

12. Zimmerman, p. 204, emphasis added. Zimmerman is here quoting from

Susan Sniader Lanser, "Speaking in Tongues: *Ladies' Almanack* and the Language of Celebration," *Frontiers*, 4,3 (1979), p. 39.

13. I borrow the phrase from Jill Johnston, *Lesbian Nation* (New York: Simon and Shuster, 1974).

14. Terry Eagleton, *Literary Theory: An Introduction* (Minneapolis: University of Minnesota Press, 1983), p. 28, emphasis Eagleton's. For another example, from French literature, see Joan De Jean, "Classical Reeducation: Decanonizing the Feminine" in De Jean and Nancy K. Miller, eds., *Displacements: Women, Tradition, Literatures in French* (Baltimore: Johns Hopkins University Press, 1991), pp. 22–36.

15. Miller, p. 342, quoting T.S. Eliot, cited in Elizabeth Janeway, "Women's Literature," in *Harvard Guide to Contemporary American Writing*, ed. Daniel Hoffman (Cambridge: Harvard University Press, 1979), p. 344. Virginia Woolf also compared American literature to women's literature, although to the detriment of both, given her modernist aesthetic: "Women writers have to meet many of the same problems that beset Americans. . . . In both cases all kinds of consciousness—consciousness of self, of race, of sex, of civilization—which have nothing to do with art, have got between them and the paper" ("American Fiction," *Collected Essays*, Vol. 2, p. 113, cited in Elaine Showalter, *A Literature of Their Own* [Princeton: Princeton University Press, 1977]).

16. Smith, p.175. Smith takes this definition from a paper delivered by Bertha Harris at the 1976 Modern Language Association Convention.

17. Bernice Johnson Reagon has a similar take on the relation between exclusionary "nationalism" and temporal progression: "At a certain stage nationalism is crucial to a people if you are going to ever impact as a group in your own interest. Nationalism at another point becomes reactionary because it is totally inadequate for surviving in the world with many peoples" ("Coalition Politics: Turning the Century" in *Home Girls: A Black Feminist Anthology*, Barbara Smith, ed., [New York: Kitchen Table, 1983], p. 358).

18. This notion of the "double" vision of the "disenfranchised" can be traced back to W. E. B. DuBois's notion of black people's "double consciousness." Zimmerman cites no reference for her phrase "double vision" and, in the context of the anthology, I am attributing it to her, especially since I purposefully displace it to mean not awareness of both dominative and dominated viewpoints but refusal to choose either the exclusive or the inclusive definition along with her recognition of the value of both.

19. p. 263. Showalter takes the phrase from Susan Lanser and Evelyn Torton Beck, "[Why] Are There No Great Women Critics? And What Difference Does It Make?" in *The Prism of Sex: Essays in the Sociology of Knowledge*, ed. Beck and Julia A. Sherman (Madison: University of Wisconsin Press, 1979), p. 86.

20. Showalter, "Women's Time, Women's Space," pp. 33–34.

3. "French Feminism"

1. I am thinking in particular of the books by Ruthven (1984), Moi (1985), and Todd (1988), but also, for example, of Showalter's 1984 "Women's Time, Women's Space: Writing the History of Feminist Criticism."

2. Cixous, Hélène, "The Laugh of the Medusa," *Signs* 1 (Summer 1976), pp. 875–93. Reprinted in Marks and Courtivron, eds. *New French Feminisms* (Amherst: University of Massachusetts Press, 1980), pp. 245–64. Page numbers in the text are from the anthology.

3. Examples include Annie Leclerc, *Parole de femme* (Paris: Grasset, 1974); Luce Irigaray, *Ce Sexe qui n'en est pas un* (Paris: Minuit, 1977), translated by Catherine Porter as *This Sex Which Is Not One* (Ithaca: Cornell University Press, 1985); Cixous, Madeleine Gagnon and Leclerc, *La venue à l'écriture* (Paris: Union Générale d'Editions, 1977); and various articles in newly formed women's journals such as *Cahiers du grif* and *Sorcières*.

4. Cixous, Hélène, "Le rire de la méduse," *L'Arc* 61 (1975), pp. 39–54.

5. Toril Moi, *Sexual/Textual Politics*, p. 98

6. Translated as "Enslaved Enclave" by Marilyn R. Shuster in Marks and Courtivron. Page numbers in the text are from this translation.

7. Adrienne Rich, "Privilege, Power, and Tokenism" (excerpted from a commencement speech at Smith College, May 7, 1979), *Ms.* Vol. 8, No. 3 (September 1979), p. 43.

8. Gayatri Chakravorty Spivak, "Explanation and Culture: Marginalia" in *In Other Worlds*, p. 107.

9. *Les temps modernes*, April–May 1974, quoted in the editors' introduction to *L'Arc*, p. 1.

10. Virginia Woolf, *A Room of One's Own* (New York: Harcourt Brace Jovanovich, 1929), pp. 68–69.

11. For my commentary on "lips" in Irigaray's work, see "Lip Service" in *Thinking Through the Body*, pp. 92–99.

12. For my commentary on the untranslatability of "jouissance," see "Beyond the *Jouissance* Principle" in *Thinking Through the Body*, pp. 119–24.

13. Sometimes a fourth name is added to the list or another name substituted for one of these three, but the composite of all references leaves us mainly with this triumvirate, the one represented by Moi's chapters on "French Feminist Theory" in *Sexual/Textual Politics*. Monique Wittig is a French feminist frequently cited but is not representative of "French feminism," that peculiar phenomenon constructed in binary opposition to "American feminism."

14. Showalter, "Feminist Criticism in the Wilderness" in *The New Feminist Criticism*, p. 243.

4. The Monster in the Mirror

1. The Editors, "Introduction," *Yale French Studies* 62, (1981), p. 2.

2. Marianne Hirsch, "A Mother's Discourse: Incorporation and Repetition in *La Princesse de Clèves*," *YFS* 62, p. 73, emphasis added.

3. Nancy Chodorow, *The Reproduction of Mothering: Psychoanalysis and the Sociology of Gender* (Berkeley: University of California Press, 1978).

4. Hirsch, p. 69, emphasis added. She is referring to Luce Irigaray, *Et l'une ne bouge pas sans l'autre* (Paris: Minuit, 1979), translated as "And the One Doesn't Stir without the Other," by Hélène Vivienne Wenzel, *Signs*, Vol. 7, No. 1 (1981), pp. 60–67.

5. Marianne Hirsch, "Mothers and Daughters," *Signs* Vol. 7, No. 1 (1981), p. 210.

6. Adrienne Rich, *Of Woman Born: Motherhood as Experience and Institution* (New York: Norton, 1976), p. 236.

7. See Jane Flax, "The Conflict Between Nurturance and Autonomy in Mother-Daughter Relationships and Within Feminism," *Feminist Studies*, Vol. 4, No. 1 (1978), pp. 171–89.

8. The original 1983 version of "The Monster in the Mirror" was published in Richard Feldstein and Judith Roof, eds., *Feminism and Psychoanalysis* (Ithaca: Cornell University Press, 1989), pp. 13–24.

9. Scharfman, "Mirroring and Mothering in Simone Schwarz-Bart's *Pluie et*

vent sur Télumée Miracle and Jean Rhys's *Wide Sargasso Sea*," *YFS* 62, p. 91, quoting from D.W. Winnicott, "Mirror-role of Mother and Family in Child Development" in *Playing and Reality* (New York: Basic Books, 1971), pp. 111–18.

10. *The Reproduction of Mothering*, p. 87.

11. Naomi Schor, "Female Paranoia: The Case for Psychoanalytic Feminist Criticism," *YFS* 62, p. 209. Schor is referring to Sigmund Freud, "A Case of Paranoia Running Counter to the Psychoanalytic Theory of the Disease" in *The Standard Edition*, Vol. 14 (London: Hogarth, 1957), pp. 263–72.

12. See Jane Marcus, "Still Practice, A/Wrested Alphabet: Toward a Feminist Aesthetic" in *Feminist Issues in Literary Scholarship*, pp. 89–90.

13. Nina Baym, "The Madwoman and Her Languages: Why I Don't Do Feminist Literary Theory" in *Feminist Issues in Literary Scholarship*, pp. 57–58.

14. Gayatri Chakravorty Spivak, "Three Women's Texts and a Critique of Imperialism" in Henry Louis Gates, Jr., ed., *"Race," Writing, and Difference* (Chicago: University of Chicago Press, 1986), p. 267. Spivak and Baym are referring to Gilbert and Gubar's *The Madwoman in the Attic: The Woman Writer and the Nineteenth-Century Literary Imagination* (New Haven: Yale University Press, 1979), pp. 360–62.

15. Spivak, "Three Women's Texts," p. 268, quoting from Jean Rhys, in an interview with Elizabeth Vreeland, quoted in Nancy Harrison, *An Introduction to the Writing Practice of Jean Rhys: the Novel as Women's Text*.

16. Spivak, "Three Women's Texts," p. 268.

17. Jean Rhys, *Wide Sargasso Sea* (New York: Popular Library, 1966), p. 46.

18. Gayatri Chakravorty Spivak, "French Feminism in an International Frame," *YFS* 62, p. 179.

5. Reading the Mother Tongue

1. Shirley Nelson Garner, Claire Kahane, and Madelon Sprengnether, eds., *The (M)other Tongue: Essays in Psychoanalytic Feminist Interpretation* (Ithaca: Cornell University Press, 1985); all further references to this work will be included in the text.

2. I owe the phrases "other as self" and "self as other" to a related use by Naomi Schor, "*Eugénie Grandet*: Mirrors and Melancholia," *The (M)other Tongue*, p. 218 n. 2. All references to Chodorow are to *The Reproduction of Mothering*.

3. In this context let us remark the phrase "Anglo-American." It is not at all obvious that English and American psychoanalytic feminists share a theory. For example, the British tend to be Lacanian. Of course object-relations theory is an English movement, but Chodorow has not been very influential in Britain. Perhaps the phrase stems rather from the fact that the English and Americans more or less share a "mother tongue." The contrast between the French and the Anglo-Americans is thus not between two different discourses but rather literally between two different languages. For another consideration of "Anglo-American" and the other within the mother tongue, see my "The Mother Tongue" in Francis Barker et al., eds., *The Politics of Theory* (Colchester: University of Essex, 1983), pp. 49–56.

4. See, for example, Barbara Johnson, *The Critical Difference: Essays in the Contemporary Rhetoric of Reading,* p. 4.

5. For exemplary instances of critical self-implication in *The (M)other Tongue*, see Schor, "*Eugénie Grandet*," pp. 236–37 and Kahane, "The Gothic Mirror," p. 340.

6. In *The Psychopathology of Everyday Life*, Freud opens the possibility of treating mistakes by copyists and compositors as psychologically motivated, that is, interpretable; see Freud, *The Standard Edition of the Complete Psychological Works*, Vol. 6 (London: Hogarth, 1960), p. 129. I have begun to notice typos in this word in other feminist texts. For example: Gayle Greene and Coppélia Kahn, eds. *Making a Difference*, p. 4—"patriarchal," p. 239—"partriarchy"; Lydia Sargent, ed., *The Unhappy Marriage of Marxism and Feminism: A Debate on Class and Patriarchy* (London: Pluto Press, 1981), p. 75—"patriarchial," p. 241—"partriarchy"; Susan Koppelman Cornillon, ed., *Images of Women in Fiction: Feminist Perspectives* (Bowling Green: Bowling Green University Popular Press, 1972), pp. 179, 204—"partiarchal"; Cheryl L. Brown and Karen Olson, eds., *Feminist Criticism: Essays on Theory, Poetry and Prose* (Metuchen: Scarecrow Press, 1978), p. 16—"partriarchal."

7. According to Jacques Lacan, "the unconscious is the discourse of the Other." See for example *Ecrits: A Selection,*, p. 312.

8. See, for example, Dorothy Dinnerstein, *The Mermaid and the Minotaur: Sexual Arrangements and Human Malaise* (New York: Harper Colophon, 1976), and Adrienne Rich, *Of Woman Born*.

9. Schor makes a similar point in *The (M)other Tongue*: "What Eugénie begins to understand is that even as she enjoyed the shelter of the symbi-

otic mother-daughter relationship, even then she lived under the sway of the Symbolic, the order in which she was inscribed before her birth" ("*Eugénie Grandet*," p. 227).

10. *The American Heritage Dictionary of the English Language*, new college ed., s.v. "fascinate."

11. See Ronnie Scharfman, "Mirroring and Mothering in Simone Schwarz-Bart's *Pluie et vent sur Télumée Miracle* and Jean Rhys's *Wide Sargasso Sea*," *Yale French Studies* 62, pp. 91, 99. Scharfman refers to D. W. Winnicott, "Mirror-role of Mother and Family in Child Development" in *Playing and Reality*.

12. Baym, "The Madwoman and Her Languages," p. 57.

13. According to Chodorow, "Alice Balint argues that the essence of 'love for the mother' is that it is not under the sway of the reality principle" (p. 79). Chodorow's source here is Alice Balint, "Love for the Mother and Mother Love," in *Primary Love and Psycho-Analytic Technique*, ed. Michael Balint (New York: Liveright, 1965), pp. 91–108.

14. "Secondary revision" is the "rearrangement of a dream so as to present it in the form of a relatively consistent and comprehensible scenario"—J. Laplanche and J.-B. Pontalis, *The Language of Psycho-analysis*, trans. Donald Nicholson-Smith (London: Hogarth, 1973), p. 412.

15. The phrase "object of service" is taken from the Introduction to *The (M)other Tongue*, p. 19.

16. In the month following my writing of the 1986 version of this chapter, I founnd myself regularly making a certain typo: "materity" for "maternity," as if I felt there was an n that did not belong in "maternity." In the previous sentence, the extra n in "founnd" was produced when I retyped the text on my new computer in 1988. I discovered it, while revising, in 1990.

6. The Coloration of Academic Feminism

1. Jane Gallop, "Annie Leclerc Writing a Letter, with Vermeer" in Nancy K. Miller, ed., *The Poetics of Gender* (New York: Columbia University Press, 1986), pp. 138–39.

2. Cf. ". . . Mr. Whistler said: 'Mauve? Mauve is just pink trying to be purple . . .'", epigraph to Thomas Beer, *The Mauve Decade: American Life at the End of the Nineteenth Century* (London: Knopf, 1926). In his account of American literary culture in the 1890s, Beer uses "mauve" to character-

ize a pretentious high female culture. Sandra Gilbert and Susan Gubar refer to Beer's *Mauve Decade* in their essay in *The Poetics of Gender*, "Tradition and the Female Talent," pp. 195–96.

3. Susan Rubin Suleiman, "Pornography, Transgression, and the Avant-Garde: Bataille's *Story of the Eye*" in *The Poetics of Gender*, p. 126. The quotation is Suleiman's translation from Georges Batailles, *Histoire de l'oeil*, in *Oeuvres complètes*, Vol. 1 (Paris: Gallimard, 1970), pp. 12–13.

4. Andrea Dworkin, *Pornography: Men Possessing Women* (New York: Perigree, 1981), p. 167.

5. Monique Wittig, "The Mark of Gender" in *The Poetics of Gender*, p. 72.

6. Elizabeth Berg, "Iconoclastic Moments: Reading the *Sonnets for Hélène*, Writing the *Portuguese Letters*" in *The Poetics of Gender*, p. 220.

7. Audre Lorde, "The Master's Tools Will Never Dismantle the Master's House" in *This Bridge Called My Back: Writings by Radical Women of Color*, eds. Cherríe Moraga and Gloria Anzaldúa (Watertown, Mass.: Persephone, 1981), p. 112.

8. Hortense J. Spillers, "Interstices: A Small Drama of Words" in Carole S. Vance, ed., *Pleasure and Danger: Exploring Female Sexuality* (Boston: Routledge Kegan Paul, 1984), p. 91.

9. Angela Y. Davis, *Women, Race, and Class* (New York: Vintage, 1983), p. 94.

10. Suleiman, p. 124; Dworkin, p. 174.

11. Dworkin, pp. 129–31.

12. Georges Bataille, *Manet*, trans. Austryn Wainhouse and James Emmons (New York: Rizzoli, 1983), p. 61.

13. Roger Hargreaves, *Mr. Dizzy* (Los Angeles: Price/Stern/Sloan, 1982) n.p.

14. Elaine Showalter, "Piecing and Writing" in *The Poetics of Gender*, p. 222.

15. "Annie Leclerc," p. 144, quoting from Gayatri Spivak, "French Feminism in an International Frame" in *In Other Worlds*, p. 150.

16. This use of the Spivak quotation ends chapter 4 above, "The Monster in the Mirror."

7. Writing About Ourselves

1. Susan Koppelman Cornillon, ed., *Images of Women in Fiction: Feminist Perspectives*, Revised Edition, (Bowling Green, Ohio: Bowling Green University Popular Press, 1973), Preface, p. xi.

2. Vivian Gornick, "Woman as Outsider"; Wendy Martin, "Seduced and Abandoned in the New World: the Image of Woman in American Fiction"; Cynthia Ozick, "Women and Creativity: the Demise of the Dancing Dog"; and Elaine Showalter, "Women Writers and the Double Standard" in Vivian Gornick and Barbara K. Moran, eds., *Woman in Sexist Society* (New York: Signet, 1971).

3. In the light of her eighties position as someone who "doesn't do theory," it is worth noting that Nina Baym may well have been the first feminist structuralist critic. Cf. Nina Baym, "The Madwoman and Her Languages: Why I Don't Do Feminist Literary Theory" in *Feminist Issues in Literary Scholarship*, pp. 45–61 and Nina Baym, "The Women of Cooper's *Leatherstocking* Tales" in *Images of Women*, pp. 135–54.

4. K. K. Ruthven, *Feminist Literary Studies*, pp. 20–21.

5. Janet Todd, *Feminist Literary History*, p. 13, quoting from Cora Kaplan, *Sea Changes: Culture and Feminism* (London: Verso, 1986), p. 8.

6. Jane Gallop, *Thinking Through the Body*, pp. 109–10. For my protection, I should extend the quotation: "These two phases are obviously schematic and the neat bipolarities betray a sinister distortion. I should add, of course, that many feminist critics devote themselves to proving various male authors (from Shakespeare to Lacan) sympathetic proto- or crypto-feminists just as other feminist critics exert themselves in vehement critique of diverse women writers. The actuality and plurality of feminist criticism has a tapestried complexity that makes my tight binary scheme of attacking male pigs and celebrating female identity what Barthes might call a 'little mythology.'"

7. In her account of the 1972 anthology, Toril Moi writes: "both sexes come in for harsh criticism for their creation of 'unreal' female characters. Indeed, the editor in her essay . . . accuses women writers of being *worse* than male writers in this respect, since they, unlike the men, are betraying their own sex" (*Sexual/Textual Politics*, p. 43).

8. Nan Bauer Maglin, "Fictional Feminists in *The Bostonians* and *The Odd Women*," p. 216; Kathleen Conway Mcgrath, "Popular Literature as Social Reinforcement: The Case of *Charlotte Temple*," pp. 21–27; Susan Gorsky, "The Gentle Doubters: Images of Women in Englishwomen's Novels, 1840–1920," pp. 28–54; and Madonna Marsden, "Gentle Truths for Gentle Readers: The Fiction of Elizabeth Goudge," pp. 68–78.

9. Florence Howe, "Feminism and Literature" in *Images of Women*, p. 266.

10. Susan Koppelman Cornillon, "The Fiction of Fiction" in *Images of Women*, p. 130 n. 2.

11. Marcia R. Lieberman, "Sexism and the Double Standard in Literature" in *Images of Women*, p. 328.

12. For a theoretical exposition of this complex, I refer the reader to Jacques Lacan, "Aggressivity in psychoanalysis" in *Ecrits: A Selection*, pp. 8–29.

13. See, for example, Helen Longino and Valerie Miner, eds., *Competition: A Feminist Taboo?* (Old Westbury, NY: Feminist Press, 1987).

14. Linda Ray Pratt, "The Abuse of Eve by the New World Adam" in *Images of Women*, p. 155.

15. René Wellek and Austin Warren, *Theory of Literature*, 3rd edition (New York: Harcourt Brace, 1977), p. 108.

16. Her balancing act may not be very different from the project of New Criticism in the first place, although her politics are presumably quite different. According to Gerald Graff, "[i]t was not a question of purging moral and social significance from literature, but of showing how that significance became a function of the formal texture of the work itself rather than something external or superadded"—*Professing Literature: An Institutional History* (Chicago: University of Chicago Press, 1987), pp. 148–49.

17. Cheri Register, "Literary Criticism," *Signs* Vol. 6, No. 2 (1980), p. 271.

18. Elizabeth Abel, "Introduction" in *Writing and Sexual Difference*, pp. 1–2.

19. Elaine Showalter, "Women's Time, Women's Space: Writing the History of Feminist Criticism" in *Feminist Issues in Literary Scholarship*, p. 36. I first heard Showalter's paper at the 1983 English Institute.

20. Elizabeth A. Meese, *Crossing the Double-Cross: The Practice of Feminist Criticism* (Chapel Hill: University of North Carolina Press, 1986), p. ix.

21. Carolyn Heilbrun and Catharine Stimpson, "Theories of Feminist Criticism: A Dialogue" in Josephine Donovan, ed., *Feminist Literary Criticism: Explorations in Theory*, 2d ed. (Lexington: University Press of Kentucky, 1989), p. 61.

22. Lillian S. Robinson and Lise Vogel, "Modernism and History" in *Images of Women*, pp. 282–83.

23. Robinson and Vogel, p. 285. The phrase "changing race" is from The Schoolboys of Barbiana, *Letter to a Teacher* (New York, 1970).

24. bell hooks, *Ain't I a Woman* (Boston: South End Press, 1982). Gloria T.

Hull, Patricia Bell Scott, and Barbara Smith, eds., *All the Women Are White, All the Blacks Are Men, But Some of Us Are Brave: Black Women's Studies.*

25. Gill Gane, Ann Kautzman, Kathleen Kelley, Nancy Jainchill, Susan Mullins, Susan Tenenbaum, "Bibliography" in *Images of Women*, p. 355.

26. Charles Blinderman, "The Servility of Dependence: The Dark Lady in Trollope" in *Images of Women*, p. 55.

27. Blinderman, p. 64. The quotation is from Leslie Fiedler, *Love and Death in the American Novel* (New York: Dell, 1960), pp. 266–67.

28. Robinson and Vogel, "Modernism and History" and Fraya Katz-Stoker, "The Other Criticism: Feminism vs. Formalism" in *Images of Women*, pp. 315–27.

8. An Idea Presented Before Its Time

1. "Editor's Preface" in Josephine Donovan, ed., *Feminist Literary Criticism: Explorations in Theory*, p. ix, speaking of Cheri Register, "American Feminist Literary Criticism: A Bibliographical Introduction" in *Feminist Literary Criticism*, pp. 1–28.

2. Editorial, *Signs: Journal of Women in Culture and Society*, Vol. 1, No. 1 (1975), p. vi.

3. Elaine Showalter, "Literary Criticism," *Signs*, Vol. 1, No. 2 (1975), p. 453.

4. Josephine Donovan, "Introduction to the Second Edition: Radical Feminist Criticism" in Josephine Donovan, ed., *Feminist Literary Criticism: Explorations in Theory*, 2d ed., p. xi. The quotations are from Elizabeth A. Meese, *Crossing the Double-Cross*, pp. 140–41.

5. Annette Kolodny, "The Feminist as Literary Critic," *Critical Inquiry* 2 (1976), p. 828.

6. Register, pp. 18–19. The layout of the essay is such that I cannot tell whether this paragraph is part of the response to the last question or not.

7. Kolodny, p. 827, quoting from Kathleen Fraser, "On Being a West Coast Woman Poet," unpublished paper presented at the 1975 meeting of the Modern Language Association.

8. Cf. Lillian Robinson on "The Critical Task": "One must begin by combatting [the ideas of the bourgeoisie] in the areas where they are most pervasive, have the widest audience, and serve the most vicious purposes.

[I] do not deny the presence of reactionary views in the works of say, D. H. Lawrence. The question is whether it matters much that they are there"—*Sex, Class, and Culture* (New York: Methuen, 1986), p. 49. Robinson, here in 1971, might disagree with Register as to which texts have influence, but she concurs that we must combat ideas not because they are there but because they are influential.

9. Toril Moi, *Sexual/Textual Politics*, p. 31.

10. Cf. Meese, p. 6: "Basically, works included in the literary canon deserve critical attention (while others don't), and critical attention needs to be paid to works in the canon because they are, by definition, important. . . . [W]hat is not valued is not studied (canonized); what is not studied is not valued."

11. Moi also dates a shift in American feminist criticism around 1975: "From about 1975, interest started to focus exclusively on the works of women writers" (p. 50).

12. Moi remarks this aspect of the difference between reading men's and women's writing, pp. 75–76: "The 'hermeneutics of suspicion', which assumes that the text is not, or not only, what it pretends to be, and therefore searches for underlying contradictions and conflicts as well as absences and silences in the text, seems to be reserved for texts written by men."

13. *Webster's Third New International Dictionary* (Springfield, Massachusetts: Merriam-Webster, 1986), p. 2289.

14. K. K. Ruthven, *Feminist Literary Studies*, p. 73.

15. Carole S. Vance, "Pleasure and Danger: Toward a Politics of Sexuality" in Carole S. Vance, ed., *Pleasure and Danger*, p. 21. All further quotations from Vance refer to this same page.

16. *Webster's Third New International Dictionary*, p. 380.

17. Echols, "The Taming of the Id: Feminist Sexual Politics, 1968–83" in Vance, ed., *Pleasure and Danger*, p. 50. Introducing another version of the same work by Echols, the editors of the anthology *Powers of Desire* write: "the theoretical assumptions of cultural feminism hardened into a set of proscriptions that sometimes excluded and even condemned other women"—Ann Snitow, Christine Stansell, and Sharon Thompson, eds., *Powers of Desire: The Politics of Sexuality* (New York: Monthly Review Press, 1983), p. 439.

18. In the Redstockings' 1975 publication, *Feminist Revolution* (reissued by

Random House in 1978), according to "The Taming of the Id," p. 67, n. 3.

19. Later, Josephine Donovan explicitly claims the label "cultural feminism": "A feminist critical theory that is focused on women's art and toward the development of a women's poetics—in other words, gynocriticism—is rooted in a feminist theory that may be labeled 'cultural feminism.' This particular branch of feminist theory . . . stresses the identification of women as a . . . separate culture, with its own customs, its own epistemology, and, once articulated, its own aesthetics and ethics. . . . I plan to draw upon these"—"Toward a Women's Poetics" in *Feminist Issues in Literary Scholarship*, p. 100.

20. Moi's description of this turn resonates with our sense of cultural feminism: "The role of the feminist critic is . . . to sit quietly and listen to her mistress's voice as it expresses authentic female experience" (p. 78).

21. Cheri Register, "Literary Criticism," *Signs*, Vol. 6, No. 2 (Winter 1980), p. 272.

22. The last phrase comes to me from Bonnie Zimmerman's article "What Has Never Been," collected both in *The New Feminist Criticism* and in *Making a Difference*. She gets the phrase from June Arnold, "Lesbian Fiction," *Sinister Wisdom* 2 (Fall 1976), p. 28.

9. A Contradiction in Terms

1. Arlyn Diamond and Lee R. Edwards, eds., *The Authority of Experience: Essays in Feminist Criticism* (Amherst: University of Massachusetts Press, 1977), and Sandra M. Gilbert and Susan Gubar, eds., *Shakespeare's Sisters: Feminist Essays on Women Poets* (Bloomington: Indiana University Press, 1979).

2. "Introduction" in *Shakespeare's Sisters*, p. xxiv.

3. "Preface" in Cheryl L. Brown and Karen Olson, eds., *Feminist Criticism: Essays on Theory, Poetry and Prose* (Metuchen, NJ: Scarecrow Press, 1978), p. xiii.

4. Annette Kolodny, "Some Notes on Defining a 'Feminist Literary Criticism'" in Brown and Olson, eds., *Feminist Criticism*, p. 37.

5. Lillian S. Robinson, "Dwelling in Decencies: Radical Criticism and the Feminist Perspective" in Brown and Olson, eds., *Feminist Criticism*, p. 35.

6. Margret Andersen, "Feminism as a Criterion of the Literary Critic" in Brown and Olson, eds., *Feminist Criticism*, pp. 5–6.

7. Robinson, "Dwelling in Decencies," p. 32.

8. Lillian S. Robinson, *Sex, Class, and Culture* (New York: Methuen, 1986; originally published: Bloomington: Indiana University Press, 1978), pp. 15, 225.

9. William W. Morgan, "Feminism and Literary Study: A Reply to Annette Kolodny," *Critical Inquiry* 2, No. 4 (Summer 1976), p. 813. Kolodny responds to Morgan in the same issue: "The Feminist as Literary Critic," pp. 821–32.

10. See note 14, chapter 5 above.

11. Paul Lauter, "Race and Gender in the Shaping of the American Literary Canon: A Case Study from the Twenties" in Judith Newton and Deborah Rosenfelt, eds., *Feminist Criticism and Social Change: Sex, Class and Race in Literature and Culture* (New York: Methuen, 1985), pp. 20–23.

12. Harold Bloom, *A Map of Misreading* (New York: Oxford University Press, 1975), p. 186. See also Harold Bloom, *The Anxiety of Influence* (New York: Oxford University Press, 1973). Pamela Di Pesa discusses the implications of Bloom's theories for women in a theoretical essay that opens the poetry section of *Feminist Criticism*, "The Imperious Muse: Some Observations on Women, Nature, and the Poetic Tradition," pp. 59–68.

13. Barbara J. Williams, "A Room of Her Own: Emily Dickinson as Woman Artist" in Brown and Olson, eds., *Feminist Criticism*, p. 87, quoting from Archibald MacLeish, "The Private World" in Archibald MacLeish, Louise Bogan, and Richard Wilbur, *Emily Dickinson: Three Views* (Amherst: Amherst College Press, 1960), p. 21.

14. Sandra M. Gilbert and Susan Gubar, *The Madwoman in the Attic*, pp. 582–83. "Judith" is the name Woolf gave to Shakespeare's imaginary sister.

15. Suzanne Juhasz, "'The Blood Jet': The Poetry of Sylvia Plath" in Brown and Olson, eds., *Feminist Criticism*, p. 111, reprinted from *Naked and Fiery Forms*.

16. pp. 162, 167, 185.

17. Ellen Morgan, "Humanbecoming: Form and Focus in the Neo-Feminist Novel" in Koppelman Cornillon, ed., *Images of Women in Fiction*, p. 188.

18. Myra Jehlen, "Archimedes and the Paradox of Feminist Criticism" in Nannerl O. Keohane et al., eds., *Feminist Theory: A Critique of Ideology*, p. 206, reprinted from *Signs* 6 (1981). Jehlen is quoting from Nina Baym,

Woman's Fiction: A Guide to Novels by and about Women in America, 1820–1870 (Ithaca: Cornell University Press, 1978), pp. 14–15, 32. Lillian Robinson uses Jehlen's reading of Baym to make a similar point in "Treason Our Text" in *The New Feminist Criticism*, pp. 110–11.

19. Juhasz, "The Feminist Poet," p. 167, quoting from Alta, *I Am Not a Practicing Angel* (Trumansburg, NY: The Crossing Press, 1975).

20. See Robinson, *Sex, Class, and Culture*, pp. 225–30.

21. Toril Moi, *Sexual/Textual Politics*, p. 69.

22. Jehlen, pp. 214–15.

23. Janet Todd, *Feminist Literary History*, pp. 60–61.

24. I take the phrase from Barbara Herrnstein Smith, *On the Margins of Discourse: The Relation of Literature to Language* (Chicago: University of Chicago Press, 1978), pp. 3, 14. Smith traces the concept to Aristotle.

25. Register, "American Feminist Literary Criticism" in Donovan, ed., *Feminist Literary Criticism*, p. 19.

26. *Sex, Class, and Culture*, p. 230.

27. Register, p. 11.

10. Tongue Work

1. Marjorie Pryse and Hortense J. Spillers, eds., *Conjuring: Black Women, Fiction, and Literary Tradition* (Bloomington: Indiana University Press, 1985), p. 22. Further references will appear in the text.

2. Alice Walker, *In Search of Our Mothers' Gardens: Womanist Prose* (New York: Harcourt Brace, 1983), p. 107.

3. *I Love Myself When I Am Laughing* (Old Westbury, NY: The Feminist Press, 1979).

4. *Conjuring*, p. 15, quoting from Walker's Foreword to Robert Hemenway's *Zora Neale Hurston: A Literary Biography* (Urbana: University of Illinois Press, 1977), which is reprinted in *In Search of Our Mothers' Gardens*, p. 86, emphasis Walker's.

5. Gloria T. Hull, Patricia Bell Scott, and Barbara Smith, eds., *All the Women Are White, All the Blacks Are Men, But Some of Us Are Brave: Black Women's Studies*, pp. xiii, 376–78.

6. *In Search of Our Mothers' Gardens*, p. 387.

7. Cf. K. K. Ruthven, *Feminist Literary Studies*, p. 128: "All the evidence suggests that a tradition . . . is created retrospectively for self-validating purposes out of the present needs of a particular group of people."

8. Walker, "In Search of Our Mothers' Gardens" in *In Search of our Mothers' Gardens*, p. 241.

9. Gloria T. Hull, "'What It Is I Think She's Doing Anyhow': A Reading of Toni Cade Bambara's *The Salt Eaters*" in *Conjuring*, p. 220. The quotations are, presumably, from Bambara's *The Salt Eaters* (New York: Random House, 1980), although Hull intersperses them liberally in her writing without specific reference.

10. Barbara Christian, "Trajectories of Self-Definition: Placing Contemporary Afro-American Women's Fiction" in *Conjuring*, p. 245. Christian is here quoting from and interpreting Toni Morrison, *Tar Baby* (New York: Knopf, 1981), p. 305.

11. Virginia Woolf, *A Room of One's Own*, pp. 117–18.

12. *Conjuring*, p. 13, quoting from Zora Neale Hurston, *Their Eyes Were Watching God* (Urbana: University of Illinois Press, 1978), p. 26.

13. Addison Gayle, Jr., *The Way of the New World* (Garden City: Anchor/ Doubleday, 1975), p. 196, as quoted in Marjorie Pryse, "'Pattern against the Sky': Deism and Motherhood in Ann Petry's *The Street*" in *Conjuring*, p. 123.

14. A decade earlier, Gloria Hull argues for the necessity of placing contemporary black women's poetry in a tradition: "the . . . spotlight which has been focused on contemporary Black women poets . . . has, ironically, tended to obscure the already shadowy literary past by suggesting that Black female poets are something new. . . . [T]he tradition of Black women poets goes back much further than the 1960s. . . . Studying [these women who wrote before the modern period] . . . gives a necessary perspective on the present poets by placing them in their appropriate, rich tradition"—Gloria T. Hull, "Black Women Poets from Wheatley to Walker," first published in *Black American Literature Forum* (Fall 1975), reprinted in Roseann P. Bell, Bettye J. Parker, and Beverly Guy-Sheftall, eds., *Sturdy Black Bridges: Visions of Black Women in Literature* (Garden City: Anchor/Doubleday, 1979), p. 70. Hull then goes on to survey "Black Women Poets from Wheatley to Walker"; only her final poet, Margaret Walker, is presented, without reservations, as excellent. Here too, although only implicitly, the predecessors are worth studying, not for their

intrinsic value, but because they form the tradition that brought forth the already-valued contemporary writers.

15. I had better here footnote: Harold Bloom, *The Anxiety of Influence: A Theory of Poetry* and *A Map of Misreading*, although at this point in time (1990), in literary academic milieux, these ideas almost seem to belong in the public domain.

16. Claudia Tate, "Pauline Hopkins: Our Literary Foremother" in *Conjuring*, p. 54.

17. Carolyn Rodgers, "It Is Deep" in *Sturdy Black Bridges*, p. 378, reprinted from Carolyn Rodgers, *Songs of a Black Bird* (Chicago: Third World Press, 1969), p. 13.

18. Bettye J. Parker-Smith, "Running Wild in Her Soul: The Poetry of Carolyn Rodgers" in Mari Evans, ed., *Black Women Writers: Arguments and Interviews* (London: Pluto Press, 1985), p. 400.

19. Toni Cade Bambara, *Gorilla, My Love* (New York: Random House, 1972), p. ix, quoted in Parker-Smith, p. 397.

20. Renita Weems, "'Artists Without Art Form': A Look at One Black Woman's World of Unrevered Black Women" in Barbara Smith, ed. *Home Girls: A Black Feminist Anthology*, p. 102.

21. *Conjuring*, p. 15, quoting from *Their Eyes*, p. 17.

22. Pryse quoting from *The Color Purple*, *Conjuring*, p. 18.

23. Thelma J. Shinn, "The Wise Witches: Black Women Mentors in the Fiction of Octavia E. Butler" in *Conjuring*, p. 204. Amber appears in the 1976 novel, *Patternmaster*. Shinn takes the phrase "uniting the feminine generations" from Annis Pratt with Barbara White, Andrea Loewenstein, and Mary Wyer, *Archetypal Patterns in Women's Fiction* (Bloomington: Indiana University Press, 1981), p. 170.

24. Lorraine Bethel, "Conversations with Ourselves: Black Female Relationships in Toni Cade Bambara's *Gorilla, My Love* and Toni Morrison's *Sula*," unpublished paper written at Yale, 1976, quoted in Barbara Smith, "Toward a Black Feminist Criticism" in *But Some of Us Are Brave*, p. 166.

25. Lorraine Bethel, "'This Infinity of Conscious Pain': Zora Neale Hurston and the Black Female Literary Tradition" in *But Some of Us Are Brave*, p. 178.

26. Christian, p. 246. I take the phrase "lesbian continuum" from Adrienne Rich, "Compulsory Heterosexuality and Lesbian Existence," first published in 1980, reprinted in Ann Snitow, Christine Stansell, and Sharon

Thompson, eds., *Powers of Desire: The Politics of Sexuality*, pp. 192–202. Rich's "continuum" runs from mother-daughter nurture through overt lesbianism. She cites Bethel's readings of Morrison and Hurston in her exemplification of the lesbian continuum.

27. Hortense J. Spillers, *"Chosen Place, Timeless People*: Some Figurations on the New World" in *Conjuring*, p. 152.

28. Minrose C. Gwin, *Black and White Women of the Old South: The Peculiar Sisterhood in American Literature* (Knoxville: University of Tennessee Press, 1985).

29. Minrose C. Gwin, "Green-eyed Monsters of the Slavocracy: Jealous Mistresses in Two Slave Narratives" in *Conjuring*, p. 48. Gwin is referring to Harriet Jacobs, *Incidents in the Life of a Slave Girl*, ed. L. Maria Child (1861; rpt. New York: Harcourt Brace Jovanovich, 1973).

30. Minrose C. Gwin, *"Jubilee*: The Black Woman's Celebration of Human Community" in *Conjuring*, pp. 134–35.

31. Elizabeth Schultz, "Out of the Woods and into the World: A Study of Interracial Friendships between Women in American Novels" in *Conjuring*, p. 80. The other novel is Allison Mills's *Francisco*.

32. *Conjuring*, p. 83. Washington, "How Racial Differences Helped Us Discover Our Sameness," *Ms.* (September 1981), p. 76.

33. *Conjuring*, p. 83. Audre Lorde, "An Open Letter to Mary Daly" in *This Bridge Called My Back: Writings by Radical Women of Color*, ed. Cherríe Moraga and Gloria Anzaldúa, p. 94.

34. Hortense J. Spillers, "Afterword: Cross-Currents, Discontinuities: Black Women's Fiction" in *Conjuring*, p. 249.

35. Barbara Christian, "The Race for Theory," first appeared in *Cultural Critique* 6 (Spring 1987), reprinted in Linda Kauffman, ed., *Gender and Theory: Dialogues on Feminist Criticism* (Oxford: Basil Blackwell, 1989), p. 235.

36. Cf. Myra Jehlen: "contradictions . . . frequently are our firmest and most fruitful grounds"—"Archimedes and the Paradox of Feminist Criticism," pp. 200–201.

37. Christian, "The Race for Theory," pp. 231–32. Nikki Giovanni, Review of Paule Marshall, *Chosen Place, Timeless People*, *Negro Digest*, Vol. 19, No. 3 (January 1970), pp. 51–52, 84.

38. *Conjuring*, p. 15; *Their Eyes*, p. 17.

11. The Attraction of Matrimonial Metaphor

1. Gayle Greene and Coppélia Kahn, eds. *Making a Difference: Feminist Literary Criticism* (New York: Methuen, 1985). Page references will appear parenthetically in the text.

2. Bonnie Zimmerman, "What Has Never Been: An Overview of Lesbian Feminist Literary Criticism," *Feminist Studies* Vol. 7, No. 3 (1981), p. 467, in Elaine Showalter, ed., *The New Feminist Criticism*, p. 215.

3. See, for example, Adrienne Rich, "Compulsory Heterosexuality and Lesbian Existence."

4. Anthologized both in Abel, ed., *Writing and Sexual Difference* and in Showalter, ed., *The New Feminist Criticism*.

5. Also published in 1985, in the New Accents series, Toril Moi's *Sexual/Textual Politics* is likewise very explicitly beyond and against Showalter.

6. The prevalence of this metaphor may find uncanny resonance with the focus on Showalter who is after all, literally, "married to English" (her husband is English Showalter).

7. Susan Gubar, "'The Blank Page' and the Issues of Female Creativity" in Elizabeth Abel, ed., *Writing and Sexual Difference*, pp. 73–94 and Elaine Showalter, ed., *The New Feminist Criticism*, pp. 292–313.

8. Sydney Janet Kaplan, *Feminine Consciousness in the Modern British Novel* (Urbana: University of Illinois Press, 1975).

9. See, for example, *Three Essays on the Theory of Sexuality, Standard Edition*, Vol. 7, p. 229: "One of the tasks implicit in object-choice is that it should find its way to the opposite sex. This, as we know, is not accomplished without a certain amount of fumbling. Often enough the first impulses after puberty go astray, though without any permanent harm resulting. Dessoir has justly remarked upon the regularity with which adolescent boys and girls form sentimental friendships with others of their own sex."

10. I have preferred to quote the 1981 version of the note (*The New Feminist Criticism*, p. 220 n. 4). The sentence in the 1985 version reads: "The sexual preference of the authors is irrelevant; this is an analysis of lesbian feminist *ideas*" (*Making a Difference*, p. 204 n. 1).

11. Gerda Lerner, *The Majority Finds Its Past: Placing Women in History* (Oxford: Oxford University Press, 1979), p. 180, emphasis Lerner's. Greene and Kahn quote this last sentence on p. 20.

12. Judith Mayne, "Walking the *Tightrope* of Feminism and Male Desire" in Jardine and Smith, eds., *Men in Feminism*, p. 70.

13. Let me also cite, in passing, a particularly blatant example (although not from a book). Margret Andersen closes the theoretical article collected in the anthology *Feminist Criticism* by asserting that traditional criticism and feminism "will have to arrive at an understanding, in order to allow the streams of male and female consciousness to converge into a river of simply human heterosexual consciousness"—"Feminism as a Criterion of the Literary Critic," p. 9. Once again Andersen makes explicit something implicit in other feminist critics (v. chapter 9 above).

14. Carol Gilligan, *In a Different Voice: Psychological Theory and Women's Development* (Cambridge: Harvard University Press, 1982), p. 174, emphasis added.

15. Virginia Woolf, *A Room of One's Own*, pp. 100–101. Further references in the text.

16. See, for example, Atina Grossman, "The New Woman and the Rationalization of Sexuality in Weimar Germany" in Ann Snitow, Christine Stansell, and Sharon Thompson, eds., *Powers of Desire*, pp. 153–71; Lisa Duggan, "The Social Enforcement of Heterosexuality and Lesbian Resistance in the 1920s" in Amy Swerdlow and Hanna Lessinger, eds., *Class, Race, and Sex: The Dynamics of Control* (Boston: G. K. Hall, 1983), pp. 75–92; and Christina Simmons, "Companionate Marriage and the Lesbian Threat," *Frontiers*, Vol. 4, No. 3 (1979), pp. 54–59.

17. Dr. David Reuben, *Everything You Always Wanted to Know About Sex* (*But Were Afraid to Ask)* (New York: Bantam, 1969), p. 272, quoted in Meryl Altman, "Everything They Always Wanted You to Know: The Ideology of Popular Sex Literature" in Carole S. Vance, ed., *Pleasure and Danger*, p. 125.

18. Ellen Bayuk Rosenman's article in *Signs* Vol. 14, No. 3 (1989) shows how much lesbianism there is behind this passage: "Sexual Identity and *A Room of One's Own*: 'Secret Economies' in Virginia Woolf's Feminist Discourse," pp. 634–50.

19. Let us also bear in mind Gayatri Spivak's warning: "I would like to remind everyone who cites *A Room of One's Own* that 'one must be woman-manly or man-womanly' is said there in the voice of Mary Beton, a persona. Woolf must break her off in mid-chapter and resume in her authorial voice. Who can disclaim that there is in her a longing for androgyny, that artificially fulfilled copula? But to reduce her great texts to *successful*

articulations of that copula is, I believe, to make a mistake in reading"—
In Other Worlds, p. 42.

20. Gayle Greene, "Feminist and Marxist Criticism: An Argument for Alliances," *Women's Studies*, Vol. 9 (1981), pp. 29–30.

21. "One striking feature of feminist metacriticism has been its attempt to describe the different types of feminist criticism not as equally available options but as constituting an evolutionary sequence"—K. K. Ruthven, *Feminist Literary Studies*, p. 20.

22. Coppélia Kahn, "The Hand That Rocks the Cradle: Recent Gender Theories and Their Implications" in Garner, Kahane, Sprengnether, eds., *The (M)other Tongue*, p. 74, quoting from Nancy Chodorow, *The Reproduction of Mothering*, p. 181.

23. Greene, "Feminist and Marxist Criticism," p. 39, emphasis added.

24. "Feminist and Marxist Criticism," pp. 34–35, ellipsis Greene's. In 1985 Judith Newton and Deborah Rosenfelt write: "For many of us a first encounter with a criticism that explicitly and demandingly asserted its engagement in the struggle for progressive social change was with Lillian S. Robinson's now classic essay, 'Dwelling in Decencies: Radical Criticism and the Feminist Perspective' (originally published in *College English* 32 (1971))"—"Preface" in *Feminist Criticism and Social Change: Sex. Class and Race in Literature and Culture* (New York: Methuen, 1985), p. xii.

25. Heidi Hartmann, "The Unhappy Marriage of Marxism and Feminism" in Lydia Sargent, ed., *The Unhappy Marriage of Marxism and Feminism: A Debate on Class and Patriarchy* (London: Pluto Press, 1981), p. 2, quoted in Cora Kaplan, "Pandora's box: Subjectivity, Class and Sexuality in Socialist Feminist Criticism" in *Making a Difference*, pp. 146–47.

26. Greene and Kahn, p. 5.

27. For a brilliant analysis of the relation of women authors to the romance institution, read Leslie Rabine, "Romance in the Age of Electronics: Harlequin Enterprises" in Newton and Rosenfelt, eds., *Feminist Criticism and Social Change*, pp. 249–67. Accepting the analogy between women writing for Harlequin and women writing in the academy, we might apply Rabine's analysis to illuminate our own institutional situation and struggle.

28. Mary Jacobus, "The Buried Letter: Feminism and Romanticism in *Villette*" in Jacobus, ed., *Women Writing and Writing about Women* (London: Croon Helm, 1979) and Judith Lowder Newton, *Women, Power, and*

Subversion: Social Strategies in British Fiction 1778–1860 (Athens: University of Georgia Press, 1981). The quoted phrase is from Kaplan, p. 152.

29. See Sandra M. Gilbert and Susan Gubar, *The Madwoman in the Attic.*

30. Advertisement for Harlequin Temptations, found in Harlequin books of July 1984, quoted in Rabine, p. 251.

31. Janet Todd writes of Cora Kaplan's "Pandora's Box": "I find Kaplan's aim to bring psychic and social together an attractive project." A paragraph later, however, Todd cites Michele Barrett, in opposition to Kaplan's breathless resolution, as "a salutary deflation of the common hope of a quick marriage—rather than some loose friendship—between materialist feminism and French-inspired formalist and psychoanalytical theory"— *Feminist Literary History*, pp. 88–89.

32. Lise Vogel, "Marxism and Feminism: Unhappy Marriage, Trial Separation or Something Else?" in *The Unhappy Marriage of Marxism and Feminism*, p. 196. In "Dwelling in Decencies," Lillian Robinson proposes a similar list of variations on this metaphor: "I began by referring to a *mésalliance* between 'feminism' and established critical modes. It might be amusing to extend the conceit to speak of oppressive relationships, bourgeois mind-fuck and foredoomed offspring. A more exact simile, however, would be the shotgun wedding" (in Brown and Olson, eds., *Feminist Criticism*, p. 35). We might recall that Robinson and Vogel co-authored the 1971 article "Modernism and History," collected in Koppelman Cornillon, ed., *Images of Women in Fiction.*

33. Reviewing a book by the feminist historian Joan Scott, Claudia Koonz, another feminist historian, writes: "Like most of us, she links gender, race and class. But then (also like most of us), she drops race entirely"—"Post Scripts," *The Women's Review of Books*, Vol. 6, No. 4 (January 1989), p. 20. Bell hooks comments: "socialist feminists focus on class and gender. . . . [T]hey make a point of acknowledging that race is important and then proceed to offer an analysis in which race is not considered"—*Feminist Theory: From Margin to Center* (Boston: South End Press, 1984), p. 14.

34. Joanna Russ, "What Can a Heroine Do? Or Why Women Can't Write" in Koppelman Cornillon, ed., *Images of Women in Fiction*, p. 11.

35. Barbara Smith, "Toward a Black Feminist Criticism," *Conditions: Two*, Vol. 1, No.2 (October 1977), anthologized in Showalter, ed., *The New Feminist Criticism*; Newton and Rosenfelt, eds., *Feminist Criticism and Social Change*; and Gloria T. Hull, Patricia Bell Scott, and Barbara Smith,

eds., *All the Women are White, All the Blacks are Men, But Some of Us are Brave*.

12. History is Like Mother

1. Ellen Carol DuBois, Gail Paradise Kelly, Elizabeth Lapovsky Kennedy, Carolyn W. Korsmeyer, and Lillian S. Robinson, *Feminist Scholarship: Kindling in the Groves of Academe* (Urbana: University of Illinois Press, 1986). The quotation is from Lillian S. Robinson, "Feminist Criticism: How Do We Know When We've Won?" in Shari Benstock, ed., *Feminist Issues in Literary Scholarship* (Bloomington: Indiana University Press, 1987), p. 143.

2. Jane Marcus, "Still Practice, A/Wrested Alphabet: Toward a Feminist Aesthetic" in *Feminist Issues in Literary Scholarship*, p. 87.

3. Shari Benstock, "The Feminist Critique: Mastering Our Monstrosity," *Tulsa Studies in Women's Literature*, 2 (Fall 1983), p. 141, emphasis added.

4. For an extremely readable account of the history of literary studies, highlighting the dialectic between "criticism" and "scholarship," see Gerald Graff, *Professing Literature*.

5. See, for example, Laurie Finke, "The Rhetoric of Marginality: Why I Do Feminist Theory," *Tulsa Studies* 5 (1986), pp. 251–72; and Elizabeth A. Meese, "(Ex)Tensions: Feminist Criticism and Deconstruction," ch. 1 of *Ex-Tensions: Re-Figuring Feminist Criticism* (Champaign: University of Illinois Press, 1990).

6. "Making—and Remaking—History: Another Look at 'Patriarchy'" in *Feminist Issues in Literary Scholarship*, p. 124.

7. Elizabeth Fox-Genovese, "To Write My Self: The Autobiographies of Afro-American Women" in *Feminist Issues in Literary Scholarship*, pp. 176–77.

8. Elizabeth Fox-Genovese, "My Statue, My Self: Autobiographical Writings of Afro-American Women" in *The Private Self: Theory and Practice of Women's Autobiographical Writings*, Shari Benstock, ed. (Chapel Hill: University of North Carolina Press, 1988), pp. 63–89.

9. Elaine Showalter, "Women's Time, Women's Space: Writing the History of Feminist Criticism" in *Feminist Issues in Literary Scholarship*, p. 31.

10. Showalter, pp. 30–31. K. K. Ruthven shares this sense of our history: "Unlike psychoanalysis and marxism, of course, feminism does not have

the equivalent of a founding 'father'—nor could it have, seeing that that in itself is a patriarchal notion of how knowledge is created and authorized"—*Feminist Literary Studies*, p. 25.

11. Jane Marcus, Introduction, *New Feminist Essays on Virginia Woolf*, ed. Jane Marcus (Lincoln: University of Nebraska Press, 1981), p. xiii.

12. *Sexual/Textual Politics*, p. 18.

13. Margret Andersen, "Feminism as a Criterion of the Literary Critic" in Brown and Olson, eds., *Feminist Criticism*, p. 1.

14. Judith Kegan Gardiner, "Gender, Values, and Lessing's Cats" in *Feminist Issues in Literary Scholarship*, pp. 119–20.

15. Judith Kegan Gardiner, "Mind mother: psychoanalysis and feminism" in Greene and Kahn, eds., *Making a Difference*, p. 139.

16. Judith Kegan Gardiner, "The Heroine as Her Author's Daughter" in Brown and Olson, eds., *Feminist Criticism*, p. 252.

17. Josephine Donovan, "Toward a Women's Poetics" in *Feminist Issues in Literary Scholarship*, p. 105. Donovan is referring to her own "Sarah Orne Jewett's Critical Theory: Notes Toward a Feminine Literary Mode" in *Critical Essays on Sarah Orne Jewett*, ed. Gwen L. Nagel (Boston: G. K. Hall, 1984). She takes the notion of women's time as repetitive or cyclic from Kathryn Allen Rabuzzi, *The Sacred and the Feminine: Toward a Theology of Housework* (New York: Seabury, 1982).

18. For a sense of how Jardine herself uses this coining, see Alice A. Jardine, *Gynesis: Configurations of Woman and Modernity* (Ithaca: Cornell University Press, 1985).

19. See Showalter, "Toward a Feminist Poetics" and Showalter, "Feminist Criticism in the Wilderness," both collected in Showalter, ed., *The New Feminist Criticism*.

20. Hortense Spillers, "Review Essay: 'Turning the Century': Notes on Women and Difference," *Tulsa Studies in Women's Literature*, Vol. 3, Nos. 1–2 (1984), pp. 178–85.

21. Finke does not explicitly counter the "prominent" with her marginal categories and the 1987 book version adds four more "prominent" feminist critics, with three additional articles and the Stimpson introduction.

22. Hortense J. Spillers, "A Hateful Passion, A Lost Love" in *Feminist Issues in Literary Scholarship*, p. 182.

23. Following gender ideology in British culture from 1798 to 1880, Newton

shows us major shifts around 1830 and 1860 in order to argue for the necessity of understanding literature in its specific historical context.

24. No one can, at this moment in academic theoretical time, play on these two senses of the word "discipline" without referring to the work and the effect of Michel Foucault.

25. Benstock, "The Feminist Critique," p. 148.

26. Alice Jardine, "Gynesis," *Diacritics*, 12 (1982).

27. William Shakespeare, *Titus Andronicus*, III, ii, 44–45.

28. Judith Kegan Gardiner, "On Female Identity and Writing by Women" in Abel, ed., *Writing and Sexual Difference*, pp. 179, 187, 191. For an early version of this, see Gardiner, "The Heroine as Her Author's Daughter" in Brown and Olson, eds., *Feminist Criticism*, pp. 244–53.

29. Nina Baym, "The Madwoman and Her Languages: Why I Don't Do Feminist Literary Theory" in *Feminist Issues in Literary Scholarship*, p. 56.

30. Nina Auerbach, "Engorging the Patriarchy" in *Feminist Issues in Literary Scholarship*, pp. 152–53.

31. Auerbach, "Engorging the Patriarchy," p. 158. Auerbach, "Why Communities of Women Aren't Enough," *Tulsa Studies in Women's Literature*, Vol. 3, Nos. 1–2 (1984), p. 156. The only difference between the two versions of this sentence is the addition of a comma after "probably."

32. Dictionary meanings gleaned from *The American Heritage Dictionary of the English Language*, p. 434 and *Webster's Third New International Dictionary*, p. 753.

33. Baym, pp. 45, 59; Auerbach, "Why Communities of Women Aren't Enough," p. 153. Auerbach's tone in 1987 is no longer angry but even-handed. She moves from calling herself a pluralist while raging at orthodoxy to speaking with pluralist tolerance.

34. See, for example, Finke, op.cit. pp. 255, 258. Finke does cite Baym's opposition to Marcus.

35. Jane Marcus, "Storming the Toolshed" in Nannerl O. Keohane et al., eds., *Feminist Theory: A Critique of Ideology* (Chicago: University of Chicago Press, 1982), p. 218.

36. Gayatri Spivak, "A Response to Annette Kolodny," unpublished paper, 1980, quoted in Marcus, "Storming the Toolshed," p. 218. We might recall that in "Still Practice," Marcus finds Spivak bad for not recognizing Woolf's authority as the mother of socialist feminist criticism but also finds her a

model ("no more perfect example of 'still practice'") feminist critic for her essay on and translation of "Draupadi" (p. 89).

37. I am indebted to my colleague Carol Quillen of the History Department, Rice University for this phrase.

38. Susan Stanford Friedman, "Modernism of the 'Scattered Remnant': Race and Politics in H.D.'s Development" in *Feminist Issues in Literary Scholarship*, pp. 218, 227. Bryher is the close friend with whom H.D. lived and traveled for many years. *HER* is a novel H.D. wrote in 1927.

39. Susan S. Lanser, "Feminist Criticism, 'The Yellow Wallpaper,' and the Politics of Color in America," *Feminist Studies*, Vol. 15, No. 3 (1989), pp. 415–42.

40. Susan Friedman, "Who Buried H.D.? A Poet, Her Critics, and Her Place in 'The Literary Tradition'" in Brown and Olson, eds., *Feminist Criticism*, pp. 93–94.

Afterword

1. Cheryl Wall, ed., *Changing Our Own Words: Essays on Criticism, Theory, and Writing by Black Women* (New Brunswick: Rutgers University Press, 1989); Joanne Braxton and Andree Nicola-McLaughlin, eds. *Wild Women in the Whirlwind: Afra-American Culture and the Contemporary Literary Renaissance* (New Brunswick: Rutgers University Press, 1989); and Henry Louis Gates, Jr., ed., *Reading Black, Reading Feminist: A Critical Anthology* (New York: Meridian, 1990).

2. Elizabeth A. Flynn and Patrocinio P. Schweickart, eds., *Gender and Reading: Essays on Readers, Texts, and Contexts* (Baltimore: Johns Hopkins University Press, 1986) and Linda Kauffman, ed., *Gender and Theory: Dialogues on Feminist Criticism* (Oxford: Basil Blackwell, 1989).

3. Elaine Showalter, ed., *Speaking of Gender* (New York: Routledge, 1989).

4. Joseph A. Boone and Michael Cadden, eds., *Engendering Men: The Question of Male Feminist Criticism* (New York: Routledge, 1990).

Index